PSYCHOLOGICAL TESTING
OF AMERICAN MINORITIES:
ISSUES AND CONSEQUENCES

UNDER THE ADVISORY EDITORSHIP OF

LINDLEY J. STILES

*Professor of Education for Interdisciplinary Studies,
Northwestern University*

PSYCHOLOGICAL TESTING OF AMERICAN MINORITIES:
ISSUES AND CONSEQUENCES

Ronald J. Samuda
Teachers College, Columbia University

HARPER & ROW, PUBLISHERS
New York   Hagerstown   San Francisco   London

Designed by Jeffrey M. Barrie

CONTENTS

Foreword by William W. Turnbull   **vii**
Preface   **xiii**

CHAPTER 1
The Testing Controversy   **1**
Introduction   **1**
The Case for the Plaintiffs   **4**
The Case for the Defendants   **9**
A Trend for Future Testing   **16**

CHAPTER 2
Technical Problems in the Appraisal of Behavior   **18**
Introduction   **18**
Reliability and Validity   **19**
The Concept of Intelligence   **25**

CHAPTER 3
Nature and Nurture   **35**
Introduction   **35**
The Hereditarian Argument   **36**
The Environmentalist Argument   **42**
Fallacies   **50**

CHAPTER 4
Environmental Factors Influencing Test Performance   **63**
Introduction   **63**
Nutrition   **64**

Self-Concept   72
Motivation   82
Anxiety   87
Test Environment   91
Language   93

CHAPTER 5
Educational and Social Consequences   101
Introduction   101
A Brief Review of the Research   104
Consequences of Ability Grouping for Blacks and Other Minorities   107
Testing and College Admission of Minority Students   116

CHAPTER 6
Alternatives to Traditional Standardized Tests   131
Introduction   131
Culture-Free and Culture-Fair Tests   133
The Culture-Specific Movement   142
Measures of the Environment   145
Criterion-Referenced Testing   147
Summary: Trends and Alternatives   152

References   159
Appendix: Compendium of Tests for Minority Adolescents and Adults   177
Name Index   207
Subject Index   213

FOREWORD

Controversy has swirled around the assessment of intellectual ability from its earliest beginnings. One might think that time would diminish the arguments—at best, because new discoveries narrowed the room for disagreement; at worst, because arguments without apparent resolution often turn stale.

The debates about intellective powers and their measurement, on the contrary, have grown in intensity, and the circle of those participating in them has widened dramatically. The reasons are not difficult to find, and Ronald Samuda has marshaled them effectively in *Psychological Testing of American Minorities: Issues and Consequences.*

As long as the *definition* of intelligence remains a matter of choice, with that choice not made explicit, the likelihood of finding agreement on any propositions about the *measurement* of intelligence is slim indeed.

To this basic dilemma, three others must be added. The first is the increasing practical importance attached to measurements, especially in education, in applications ranging from earliest school placement through college admission and beyond. The definition of intelligence and its measurement have thus become pervasive gut issues of modern life, not academic abstractions. The second is the new and assertive self-awareness of minorities: the growing pride in their own cultures and the corresponding refusal to be measured in relation to white middle-class standards. The third is the recurrence of interest in the "heritability" question, largely dormant for years, but suddenly elevated to a new significance as hereditarians (all of them white) have sought recently to prescribe social solutions predicated on a doctrine of racial inferiority.

Those who put forward the genetic theory of intellect find their views disputed by their scientific colleagues and fiercely rejected by those who see this assertion as gratuitously insulting on its face and pernicious in its practical implications for action. But the debate continues and escalates, in part because its premises keep shifting from biology to education to politics and back again.

Since World War II, much of the concern about the social effects of testing has been focused on the use and misuse of the scores as predictors of success in college—whether they were used, as intended, as one of many sources of information about a student or misused as a sole and sufficient source of information. During the 1950s and 1960s, with pressure for admission mounting as demand for college places outran supply of seats in the freshman classes of the high-prestige institutions, the spotlight was turned on the admissions hurdles as never before. Questions were raised about all aspects of college entrance tests and especially about their usefulness as predictors of success in college for both majority and minority students.

The evidence about college entrance tests as predictors is no longer a subject of legitimate dispute. The studies have been widespread, they number in the thousands, and the results are consistent. By and large, the higher the test scores, the more successful the students are in college. It is true that the prediction is imperfect at best and that dramatic reversals of prediction do indeed occur. But the reversals are the exceptions, not the rule, and they occur with about the same frequency among minority and majority students. There is no ethnic monopoly on making it against the odds or on blowing an apparently fine set of chances.

The tests now in most common use require students to show their facility with word problems and number problems. The mental tasks that they pose are not trivial, and their solution requires difficult and precise thought. The medium in which the questions are presented and in which the solutions are required is that of the majority culture. Since college and university work is embedded in the same culture, the test scores represent quite well the degree to which the student is prepared to cope in the immediate future with the demands of higher education.

Like any other test scores, those resulting from the use of college entrance tests describe the individual's developed ability in a particular area, narrow or broad, at a given time. The stage of his or her developed ability inevitably reflects past opportunities to learn material of the kind used in the test.

The fact that a test is called an aptitude test ordinarily indicates its relative freedom from material depending on a short-term or specialized course of study (geometry or a foreign language, for example). Nonetheless, if the test draws upon the concepts and the language that are common to a broad segment of society, the degree of success in taking it represents the taker's developed ability to cope with the intellectual tasks as they are posed within that segment of society. It does not and cannot accurately portray pure aptitude in the sense of genetic endowment. There is *no* test score that can tell you ex post facto the native potential that a student may have had at birth.

Scores on a test of scholastic aptitude—or developed ability to reason with words and numbers posing college-like problems—tell you something about how much trouble a student may expect to have in moving immediately into college work. They tell you nothing about the odds against which he or she has had to struggle in developing those particular abilities or about the energy and determination the individual will put into his college work. His ability to solve problems posed in a different language or cultural context may or may not be reflected in the scores, depending on how widely divergent the two cultures at issue may be. But the tasks posed by the tests and by the typical college course have a great deal of similarity, and overall success on one set of such problems relates fairly well to probable success in the other.

I have said that the proportion of "misses" among minority students—the cases in which students do well or poorly in relation to the predictions—is just about the same as for majority students. Can we then conclude that all's well? Emphatically not, because of one galling and persistent fact: Black and brown people score lower, on the average, than do whites. The fact that they also have a harder time in college may tend to vindicate the tests, but it compounds the social and human problems. If school and college work is culture bound and if tests are devised mainly to predict success in such work, then it follows that culture-bound tests will do the best job of prediction. On such tests the student from a different cultural heritage will do poorly. His college performance will, on the average, confirm the prediction. Colleges, noting the predictive validity of the test scores, will come to place some reliance on them, and if no other information about such students is brought to bear on the college's decision, such a student from a minority culture may be denied admission to selective institutions. A tight circle seems to be drawn around his chances.

In the 1970s, of course, there is no shortage of college places for any student who graduates from high school: There are, in fact, hundreds of colleges eagerly seeking such students, regardless of their secondary school grades or test scores. But that answer is not enough.

What can be done about the fact that when test scores alone are used in selection, the minority student has a narrower range of opportunities available to him than the student from the majority culture?

The first thing to be said as clearly and forcefully as possible is that test scores should *never* be used alone in selection. Much of the significance of the score lies not in what it is but in what the particular student had to do to attain it. For a student whose schooling has been poor or whose home and perhaps predominant community language is other than English, a mediocre score may represent a triumph of ability, devotion to study, and persistence. The test scores, by themselves, are not designed to reflect these characteristics, not because the qualities themselves are unimportant but because testing has not yet produced ways to measure them. The student's biographical record, demonstrated interest, and long-term perseverance as reflected in school grades, especially as further illuminated by the comments of those who know his or her history, are the indispensable bases for understanding the meaning of the scores resulting from the test.

A great deal of research is going forward on inventing or discovering the elusive measures of motivation. Meanwhile, there are other possibilities to be pursued, and Ronald Samuda points to them. He discusses well the experience with attempts to devise "culture-fair" tests, and he documents the disappointments of those who have hoped to be able to strip off the overlay of culture to reveal the "true" ability of the child. This approach is, I believe, doomed to failure if the goal is indeed to find a way to display ability unalloyed by the past experience of even the youngest child. But one need not adhere to an all-or-none view: If through research we can find ways of moving partially toward culture fairness, we will have gained significantly, since any progress would be worthwhile. Indeed, the use *in combination* of ability indices drawn from tests of different cultural emphases taken by the same child could prove extremely useful. One can hypothesize that the magnitude of the difference—especially a difference that showed for any ability a superior performance of the "fairer" test—could provide a valid index of the degree to which a student's performance on a whole range of traditional culture tests might be open to question and in need of interpretation in the light of the student's particular background.

Criterion-referenced tests, also discussed by Dr. Samuda, offer important advantages in that they shift the mind set of the interpreter of the scores away from making comparisons among people and toward gauging the specific accomplishments of the individual. This is an important gain. And yet, as long as the criterion tasks are drawn from the majority culture, the problem for the minority student remains the same: Those are not the tasks that he or she can perform to best advantage.

In a society that is coming to accept the rhetoric of pluralism, if not yet the fact or desirability of multiethnicity, it seems inescapable that ways must be found to put measurement at the service of diversity. Ideally, each individual should be able to demonstrate his or her developed ability across a wide spectrum of talents with respect to concepts and in a mode of expression pertinent to the student's own background. Clearly, such an ideal can never be attained in its ultimate form: The multitude of combinations of culture and experience to be found in individuals across this country defy the precise tailoring of tests to each person's prior circumstances. But it should indeed be possible to move substantially away from the concept of a single stream of academic development and toward the recognition of pluralism, both in the educational process and in the testing systems that are part and parcel of it.

In Dr. Samuda's even-handed treatment of the main controversies surrounding testing as it has developed to date, one finds much that is provocative and illuminating. The "two sides" presented on each of the issues condense a world of passionate and usually inconclusive debate. In his final suggestions for paths out of the wilderness there is hope for a future in which minority students receive the recognition and respect that their genuine intellectual accomplishments deserve.

WILLIAM W. TURNBULL
President, Educational Testing Service
Princeton, New Jersey

PREFACE

The idea for this book occurred as early as August 1971 when I undertook the position of director of the first Institute for the Assessment of
Minorities at the Educational Testing Service in Princeton. As an
essential part of that task, I began a systematic search of the literature in
an attempt to pull together all of the research reports and theoretical
positions bearing upon the assessment of minorities. It became increasingly apparent that (despite a great mass and variety of sources) in no
one place had anyone attempted to present a comprehensive summary
and synthesis of the various perspectives, findings, issues, instruments,
and references in one single volume.

Two other sets of experiences convinced me of the urgency for
such a book: One was a series of courses which I taught at Teachers
College, Columbia University; and the other was my involvement as a
member of the steering committee of the first National Conference on
Testing in Education and Employment held at Hampton Institute,
Virginia, in April, 1973.

Consequently, the main purpose in writing this book was to fill a
real social and educational need. It is my hope that this work will meet a
demand in education, psychology, sociology, and social work. But, it
should also be appropriate as a reference source or text for departments
and programs dealing with ethnic studies or the implications of
psychological testing within the context of cultural, socioeconomic, or
ethnic subgroup membership at the graduate, undergraduate, or community college levels. It should also be valuable for practitioners—as a
source for the inservice training of teachers, administrators, counselors
and all who are concerned with the use and interpretation of standar-

dized tests with those minorities who have been disequalized by the system.

Let me emphasize that this book is not intended as a technical piece of work in the sense of psychometric innovation. Rather, it is a synthesis and summary of over four hundred highly selected reference sources. My overriding objective has been to present a sort of gestalt of the perspectives, pitfalls, fallacies, issues, consequences, and trends in the use of standardized norm-referenced tests with American minorities. Experience as a counselor, university professor, and administrator has persuaded me that statistical data and reference materials are often imprecise and should be treated with caution. My purpose has been to present an overview and the reader is urged to bear that in mind.

A word needs to be said about the compendium of tests included as an appendix at the end of the book. This piece of work was specifically designed as an essential element of the training materials for the ETS Institute for the Assessment of Minorities. The compendium was written by Ms. Eleanor Horne with the help of the Test Collection Center of which she was the director. The word "minority" was substituted for "disadvantaged" since the latter term tends to have pejorative and objectionable connotations for blacks, Hispanic Americans, and other ethnic minorities. Essentially, the compendium comprises a collection of all instruments designed for those persons who, by virtue of cultural or socioeconomic difference, veer from the white Anglo-Saxon mainstream of American society. However, the use of the word "minority" does not mean to imply that such tests are intended for *all* minority adolescents and adults. For there are many minority adolescents and adults whose life style and background approximate the WASP norm and, therefore, will not fall under the rubric of the compendium.

In essence, this book deals more with social justice than with psychometrics. It is intended to signify and delineate in summary form the important ways in which psychological testing can and does impede the parity of American minorities and deny them access to and participation in the goods of the society.

I wish to acknowledge the help accorded by Mrs. Priscilla Lindsley, the ETS librarian, and her staff. Without them, I would not have had access to the relevant resources. And finally, my recognition and gratitude to my wife, Madeleine, whose editing, reviews, and painstaking efforts helped to make this book a reality.

RONALD J. SAMUDA

PSYCHOLOGICAL TESTING OF AMERICAN MINORITIES: ISSUES AND CONSEQUENCES

Introduction
The Case for the Plaintiffs
The Case for the Defendants
A Trend for Future Testing

THE TESTING CONTROVERSY

1

INTRODUCTION

Several studies of testing made during the past half century have demonstrated that the mean score of blacks is one standard deviation below that of whites, especially on tests that purport to measure levels of intellectual function. This fact, which psychologists, psychometricians, geneticists, and sociologists have known well, especially since the introduction of mass objective-type testing during World War I, did not by itself anger minorities and divide the ranks of educators. Rather, it was the interpretation placed on the differences between the black and white averages and the comparative distribution of scores that has led to the more recent embittered controversy.

The Coleman Report (1966), contrary to expectations, had failed to prove that schools do make a difference (Hodgson 1973). This survey, which was provided for by Section 402 of the Civil Rights Act of 1964, did not show that differences in IQ scores and in test results of basic academic achievement between blacks and whites were significantly related to differences in the physical facilities, curricula, and teacher characteristics of the schools attended by the two groups. Coleman and his associates arrived at the surprising conclusion that, in fact, the educational provisions throughout the country were not too discrepant. They remarked:

1

The first finding is that the schools are remarkably similar in the way they relate to the achievement of their pupils when the socioeconomic background of the students is taken into account. It is known that socioeconomic factors bear a strong relation to academic achievement. When these factors are statistically controlled, however, it appears that differences between schools account for only a small fraction of differences in pupil achievement (Coleman et al. 1966, pp. 21–22).

If the cause of the difference could not be found in the educational environment, then where else could it be? If the direction indicated by nurture proved to be a dead end, why not try nature? Thus the pendulum swung: Some highly publicized papers (Jensen 1969; Herrnstein 1971) argued that heredity and genetic endowment—not environmental factors—were the preponderant determinants in explaining the consistent differences in obtained means between test results of blacks and whites.

To say that blacks score lower than whites because blacks are enslaved by genetic inferiority or because they are the victims of social, economic, and cultural deprivation, which a biased testing system helps to aggravate, is not new. Indeed, in the test performance of black children the part played by heredity, on the one hand, and by environment on the other, has been investigated for a number of years. Long before the works of Shuey (1958) and Dreger and Miller (1960), attempts were made to compile the existing studies on the subject. Among the major reviewers were those, like Pintner (1931), who interpreted blacks' lower scores as a sign of racial inferiority, and others who maintained that these differences were due to the influence of nurture and selection. In the nature-versus-nurture debate Peterson (1923) reconciled both positions by recognizing that environment as well as race accounted for the differences between the scores of blacks and whites. Canady (1946) concerned himself with the problem that tests of mental abilities, standardized almost without exception on samples of white subjects, could not be regarded as adequate measures for comparing blacks and whites. In his pioneer work on test bias Klineberg (1935b) found that various factors such as socioeconomic status, language, amount of schooling, motivation, and speed affected to a lesser or greater degree the scores of black children. Subsequently, his review of the literature in 1944 and North's in 1957 led to the conclusion that there seemed to be no genetic basis for racial differences in intelligence.

However, not before Shuey's *The Testing of Negro Intelligence*, published in 1958 and revised in 1966, was there a complete and thorough review of the intelligence test scores and studies of blacks. In this work Shuey drew upon more than 500 studies covering a period of 50 years, taken from books, articles, published and unpublished monographs, theses, and dissertations which had used 81 different tests of intellectual ability. A careful evaluation of the assembled data convinced Shuey that "all taken together inevitably point to the presence of native differences between Negroes and whites as determined by intelligence tests" (1966, p. 52).

The fundamental issue of the testing controversy was expressed well by Roger Lennon at the 1969 Invitational Conference on Measurement in Education. "There is a deep-seated conviction" Lennon said, "that the performance of poor black, Puerto Rican, Mexican-American or just poverty-stricken examinees on these tests will be relatively poor; that because of this poor performance, inferences will be made as to the ability of these examinees, which inferences will lead to treatment, either in school or on jobs, that will in effect constitute a denial of opportunity" (1970, p. 42). Basically, one can say that the 1960s and early 1970s have raised a new concern. As Lennon also remarked:

> The discussion has moved off the pages of educational and psychological journals onto the pages of mass media. Its forum has moved from the classroom and the psychological laboratory to City Hall and the courtroom. The tone of the discourse has become strident and emotional. The matter of bias and relevancy of test results has become political and central to a great many other concerns in the entire civil rights movement (1970, p. 43).

The debate concerning standardized tests, and especially the interpretations placed on the results or scores of minorities, has intensified in recent years. The public has been alerted to the social, economic, educational, and psychological implications of testing that preserves the status quo and thus relegates blacks and other minorities to an inferior position in the larger society. A cadre of Hispanic-American and black social scientists has spearheaded the attack on the testing industry; many eminent white psychologists, sociologists, and educators have joined the ranks of those who claim that testing serves a gatekeeping function and represents the chief element in retarding the social mobility of minorities and in blocking the path for the poor and deprived to share in the educational opportunities and, by extension, the goods of society.

So far, though, relatively unopposed and unchallenged in their selective and censoring function, the testing organizations have been subjected to a national wave of disenchantment, skepticism, and hostility as evidenced by the numerous lawsuits and court rulings, as well as by the positions taken by the Association of Black Psychologists (ABP) and the American Personnel and Guidance Association (APGA).

THE CASE FOR THE PLAINTIFFS

In 1968 the ABP called for a moratorium on testing, to remain in effect until intelligence tests appropriate for use with black children had been developed. Such a stand was reaffirmed more recently by the Bay Area ABP in the deposition given in connection with the case of *Larry P. et al.* v. *Wilson Riles et al.* (1972) in California. The deposition was stated as follows:

> We, as members and representatives of the Bay Area Association of Black Psychologists strongly affirm that the ability and intelligence tests which are part of the set of criteria mandated by the State Department of Education are inappropriate and inadequate techniques. They are based on white, middle-class norms, values, and experiences and hence are culturally biased against black children. . . . It is thus imperative that we stop whatever enterprise that victimizes, oppresses and denies the full realization of black children's potential. In conclusion, we the members and representatives of the Bay Area Association of Black Psychologists reiterate our unequivocal stand and call for an immediate moratorium on the use of the current tests of intellectual ability in use in the State of California.

After this call for a moratorium on testing, other organizations proceeded to pass similar resolutions. On March 25, 1970, for example, the Senate of the APGA issued the following declaration:

> BE IT RESOLVED: That the American Personnel and Guidance Association through the Association for Measurement and Evaluation in Guidance develop and disseminate a position paper stating the limitations of group intelligence tests particularly and generally of standardized psychological educational and employment testing for low socioeconomic and underprivileged and nonwhite individuals in educational business and industrial environments.
>
> BE IT ALSO RESOLVED: That if demonstrable progress in clarifying and rectifying this situation cannot be achieved by this time next year, proposals for a moratorium on the use of group intelligence tests with these groups be presented.

On July 5, 1974, the NAACP adopted the following resolution at its 65th annual convention:

> WHEREAS, a disproportionately large number of black students are being misplaced in special education classes and denied admissions to higher educational opportunities,
>
> WHEREAS, standardized tests, e.g., Stanford-Binet and the Wechsler Scale for Children exclude blacks, Puerto Ricans and Mexican-Americans from the representative sample, and,

WHEREAS, such tests label black children as uneducable, assign them to lower educational tracks than whites; deny black children higher education opportunities; perpetuate inferior education; place black children in special classes and destroy growth and development of black children, and,

WHEREAS, students who fail to show a high verbal or numerical ability, score low on the Scholastic Achievement Test (SAT), the Law School Admissions Test (LSAT), the Graduate Record Examination (GRE), etc., and are routinely excluded from college and graduate or professional education,

BE IT RESOLVED, that the NAACP demand a moratorium on standardized testing wherever such tests have not been corrected for cultural bias and direct its units to use all administrative and legal remedies to prevent the violation of students' constitutional rights through the misuse of tests, and,

BE IT FURTHER RESOLVED, that the NAACP calls upon the Association of Black Psychologists to assert leadership in aiding the College Entrance Examination Board to develop standardized tests which have been corrected for cultural bias and which fairly measure the amount of knowledge retained by students regardless of his or her individual background.

BE IT FINALLY RESOLVED, that the NAACP directs its units to use all administrative remedies in the event of violation of students constitutional rights through the misuse of tests and directs National Office staff to use its influence to bring the CEEB and ABP together to revise such tests.

Briefly stated, the ultimatum contained in the APGA and NAACP resolutions and the stand taken by the ABP with regard to the testing of minorities were the inevitable results of long and repeated abuse. As Robert Williams points out: "The single, most salient conclusion is that traditional ability tests do systematically and consistently lead to assigning of improper and false labels on black children, and, consequently to dehumanization and black intellectual genocide" (1971, p. 62).

The most common individually administered instruments for measuring the intelligence of children in the United States are the Stanford-Binet Intelligence Scales and the Wechsler Intelligence Scale for Children (WISC). Brief examinations of both tests reveal that their standardization samples included no black children. Among the various American versions of the Binet-Simon Intelligence Scales, the Stanford revision emerged as the standard test of intelligence. First developed at Stanford University in 1916 and revised in 1937 by Lewis Terman in collaboration with Maud Merrill, the Stanford-Binet was standardized on a sample comprising 3184 boys and girls ranging in age from one-and-a-half to eighteen years, drawn from 11 states and from urban and rural, high and low socioeconomic environments. In *Measuring Intelligence* Terman and Merrill emphasized that "all subjects are American-born and belong to the white race" (1937, p. 12). Therefore, one must inevitably conclude, along with Kimble and Garmezy, that "the test proved to be of doubtful validity in evaluating the intelligence of foreign-born or Negro children or for comparing their intelligence with that of native white children" (1968, p. 508). A similar statement could be made about the WISC, for the manual issued in 1949 by the Psychological Corporation mentioned that only white children were examined. The chosen sample included 2200 children (1100 boys and 1100 girls) ranging from five to fifteen years of age, who had been carefully screened according to geographical distribution and socioeconomic status. Among those researchers who used the WISC, Dreger and Miller (1960) cited Young and Bright (1954) and Caldwell (1954), who encountered difficulties with the instrument when testing Southern black children. Regarding Young and Bright's study, Dreger and Miller commented: "Not surprisingly in view of its standardization, the WISC was found inappropriate for testing Southern Negro children from 10 to 13 years of age" (p. 367). In the case of the second study (Caldwell 1954), the reviewers remarked: "In this investigation the suggestion is also made that cultural bias results from using the WISC, standardized as it was on a white population" (p. 368).

Group tests of intelligence such as the Otis-Lennon and Lorge-Thorndike were standardized on much larger and more representative samples of the school population. The manual for the Otis-Lennon, for example, states that:

> Procedures used in the selection of school systems for the national standardization program were designed to yield a stratified random-cluster sample of pupils representative of United States school pupils enrolled in grades K-12. . . . In total, approximately 200,000 pupils in 117 school systems drawn from all 50 states participated in the various phases of the national standardization program (1967, p. 23).

The Lorge-Thorndike also was standardized on a large sample comprising more than 180,000 children enrolled in 70 school systems across 42 states and representing very low to very high socioeconomic levels. However, the weakness of such procedures is that they presumed a fairly homogeneous distribution of population within the various social classes; hence they ignored the heavy concentration and overrepresentation of blacks in the lower socioeconomic levels. In both cases, then, norms were established on samples that, despite their appearance, did not provide for an adequate representation of the black population.

Minority psychologists question the validity of individual or group tests like these when they are used with subjects who do not correspond with the ethnocentric, white, middle-class sample upon which these instruments are standardized. They do not feel that such tests measure the intellectual level and potential of minority subjects. As was mentioned earlier, Canady regarded the lack of an adequate instrument to assess the intelligence of blacks as a problem of paramount importance. He wrote:

> It is significant that, almost without exception, all measurements of the Negro have been made with tests standardized chiefly on Northern urban whites. Such a procedure is unjustifiable, for tests are applicable only to individuals similar in their experiential background to the group upon whom they were standardized. . . .
> The unsuitability of attempting to evaluate the intelligence produced by one culture in terms of another and the decided advantage to the group in which the tests arose is obvious. . . . If, therefore, it can be demonstrated that the experiential background of the American Negro child differs appreciably from that of the whites upon whom the tests were standardized the test results may not be used as a measure of the relative innate ability of the two groups (Canady 1946, pp. 411–412).

The most salient objection to testing as it presently exists stems from the fact that, indeed, "the experiential background of the American Negro child differs appreciably from that of the whites upon whom the tests were standardized"; consequently, a grave injustice is done to those who are evaluated by means of standards that are foreign to them. Aside from postulating a normal distribution of the population, standardization procedures have also been based on the assumption that the white, middle-class standards, values, attitudes, beliefs, experiences, and knowledge are the only correct ones, thereby denying minority groups and poor whites the recognition of their cultural distinctiveness. In other words, minority children have been forced to compete on unequal terms with white, middle-class children, giving the latter a marked advantage. It is not surprising, then, that the scores on aptitude and achievement tests are consistently lower for those subjects who differ from the white sample for, as Shimberg (1929) demonstrated, when a test designed for one cultural group is administered to a different cultural group, the test automatically favors the first group and gives low results for the other group.

Thus the black intellectual genocide of which Williams (1971) spoke is being perpetrated when, on the basis of intelligence test scores, minority children are relegated to slow-learners' tracks, educable mentally retarded (EMR), and mentally retarded (MR) classes. The recent case of *Larry P. et al.* v. *Wilson Riles et al.* (1972), the court ruling in the case of *Hobson* v. *Hansen* (1967), and Mercer's study (1971) of mental retardation in Riverside, California—all these emphasize the fact that, in the language of the court, "irreparable harm and injury" are inflicted upon those children who are wrongfully labeled and placed into EMR, MR, or slow-learners' classes (see the section on ability grouping in Chapter 5).

It has been demonstrated experimentally that children tend to behave the way they are expected to behave—that is, they try to meet the expectations of parents, peers, and teachers—thereby consolidating the opinion that teachers, in particular, have of them. Rosenthal and Jacobson (1968), in a widely publicized study,* attempted to demonstrate the validity of the hypothesis that the perceptions and attitudes of the experimenter, the examiner, or the teacher may serve as self-fulfilling prophecies in their interaction with pupils. Although subsequent studies of a similar nature failed to produce corroborative results (Fleming and Anttonen 1970; Gozali and Meyer 1970; Haberman 1970; José and Cody 1971), perceived examiner attitudes and social stereotypes are still believed to be major factors influencing the results of tests and the learning process itself. In a more recent investigation, Rist (1970) reported the observations of an all-black kindergarten class of children who were followed up over a period of two-and-a-half years. In the first and second grades it was found that the organization of the original kindergarten reading groups was largely determined by subjectively interpreted characteristics (such as clothing, body odor, general appearance, and manners) of the students and that the composition of the various groups within the class resembled that of the social structure of the larger society. Rist observed that the placement of a child in one or another reading group was related more to the teacher's perceptions of social stereotypes than to the actual achievement levels of the child. Thus the teacher served unwittingly as a social agent for ensuring that proper "social distance" was maintained among the various strata of the society represented by the children (Rist 1970, p. 444). The picture emerging from this study is one in which "the school strongly shares in the complicity of maintaining the organizational perpetration of poverty and unequal opportunity. This, of course, is in contrast to the formal doctrine of education in this country to ameliorate rather than aggravate the condition of the poor" (p. 447).

Test results can also serve to reinforce social roles by trapping poor and minority students in a vicious circle. At the very outset of their educational careers, on the basis of low test results these students are

* Questions have been raised as to the validity of their data (Snow 1969, Thorndike 1968).

placed in classes for poor performers; when they fail to make progress, which is again measured in terms of tests not geared for them, they fall further and further behind their white peers (Coleman 1966; Deutsch's cumulative deficit phenomenon). Doomed from the very beginning to an inferior education, the socioeconomically deprived student tends to drop out of school early, to accept his role in the larger society as an unskilled worker, and thus maintains a life dependency on menial wages or, possibly, public welfare.

THE CASE FOR THE DEFENDANTS

Since the beginning of psychometrics it has taken many decades for the American public to realize that tests are not infallible but require care and judgment in their use. Objective intelligence testing was pioneered by Arthur Otis, whose paper-and-pencil version of the individually administered Stanford-Binet test was given to millions of servicemen during World War I. The aftermath of the army testing program was the speedy adoption of the objective item in standardized tests of intelligence, aptitude, and educational achievement and in measurement of personality and interests (DuBois 1972, p. 55). Even during that early boom phase of intelligence testing between the two world wars, there were many psychologists and educators who seriously questioned the validity of test results, but there were also many reputable social scientists who subscribed to the notion that IQs represented accurate and absolute measures of innate capacity wholly "apart from any consideration of an individual's environmental opportunities" (Linden and Linden 1968a, p. 52).

Nevertheless, despite the critical reappraisal of intelligence tests since World War II, the publication of test materials has become bigger and bigger business. At least three-fourths of the public school systems in the United States and a large proportion of the private schools have regular testing programs. And, as testing instruments have become more refined, their use has increased and their influence has become more potent and pervasive.

The attack on objective testing, especially IQ testing, culminated in a series of publications during the early 1960s (Hoffman 1962; Gross 1962; Black 1963). The principal criticisms have been reviewed, summarized, and identified by Ebel (1963), Anastasi (1967), and Goslin (1968). In general, critics have suggested the following harmful consequences of educational testing: (1) permanent classification of individuals; (2) invasion of privacy; (3) lack of confidentiality of test scores; (4) limited conceptions of intelligence and ability; (5) domination by the testers; (6) too much testing; and (7) cultural bias (see also Pasanella, Manning, and Findikyan 1967).

In the wake of what Anastasi calls the antitest revolt, responsible test publishers, as well as social scientists in the academic world, have undertaken to reexamine testing instruments in the light of the criticisms. Writers such as Hoffman and Black did less to create the recent furor concerning IQ testing than those psychologists who reaffirmed the genetic argument that IQ results do, indeed, provide a real and relatively accurate estimate of an individual's innate mental ability. The inference that the relatively low scores of blacks and other minorities on standardized tests represent an inherited genetic inferiority brought IQ testing, in particular, and aptitude testing, in general, under the sharp and critical scrutiny of both minority and white social scientists in the United States and other parts of the world.

The CEEB commissioned a task force "to undertake a thorough and critical review of the Board's testing function in American education and to consider possibilities for fundamental changes in the present tests and their use in schools, colleges and universities." Late in 1970, after serious deliberation, the commission presented the board and the public with its recommendations: It stated that the "Board's current tests and associated services are in need of considerable modification and improvement if they are to support equitable and efficient access to America's emerging system of mass post-secondary education" (1970a, p. 63). At the opening of the Thirty-Second Invitational Conference on Testing Problems, William Turnbull, president of Educational Testing Service, also recognized that "we must not only bring education and measurement more in tune with each other but . . . we must insist that both become more attuned to the real needs of our time" (Turnbull 1972). Undoubtedly, there is a willingness on the part of test makers to listen to their critics and help "right the balance" (see Report of the Commission on Tests 1970a) whenever it is found that tests do not serve the interests of the public effectively. On the other hand, the testing industry is not prepared to capitulate to those who demand the abolition of tests. Henry Dyer (1961) pertinently remarked:

> Some of our brasher critics have argued that, since tests are so widely misused, they do constitute a menace to sound education and therefore should be abolished. This argument is specious. It is the same as saying that automobiles should be abolished because they are a menace to human life when reckless drivers are at the wheel. Or it is the same as saying that teachers should be abolished because too many of them make psychometric hash out of marks and test scores (in Chase and Ludlow 1966, p. 45).

The ranks of the defendants of testing comprise many eminent test makers, psychologists, psychometricians, educators, and sociologists who have reacted to the attack by reaffirming unequivocally their positions concerning intelligence testing. Simply stated, the respondents have outlined a number of commonly held misconceptions about tests, in general, and IQ tests, in particular, as the main cause of the problem. In addition, they have attempted to expose what they regard as the fallacy behind a position that advocates abandoning standardized tests. Ebel remarked that:

> Many of the popular articles critical of educational testing that have appeared in recent years do not reflect a very adequate understanding of educational testing, or a very thoughtful, unbiased consideration of its social consequences. . . . What appears in print often seems to be only an elaboration and documentation of prejudices and preconceptions, supported by atypical anecdotes and purposefully selected quotations. Educational testing has not fared very well in these articles (1963, pp. 130–131).

Laymen as well as experts still commonly confuse the measure called IQ with the concept of intelligence. Confusion is rife over the meaning of "intelligence" for lack of a consensual definition of the term; yet over the years many definitions have been proposed (see Chapter 2). And whether they are the definitions proposed by Binet, Terman, Boring, Stoddard, Goddard, Wechsler, Burt, Vernon, Guildford, or Hunt, all differ in some more or less marked degrees. Moreover, there has been a tendency to regard intelligence as an entity and to assume that it "lies buried in pure form deep in the individual and needs only to be uncovered by ingenious mining methods" (Wesman 1968a, p. 269).

The belief that intelligence tests measure something innate —fixed at the moment of conception and for all time—still persists. This is not to say that such a notion is altogether nonsensical and that Helvetius' claim *l'éducation peut tout* ("education is all important") is altogether acceptable. What is absurd is to think that intelligence tests measure anything else but psychometric intelligence, or simply, what the individual has learned. For Wesman, intelligence refers to the sum total of all the learning experiences that an individual has uniquely had at any moment in time (1968a p. 273). "It is absurd to suppose," Dyer (1961) asserts, "that a child's score on an intelligence test . . . gets directly at the brains he was born with" (in Chase and Ludlow 1966, p. 41). Thus what an intelligence-test score indicates is "the quality of a pupil's performance on a number of mental tasks. It tells how well he can cope with tasks like those on the test at the time he takes the test, and it tells nothing more" (Dyer 1960, p. 395). Addressing administrators and teachers of the Boston Schools, Lennon expressed the same view:

Intelligence, for the man in the street, and indeed even for professionals, carries connotations that are not sustainable in the application of the test score to an understanding of a child. Particularly, there persists a tendency to regard the score as an index of native endowment, and to ascribe to it a mystical constancy or fixity-notions that the test-makers are the first to disavow. Why not regard a child's score on a mental ability test as merely the best index of his present state of readiness to cope with the classroom learning tasks and, as such, a vital guide in planning appropriate instruction? (1964, pp. 8–9).

An illustration of the possible damage that can result from the comparisons of IQs yielded by different tests is given by Good (1954). He called attention to the fact that the standard deviations used by different intelligence tests vary from about 10 to 26. For instance,

... a very bright youngster might have, taking extremes, an IQ of 130 on one test and an IQ of 178 on another. Or a child might have an IQ of 80 on one test and be judged a bit subnormal and have an IQ of 48 on another and be classified as an imbecile by the scoring (in Chase and Ludlow 1966, p. 178).

Thus Good advocates that teachers be aware of some elementary statistics in order to avoid such disastrous consequences.

To prevent further confusion and further misinterpretations as to what an IQ test really measures, many requests have been made that the term "intelligence" or "IQ" be abandoned altogether (Le Sage and Riccio 1970; Anastasi 1967; Lennon 1964; Ebel 1963; Dyer 1961; Good 1954). Ebel recommended that:

One of the important things test specialists can do to improve the social consequences of educational testing is to discredit the popular conception of the IQ. Wilhelm Stern, the German psychologist who suggested the concept originally, saw how it was being overgeneralized and charged one of his students coming to America to "kill the IQ." Perhaps, we would be well advised, even at this late date, to renew our efforts to carry out his wishes (1963, p. 135).

Moreover, the defendants of testing have repeatedly emphasized that tests are being misused and scores misinterpreted by teachers, counselors, administrators, admission officers, and the public at large. In response to the question of unfairness in testing, the authors of the *Standards for Development and Use of Educational and Psychological Tests* suggested that denial of equal opportunity "more often seems due to misuses of tests" (1973, p. II) than to the test themselves. Similarly, Goldman emphasized the frequent misinterpretations of test results:

Sometimes, the interpreter implies a degree of precision that does not exist (such as, "his IQ is 119"); sometimes, he compares scores which are not comparable because of differences in norm groups; sometimes, he implies a prediction for which there is absolutely no basis in either "statistical" or "clinical" validation. . . . It is becoming clear that we need to be much more concerned than we have been in the past with the *use* of tests and with the *users* (1961, p. 2).

In other words, what is needed is more and better education and training in the proper methods of test selection, administration, and interpretation (Karmel 1970; Mehrens and Lehman 1969; Messick and Anderson 1970; Clemans 1970; Bennett 1970; Sommer 1970). The test can only answer for its meaningfulness: Does it do what it purports to do? One cannot hold a test accountable for the ways in which it is used. Ebel (1968, p. 385) contends that it is the responsibility of the teacher or counselor to ensure that tests are used as well as they possibly can be, so that they become useful and valuable tools for the facilitation of learning. The burden of responsibility shifts, therefore, onto the test user, whose duty it is to be alert to and eliminate unfair circumstances, biased items, and inappropriate questions. A test is a tool, and as such not a bad device per se. To say that a test is fair or unfair is inaccurate, for "it is the particular use of a test, not the test itself, which is fair or unfair. A test may be fair for one use and not for another" (Darlington 1971, p. 72). For Darlington, the fair use of a test involves consideration of test scores as well as differences in socioeconomic and cultural backgrounds.

Some educators claim that IQ tests, especially, are used as sorting devices for group placement, and, as stated previously, such practices lead to frequent mislabeling and poor learning environments that divert the education of blacks and other minorities into a barely elementary and functional level. Those who manage to survive the hurdles and reach the top grades of the high school must face another barrier—the Scholastic Aptitude Test (SAT). Though the SAT is not strictly an IQ test, it is frequently regarded by both taker and user as if it were a test of capacity to reason abstractly and therefore as a determinant of the fitness of an individual to undertake higher education. The SAT has been blamed for keeping minority students out of college, for serving a gatekeeping function, and for holding back many minority students —especially blacks—who might have succeeded in completing college had the criteria for entrance been determined differently (Davis and Temp 1971). In an effort to investigate item bias, Cleary and Hilton defined bias as follows:

An item of a test is said to be biased for members of a particular group, if on that item, the members of the group obtain an average score which differs from the average score of other groups by more or less than expected from performance on other items of the same test. That is, the biased item produces an uncommon discrepancy between the performance of members of the group and members of other groups (1968, p. 61).

In a subsequent article Cleary gave another possible definition of bias:

A test is biased for members of a subgroup of the population if, in the prediction of a criterion for which the test was designed, consistent nonzero errors of prediction are made for members of the subgroup. In other words, the test is biased if the criterion score predicted from the common regression line is consistently too high or too low for members of the subgroup. With this definition of bias, there may be a connotation of "unfair" particularly if the use of the test produces a prediction that is too low (1963, p. 115).

On the basis of the preceding definitions, Preliminary Scholastic Aptitude Test (PSAT) items were investigated and found to be fair or unbiased; that is, "there were few items producing an uncommon discrepancy between the performance of Negro and white students" (Cleary and Hilton 1968, p. 70). The second study by Cleary (1968) examined the possibility that the SAT—as a whole—might not be a valid predictor of the performance of blacks in integrated colleges. Such a possibility had been suggested by Clark and Plotkin (1963). In the three colleges she studied—two Eastern and one Southwestern, with a total of 21,000 students—

. . . there was little evidence that the Scholastic Aptitude Test is biased as a predictor of college grades. In the two eastern schools, there were not significant differences in the regression lines for Negro and white students. In the one college in the southwest, the regression lines for Negro and white students were significantly different: the Negro students' scores were overpredicted by the use of the white or common regression lines (Cleary 1968, p. 123).

According to Cleary's definition of test bias, the last investigation suggested a slight bias in favor of blacks; that is, it was predicted that they would do better than they actually did. Previous evidence had also been obtained suggesting that the predictive validity of the SAT for blacks in black colleges was as high as that of whites (Biaggio 1966; Hills, Klock, and Lewis 1963; Stanley and Porter 1967; Roberts 1962). Also, "differences in score distributions do not, per se, constitute evidence of unfairness" (Thorndike 1971, p. 64). What the discrepancy may very well record, instead, is the unfairness of some human conditions. As Wechsler (1966) wrote: "It is true that the results of intelligence tests and of others too, are unfair to the disadvantaged, deprived and various minority groups, but it is not the IQ that has made them so. The culprits are poor housing, broken homes, a lack of basic opportunities etc., etc." (in Spielberger, Fox, and Masterton 1968, p. 309).

One persistent point made by the defenders of the IQ test is that unless children enjoy equality of opportunity to learn what is required to perform on intelligence tests, differences will inevitably recur because of the varied backgrounds of the children (Good, 1954). In fact, tests are regarded as being good indicators of who is "disadvantaged." They help sort out those who need educational guidance from those who do not.

Test defenders also say that, just as tests cannot be blamed for the deficiencies of the child, neither can they be accused of reflecting white, middle-class values, standards, experiences, and language. Nor, for that matter, can the school bear the weight of the accusation, for what else could it be but middle class? Some contend that to condemn the American educational system for its ethnocentric view of human life is to lack historical judgment. Indeed, neither European nor American schools were initially designed for the populace. Education was traditionally the prerogative of the elite; the New England grammar schools, for example, and Benjamin Franklin's Academy, were institutions reserved for a few—the boys of the upper middle and the upper classes. Nor were American schools intended to accommodate black children and allow for the coexistence of a plurality of values, experiences, and languages that millions of immigrants brought along with them. The melting pot theory and the Americanization process became one of the major tenets of the school system. Today, however, that very tenet is being challenged.

Finally, those who entertain the notion that tests must be abandoned are, in the opinion of Lennon (1964), guilty of trying to burn the barn to catch the mouse. The elimination of all testing would not, ipso facto, eradicate the needs that it presently serves. Therefore, in lieu of tests, another means would have to be provided. It is not unlikely that subjective appraisals would surface again and thus increase the likelihood of bias and discrimination (Messick and Anderson 1970). Ebel, among others, has enumerated what some of the social consequences of not testing would be:

> If the use of educational tests were abandoned, the distinctions between competence and incompetence would become more difficult to discern . . . the encouragement and reward of individual efforts to learn would be made more difficult. Excellence in programs of education would become less tangible as a goal and less demonstrable as an attain-

ment. Educational opportunities would be extended less on the basis of aptitude and merit and more on the basis of ancestry and influence; social class barriers would become less permeable. Decisions on important issues of curriculum and method would be made less on the basis of solid evidence and more on the basis of prejudice or caprice (1963, pp. 142–143).

Messick and Anderson (1970) seem to concur with Ebel's view that "the social consequences of not testing . . . are potentially far more harmful than any possible adverse consequences of testing" (Ebel 1963, p. 143). In addition, they warn against the prospect of time-consuming methods of collecting information about students, the increase in parochialism due to the loss of national norms and standards, and the loss of educational accountability.

Those who help to construct tests and who earn a living from the testing industry are, understandably, against any hint of the abolition of tests. Though they acknowledge that tests are not perfect and infallible instruments, they point out that tests have allowed merit to shine through and opened the door to a more equitable distribution of opportunities. In his address to the 1971 Invitational Conference on Testing Problems, DuBois reiterated that measurement has increased human opportunity and revealed unsuspected talent. "We may not have turned many of the mute and inglorious into Miltons," DuBois said, "but in some instances at least the mute and inglorious have become physicians, lawyers, engineers, scientists and educators" (p. 54).

A TREND FOR FUTURE TESTING

Though it is too early to know the outcome of the testing debate, a general trend can be discerned. The attacks upon the testing industry probably will not result in the abolition of objective testing, nor is it certain that the example of the New York City school system, which discontinued and subsequently banned the use of group intelligence tests (Loretan 1966), will be followed en masse. Rather, it seems that the tide is turning more toward an expansion and an elaboration of psychometrics. But if test makers and users are to discharge their functions responsibly, changes are indeed mandatory.

Such was the opinion of the drafters of the "Guidelines for Testing Minority Group Children" (Fishman et al. 1964). Basically, the message conveyed by the authors reflected the old adage: "Don't throw out the baby with the bath water." Although tests have not proved to be the panacea everyone hoped for, they are, nonetheless, "among the most important evaluative and prognostic tools that educators have at their disposal" (p. 143). In an attempt to clarify the situation, Fishman and his associates outlined what, in their view, constitutes the principal source of difficulty when using standardized tests with minority groups. Three major problems were identified: (1) tests may lack reliable differentiation in the range of minority-group scores, which tend to cluster at the lower end of the total range; (2) tests may not predict for the minority child what they predict for the white, middle-class child; (3) test results should be interpreted by professionally trained personnel who possess a thorough understanding of the sociocultural background of the group being tested. In addition, the authors suggested certain possible modifications to be introduced into the structure of existing tests and into the procedure for administering tests. Reiterating their belief that good test usage depends upon conscientious, methodical, and critical examination of test scores, Fishman and his associates concluded:

> Many comparisons depend upon tests, but they also depend upon *our* intelligence, our good will, and our sense of responsibility to make the proper comparison at the proper time and to undertake proper remedial and compensatory action as a result. The misuse of tests with minority group children, or in any situation, is a serious breach of professional ethics. Their proper use is a sign of professional and personal maturity (1964, p. 144).

The essential philosophy of the "Guidelines" views the disadvantaged from a cultural-deprivation perspective, that is to say, the environment, not the genes, has failed him. But even this seemingly more equalitarian view has been attacked on the ground that it explains the intellectual behavior of minorities in the same terms as the hereditarians, that is, as deficiency or deviance from the white norm (see Chapter 3). Having assumed successively the characteristics of the genetically deficient model and culturally disadvantaged or deprived model, the minority child is now being described in the light of the culturally different model.

TECHNICAL PROBLEMS IN
THE APPRAISAL OF BEHAVIOR

2

INTRODUCTION

Almost without exception, articles and textbooks concerned with educational and psychological testing take great pains in recommending that test buyers and users exercise the utmost judiciousness when selecting and administering tests and interpreting test scores. More recently, this good advice has been reiterated emphatically with respect to the testing of minority groups. As mentioned in Chapter 1, psychologists and psychometricians, in general, and test makers, in particular, have associated the source of the present discontent of minority educators with the assessment (especially intellectual assessment) of minority individuals with the long and repeated abuses perpetrated by teachers, counselors, admission officers, and so on. Goldman quotes a *Newsweek* special report on testing in which Harold Seashore, vice-president of Psychological Corporation, remarked that:

> The biggest problem today is not the tests themselves. . . . It is getting a supply of competent professionals to interpret and make proper use of the tests. For every $500.00 a school spends on the tests themselves, it should spend $15,000.00 on salaries for personnel to supervise and interpret the tests (in Goldman 1961, p. 2).

In the introductory section of the "Guidelines," Fishman and his associates expressed the same sentiment:

Responsible educational authorities recognize that it is as unwise to put tests in the hands of untrained and unskilled personnel as it is to permit the automobile or any highly technical and powerful tool to be handled by individuals who are untrained in its use and unaware of the damage that it can cause if improperly used.

The necessity for caution is doubly merited when educational and psychological tests are administered to members of minority groups (1964, p. 130).

RELIABILITY AND VALIDITY

The most important aspect of a test is, undoubtedly, the degree to which it is valid—that is, the extent to which it measures what it was intended to measure. Ebel (1961) has called validity "one of the major deities in the pantheon of the psychometrician" (p. 640). Another essential one is reliability.

Reliability and validity are the two most important technical characteristics of a test. They are also the two necessary conditions for the existence of a test as a viable tool of measurement, for of what use is a test that does not fulfill its function? Of what use is a test that does not provide consistent measurements? Clearly, "no test can be valid unless it is reliable" (Wesman 1952); conversely, although reliability is a highly desired quality, it does not, however, ensure the validity of a test. Gronlund has illustrated the nature of the relationship between reliability and validity as follows:

As with a witness testifying in a courtroom trial—the fact that he consistently tells the same story does not guarantee that he is telling the truth. The truthfulness of his statements can be determined only by comparing them with some other evidence. Similarly, with evaluation results, consistency is an important quality but only if it is accompanied by truthfulness, and truthfulness, or validity, must be determined independently. Little is accomplished if evaluation results consistently provide the wrong information (1971, p. 76).

As the term indicates, "reliability refers to the consistency of scores obtained by the same individuals when re-examined with the same test on different occasions, or with different sets of equivalent items, or under other variable examining conditions" (Anastasi 1968a, p. 71). Thus if an intelligence test yields a score of 116 for a particular individual and two weeks later the same individual scores 84 when the same test is administered under the same conditions, then it follows that the reliability of the test is highly suspect. No test, however, can be perfectly reliable, for psychological measurements, unlike physical measurements, are affected by a number of sources of variance or error, which Mehrens and Lehmann identified as trait instability, sampling error, administrator error, scoring error, health, motivation, degree of fatigue of the person, good or bad luck in guessing (1969, p. 33). Thus it is essential for a test to state how reliable it is so that users are aware of the degree to which it will provide accurate measurements. A measure of reliability is given in the form of a reliability coefficient ranging from 0 to 1.0, with the most typical value being somewhere between 0.85 and 0.90.

It is not the purpose of this present discussion to examine in any detail the different types of reliability coefficients. It is enough to say that there are various ways of estimating reliability, including internal consistency, test-retest, and interform techniques (see Anastasi 1968a, pp. 78–85). Rather, attention will focus on those factors affecting reliability coefficients and their implications for the test results of minority-group members.

A variety of factors are known to influence the reliability of a test. Durost and Prescott (1962) have categorized them according to their effect on the different types of reliability coefficients. It is apparent that test length (the fewer the items, the lower the reliability), item difficulty, group heterogeneity (the more heterogeneous the group, the higher the reliability), and, most important for the purposes of this discussion, spread of scores, all affect the reliability of a test. Although the range of minority test scores comes close to overlapping that of whites, whose scores are spread across the entire distribution, the test results of minorities tend to cluster at the lower end of the scale with little differentiation among them. Wesman (1952), notably, has shown that the narrower the range of scores, the lower the coefficient of reliability. He concluded that:

> A test may discriminate with satisfactory precision among students with wide ranges of talent but not discriminate equally well in a narrow range of talent. A yardstick is unsatisfactory if we must differentiate objects varying in length from 35.994 to 36.008 inches. . . . It should be obvious, then, that no reliability coefficient can be properly interpreted without information as to the spread of ability in the group on which it is based (in Gronlund 1968, p. 197).

Consistently, then, minority children are assessed by means of tests that do not indicate the value of the reliability coefficient for their group. They only tell how reliable tests are with the sample groups upon whom reliability was first established. As a result, for those groups that differ from the sample group, that is, for minorities, the "actual effectiveness of the test will tend to be lower than the reported reliability coefficient appears to promise" (Fishman et al. 1964, p. 131). High reliability coefficients are only high for the reliability sample and those groups that approximate it. They will tend to be much lower for groups that are more homogeneous and have a smaller range of talent than the reference group. In its set of recommendations the "Guidelines" emphasizes the fact that:

> The sensitive test user should be alert to reliability considerations in regard to the particular group involved and the intended use of the test. In assessing reports . . . he will not be satisfied with high reliability coefficients alone. He will consider not only the size of the reliability samples, but also the nature and composition of the samples and the procedures used to estimate reliability. He will try to determine whether the standard error of measurement varies with score levels and whether his testing conditions are similar to those of the reliability samples. He will ask whether the evidence on reliability is relevant to the persons and purposes with which he is concerned. He will know that high reliability does not guarantee validity of the measures for the purpose in hand, but he will realize that low reliability may destroy validity (Fishman et al. 1964, p. 133).

Although the concept of validity has always been recognized as an essential and indispensable characteristic of a test, it has suffered from a lack or, more precisely, from an abundance of definitions (Ebel 1961). What constitutes a valid test and how is its validity to be measured? In order to answer this question a joint committee of the American Psychological Association, the American Educational Research Association, and the National Council on Measurement and Education proposed guidelines in 1954, which were revised in 1966, and then extended in 1973 as the *Standards for Development and Use of Educational and Psychological Tests*. The validity of a test refers to "the degree to which the test is capable of achieving certain aims" (French and Michael, in Gronlund 1968, p. 166). Thus if one of these aims is to measure Johnny's ability to spell, the test he is given must have good content validity; if another aim is to establish Johnny's chance of entering college, the test he is given must have good predictive validity; finally, if the test user wants to know how creative Johnny is, the test the child is given must have good construct validity. This does not mean, however, that a test may fulfill only one aspect of validity, but rather, depending upon its purpose, one facet of a test's validity will be emphasized over the others. The *Standards* recognizes three types of validation procedures: content validity, criterion-related validity, and construct validity.

    Content Validity. This type of validation "is demonstrated by showing how well the content of the test samples the class of situations or subject-matter about which conclusions are to be drawn" (French and Michael, in Gronlund 1968, p. 166). Thus a test has good content validity if its items relate well to the particular objectives to be assessed. The appropriateness of a test item can only be determined by careful and critical examination. Furthermore, in the selection of test items, efforts must be made to ensure that all possible relevant sources (textbooks, curricula, experts, and so on) have been sampled so as to cover all major aspects of the area under consideration and to avoid the intrusion of extraneous factors that could lower the test's content validity. Such a validation procedure is particularly essential for evaluating achievement tests.

Two major assumptions are made in this validation procedure with respect to scholastic aptitude or mental ability: (1) test takers have been exposed to and are familiar with the universe of information from which test items are drawn; (2) the language of the test is the language of the test takers. In the case of the Stanford-Binet, for instance, children are asked to identify "common objects" presented in the form of pictures or toy models, to explain why certain objects are employed in daily living, and to interpret pictorially presented situations (Anastasi 1968a). Yet a quick glance at the so-called common objects reveals that children of cultural backgrounds that differ from that of the norm group may not be completely familiar with some of the content of the test items. While books, periodicals, and objects of art, especially, are frequent and common in the world of the white middle-class, they are almost nonexistent in the ghetto milieu. A child of the slums who is asked to respond to the question "Why do we have books?" may very well be at a serious disadvantage. Taylor (1971) has emphasized the fact that many common words have very different meanings for blacks than they have for whites. Angoff and Ford (1973) have found that blacks can answer correctly more items that deal with modern culture. Klineberg reports that when West Virginia rural blacks were asked to give the opposite of a word, no answer was given because they did not know the meaning of "opposite." He remarked: "If they were required to take the Otis test as a written examination, in the usual manner, they would naturally make a zero score on all the 'opposite' items" (1935b, p. 169).

Furthermore, strong emphasis is placed in the Stanford-Binet and in many standardized group intelligence tests on the definition of abstract words, on sentence completion, on analogies, and so on, which all presuppose a certain mastery in the comprehension and usage of standard English and a certain ease with the subtleties of grammar. Many instances have been reported in which the speaker of the black vernacular gave "nonsensical" answers because he did not understand what was required of him or because he was not familiar with the examiner's pronunciation.

Criterion-Related Validity. This type of validity "is demonstrated by comparing the test scores with one or more external variables considered to provide a direct measurement of the characteristic or behavior in question" (French and Michael, in Gronlund 1968, p. 167). Criterion-related validity is generally predictive in nature. In intelligence tests academic achievement is the criterion against which test scores are validated. It is predicted, therefore, that a high test score forecasts success at school or college and that, conversely, a low test score indicates a relatively low chance of success in the pursuit of academic enterprises. The degree to which intelligence tests have good predictive validity depends upon the degree to which both the criterion and the test score are devoid of contaminants. Fishman and his associates (1964) identified three categories of factors that impair a test's predictive validity with respect to minority test takers.

The first category concerns those factors that influence test scores. The literature abounds in studies that have demonstrated that external variables such as nutrition, self-concept, anxiety, and motivation can affect the performance of minority children on tests purporting to measure their intellectual functioning (see Chapter 4). Klineberg has illustrated the fact that speed, upon which the large majority of tests depend in more or less pronounced degrees, is basically a culturally oriented concept. He states:

> The attitude toward speed varies greatly in different cultures and not all peoples will work on the tests with equal interest in getting them done in the shortest time possible. Peterson and his associates (1925) have noted this relative indifference to speed among Negroes and the writer found that the injunction to "do this as quickly as you can" seemed to make no impression whatsoever on the American Indian children on the Yakima reservation in the state of Washington (1935b, p. 159).

Additionally, scores have been shown to increase when good rapport exists between the examiner and the examinee. In the case of black children, especially when they are being tested for intelligence, the race of the examiner greatly influences their subsequent performance (see Chapter 4). Likewise, familiarity with testing procedures, the testing center, test format, test instructions, and test-taking skills also affect, to a certain extent, the test results (see Chapter 4).

The second category of factors considered by Fishman and his associates relates to the criterion itself—that is, school grades. Do school grades give a true and accurate measure of a child's, and particularly a minority child's, scholastic aptitude? Or are they subject to the influence of some other variables that are unrelated to success at school? "Grades are likely to reflect motivation, classroom behavior, personal appearance, and study habits, as well as intelligence and achievement" the authors assert (Fishman et al. 1964, p. 136). Additionally, other variables such as knowledge of IQ scores, financial status of the family, dwelling area, number of siblings, and so on, all contribute, to a large extent, to the formation of stereotyped notions about a given individual's expected performance in school and his potential to achieve and to the determination of his rating. Subsequent to the Rosenthal and Jacobson (1968) study of educational self-fulfilling prophecies, a number of studies have documented the fact that teachers' expectations not only color their judgments of their students but also influence the students' perceptions of themselves, their attainments, and their aspirational levels (see Chapter 4).

Finally, according to Fishman's third factor, criterion validity is lowered whenever the period between the administration of the test and the obtainment of the criterion measure is lengthy. Fishman et al. state:

> An illness, an inspiring teacher, a shift in aspiration level or in direction of interest, remedial training, an economic misfortune, an emotional crisis, a growth spurt or retrogression in the abilities sampled by the test—any of these changes intervening between the testing and the point or points of criterion assessment may decrease the predictive power of the test (1964, pp. 136–137).

Construct Validity. This type of test validity "is evaluated by investigating what qualities a test measures, that is, by determining the degree to which certain explanatory concepts or constructs account for performance on the test. . . . Essentially, studies of construct validity check on the theory underlying the test" (French and Michael, in Gronlund 1968, p. 167). Because traits such as intelligence, motivation, interest, creativity, are not observable and thus cannot be measured directly, it is essential in order to obtain information as to whether individuals possess these traits to build a theory specifying the characteristics of the trait in question. It is generally hypothesized that those who possess a particular construct, like intelligence, behave differently from those who do not. By observing the two extremes—an extremely intelligent person and an extremely stupid person—a list of differentiating characteristics can be established. Maslow has provided an extensive picture of the respective behavior of the intelligent man and the unintelligent man. Generally speaking, "an extremely intelligent man, when compared with an extremely stupid man, solves his problems, intellectual and personal, more rapidly ·. . . he behaves generally in a manner that we call more efficient, more functional, more intelligent" (Maslow 1944, p. 85). Thus a theory is built specifying how intelligent people behave, and individuals are classified accordingly. Because the concept of intelligence has been and still is a concern of major importance, a detailed examination is necessary.

THE CONCEPT OF INTELLIGENCE

The advent of World War I made large-scale intelligence testing a reality of civilian life. Due primarily to the pioneer work of Otis, Terman's student, the army psychologists developed tests that came to be known as the Army Alpha and Beta, which they administered to over 1 million soldiers to sort and classify them according to intellectual levels and capacities. By the time World War II began, mass testing had become an established practice everywhere in America and its production was a booming and lucrative business. Used extensively by schools, colleges, and employers (Goslin 1965), intelligence tests play a vital part at all stages and in every aspect of a person's life. From preschool days through postgraduate years, tests are administered for grouping and course-selection purposes, for placement in special education classes or special institutions, for career orientation, for college entrance, and for admission to the professions. A person's IQ score largely determines the kind of education he receives and, ultimately, the kind of position he occupies within society. Therefore, the concept of intelligence, whether stated in terms of mental ability, intelligence quotient, or scholastic aptitude, is central to an individual's life.

What Is an Intelligence Test?

An intelligence test provides in the form of a symbol such as the IQ a global, overall estimate of a person's intellectual ability. In the case of the original intelligence test developed by Binet and Simon the score was a relative one expressed in terms of mental age. As Maslow remarked, "it could say only that little Jacques had more intelligence than little Pierre and less intelligence than Anatole" (1944, p. 89). It was Stern who introduced the notion of intelligence quotient, the quotient of the child's mental age (MA) and his chronological age (CA). The following formula was derived:

$$IQ = \frac{MA}{CA} \times 100 \text{ (decimals eliminated)}$$

Tyler compared mental age to "the size of a boy's suit or a girl's dress. We tell people how big Susie is physically when we say that she wears a size 10. We tell them how big she is mentally when we say that her MA is 10" (1963, p. 44). The 1960 revision of the Stanford-Binet provided, among various refinements, for a similar computation of the IQ as the one used in the case of group intelligence tests. The IQ is no longer merely a quotient, but rather a standard score with a mean of 100 and a standard deviation of 15. Therefore, "what an individual IQ really tells us is how many standard deviations above or below average a person is" (Tyler 1963, p. 45). The excessive popularity that the IQ has received over the years is to be deplored, for it was and still is frequently misused, and its meaning is repeatedly misinterpreted.

The Various Definitions of Intelligence

Intelligence is a concept that has always been a major concern of psychology. Given such a degree of importance, one is stunned that, to date, there is no consensual definition of what is meant by the term "intelligence." Yet over the years many definitions have been proposed; so many, in fact, that Spearman (1927) felt that it had become "a mere vocal sound, a word with so many meanings that finally it had none." When in 1921 the *Journal of Educational Psychology* published a series of articles on intelligence, all written by prominent psychologists, little agreement could be found among the fourteen distinct definitions that emerged (Tyler 1969). If the experiment were to be replicated today, the same ambiguity that existed some 50 years ago would still be apparent, for one need only look at the more common definitions of intelligence in order to realize that psychologists still have not characterized explicitly and universally what it means. The following is a list of some of the ways in which intelligence has successively been defined:

1. The capacity to judge well, to reason well, and to comprehend well (Binet and Simon)
2. The ability to carry on abstract thinking (Terman)
3. The capacity to do well in an intelligence test (Boring)
4. The ability to undertake activities that are characterized by difficulty, complexity, abstractness, economy, adaptiveness to a goal, social value, emergence of originals, and to maintain such activities under conditions that demand a concentration of energy and of resistance to emotional forces (Stoddard)
5. The aggregate or global capacity of the individual to act purposefully, to think rationally, and to deal effectively with the environment (Wechsler)

6. The degree of availability of one's experiences for the solution of immediate problems and the anticipation of future ones (Goddard)
7. Innate, general, cognitive ability (Burt)
8. The outcome of the interplay of innate potentiality and of such conditions as good emotional adjustment and appropriate educational stimulation (Vernon).

Such a plethora of definitions suffers from a number of evident weaknesses. First, in their efforts to be all encompassing, most of the definitions use undefined and often undefinable terms, are vague, and therefore reveal very little. Second, overemphasis is placed on the ability to reason abstractly. Third, all tend to regard intelligence as an entity. As Wesman remarked: "We have all too often behaved as though intelligence is a physical substance, like a house or an egg crate composed of rooms or cells; we might better remember that it is no more to be reified than attributes like beauty or speed or honesty" (1968a, p. 267). Finally, most of the definitions of intelligence fail to recognize that what constitutes an act of intelligent behavior is inescapably linked to and determined by the values and standards of society. Intelligence, therefore, is a culture-bound concept inseparable from any given setting or environmental milieu. For the aborigine of Australia, for example, intelligence within the context of his environment will be defined as the composite of those various skills and knowledge of folkways that promote survival—accuracy in the use of a boomerang, the ability to find water, and so on. Likewise, a society geared toward a more naturalistic and primitive mode of life than that found in the West will, inevitably, place greater emphasis on specialized manual skills than on technical and scientific accomplishments. To say that one acts more intelligently than the other would seem absurd, since the environmental stimulation for the development of technology within the primitive society, for instance, simply does not exist.

The Various Theories of Intelligence

From Plato's Chariot with its horses and charioteer,[1] to Guilford's cube (see p. 28), there have been many theories of intelligence. Basically, attempts at defining the nature of intelligence can be classified into two groups: the two-factor theory and the multifactor theory.

---

[1] In *Mental Capacity and Its Critics*, Burt indicates that the word "intelligence" came into everyday parlance rather late—1905 or thereabouts. Popularized by Spencer and Galton, it derived from Cicero's "Intelligentsia" itself a literal translation of the Greek term used by Aristotle to express Plato's "Chariot drawn by a pair of restive horses and steered or guided by a charioteer" (1968, p. 12).

Briefly stated, the first approach can be traced back to Galton's distinction between what he called general ability and special abilities (Burt 1958 and 1968). This theory was based on the belief that mental tests measure, to some extent, one basic intellectual ability, which Spearman called g. Reasoning tests or tests requiring the individual to establish relationships among things were thought to measure g most efficiently (Tyler 1956). The more intelligent a person is, the more g he possesses. Besides this universal or general capacity, which was believed to be true and pure intelligence, there was a specific factor, s, for each different minor type of ability. Spearman's followers, Burt and Vernon in England and Humphreys in the United States, devoted most of their efforts to organizing the multiplicity of specific factors discovered by various investigators into some kind of logical system. Hence we have the hierarchical models of Burt and Vernon, with Spearman's g at the top of the pyramid and various levels of subdivisions (Guilford 1967, pp. 58–59).

As the name suggests, the second approach departs from a theory that links all mental abilities to a common factor. Among the proponents of the multifactorial theory of intelligence, Thurstone, the leading exponent, claimed that intelligence was multifaceted.* He identified seven or eight of these aspects or specific independent abilities, which he called primary mental abilities (PMA), and listed them as follows: verbal comprehension, word fluency, number, space, memory, general reasoning, and speed. Thurstone noticed, however, that there existed some degree of intercorrelation among the primary abilities, for those who excelled at verbal comprehension also tended to evince a high facility for word fluency (Linden and Linden 1968a, pp. 71–74). Espousing Thurstone's approach, Guilford proposed the now famous structure of intellect model (SI) in the shape of a cube (Guilford 1967). The SI model comprises three dimensions: (1) content—four categories; (2) operations—five categories; (3) products—six categories. The cube contains 120 ($4 \times 5 \times 6$) possible cells, each one representing a hypothetical mental ability. By 1967 Guilford announced that out of the 120 factors 82 had already been identified. This brief summary of the two major schools of thought concerning the structure of intelligence is by no means exhaustive, and the reader is advised to refer especially to the aforementioned books and articles in order to get a more comprehensive view of a rather complex notion.

It is not surprising that the editor of the 1969 symposium *On Intelligence*, W. B. Dockrell, found that "intelligence as a concept is

---

* To use Tyler's words (1969), intelligence was essentially a plural word.

alive and well," when the participants of the conference included the famed Burt, Vernon, and Jensen. Yet such an assumption is highly debatable, especially in the light of the recent race-IQ controversy, which, if nothing else, will have uncovered the fallacies of the present IQ tests. First among them is the claim that intelligence tests measure intelligence—a concept that, as shown earlier, has not yet been uniquely or satisfactorily defined—when, at best, such tests reflect the constructor's personal view of what constitutes intelligent behavior. Furthermore, as the debate intensifies, the question becomes not whether Burt or Guilford's model or Boring's definition is correct, but rather whether the whole concept of intelligence is appropriate and useful. Guilford answers positively but qualifies his statement:

> The term "intelligence" is useful, nonetheless. But it should be used in a semi-popular, technological sense. It is convenient to have such a term even though it is one of the many rather shifty concepts we have in applied psychology. It would be very desirable, for purposes of communication and understanding, to specify a number of intelligences —intelligence A, intelligence B and so on. This could be done in terms of the combination of certain intellectual factors and their weighting in the combinations (1956, p. 290).

The Concept of Intelligence in Its Historical Perspective

How did intelligence tests come into existence? How does one explain the fact that IQ tests as they currently exist have, undeniably, been designed with the implicit notion that they measure innate potential, which remains fixed and constant throughout an individual's lifetime? The answers to these questions can only be found in the archives of psychology, which acquired the status of science with the opening of the first psychological laboratory by Wilhelm Wundt at Leipzig in 1879.

The legacy left by the early psychologists was mainly one of methodology, for they contributed little to the testing of intelligence as we understand it now. It is Sir Francis Galton who has been credited with the paternity of individual psychology and mental measurement. An eminent explorer, scientist, and scholar, Galton was undoubtedly one of the most versatile men of his time and left a variety of valuable contributions as diverse as the Galton whistle for detecting sensitivity to high tones, composite pictures, and fingerprint identification. Not surprisingly, in view of the fact that Galton came from a family of long-standing wealth and prominence, he developed an early and intense interest in the study of heredity—specifically the hereditary aspects of what he called genius. In 1869, Galton published his first major work, *Hereditary Genius: An Inquiry into Its Laws and Consequences*, which undisputedly bore the influence of his cousin

Charles Darwin, whose *The Origin of Species* (1859) had become the subject of heated controversy. In *Hereditary Genius*—a title that he explained in the prefatory chapter to the 1892 edition as an "ability that was exceptionally high and at the same time, inborn"—Galton proposed to show that genius tends to run in families (a small number of families) and hence that it is determined by inheritance and influenced only insignificantly by the environment.

> The arguments by which I endeavour to prove that genius is hereditary consists in showing how large the number of instances in which men who are more or less illustrious have eminent kinsfolk. I feel convinced that no man can achieve a very high reputation without being gifted with very high abilities; and I trust that reason has been given for the belief that few who possess these very high abilities can fail in achieving eminence (p. 49).

Galton's conviction of nature's absolute power in determining man's development was in complete opposition to the stand taken by the eighteenth-century French thinker Helvetius and his followers, who firmly believed that differences in people were due to differences in education *(l'education peut tout)*. Galton exemplified the facts of heredity with his studies of one-egg and two-egg twins, which he later included in his second major work, *Inquiries into Human Faculty and Its Development* (1883). Both books unequivocally reflect the belief that since man's mental traits are inherited and remain unaltered by environmental forces, only those superior persons should reproduce and survive in order to improve the human race. In the introductory chapters to *Hereditary Genius* and *Inquiries into Human Faculty,* one reads successively:

> I propose to show in this book that a man's natural abilities are derived by inheritance, under exactly the same limitations as are the forms and physical features of the whole organic world. Consequently, as it is easy, notwithstanding those limitations, to obtain by careful selection a permanent breed of dogs and horses gifted with peculiar powers of running, or of doing anything else, so it would be quite practicable to produce a highly gifted race of men by judicious marriages during several consecutive generations (p. 45).

and

> My general purpose has been to take note of the varied hereditary faculties of different families and races, to learn how far history may have shown the practicability of supplanting inefficient human stock by better strains, and to consider whether it might not be our duty to do so by such efforts as may be reasonable, thus exerting ourselves to further the ends of evolution more rapidly and with less distress than if events were left to their own course (quoted in Peterson 1925, p. 74).

In 1884 Galton set out to classify people at his laboratory at the Kensington Museum in London. There were over 9000 persons were tested by means of simple sensory and motor tests, for Galton believed that the ablest (hence the most intelligent) individuals would demonstrate the highest sensory discrimination. For a small fee, a person could get information concerning his height, weight, breathing power, keenness of vision and hearing, memory, strength of pull and squeeze, and reactions to color, time, and the like. These tests did not prove as successful as Galton had anticipated, however, for they did not allow him to make any important generalizations concerning individual differences. As Hunt remarked: "Had Galton's types of tests proved efficient in differentiating those who would achieve with distinction from those who would not, the use of tests to determine those who should reproduce themselves would have been only a short step" (1961, p. 12). It was in Galton's anthropometric laboratory that psychometrics began. From Quetelet—the Belgian mathematician who introduced the concept of the average man—Galton borrowed and applied the normal law of error to psychological traits, notably, to the measurement of intelligence. Assisted by his student and biographer-to-be, Karl Pearson, Galton introduced such statistical concepts as the standard-deviation units to represent all possible scores, the theory of correlation, and the principle of regression to the mean (or regression to mediocrity as he called it).

Meanwhile, on the other side of the Channel, the French were concentrating their attention and efforts on the study of mental retardation and emotional and social maladjustment. Especially creditable is the work of the physician Esquirol, the psychiatrist Itard, and the creator of the Vineland Training School for the mentally retarded, Edouard Seguin, who had established a similar institution in Paris but was forced to leave his country for political reasons. The reader is already familiar with the names of the psychologist Binet and the physician Simon, who together published the first successful test of intelligence. From its very beginning the Binet-Simon scale answered the practical and urgent demand of the French minister of public instruction for the creation of special education classes for those children who could not benefit from regular classroom instruction. To identify the defective, mentally retarded child from the normal child was the aim of the 1905 scale of intelligence devised by Binet and Simon. They wrote:

> Our purpose is by no means to study, to analyze and to disentangle the aptitudes of persons inferior in intelligence. That will be the object of a later work. Here we limit ourselves to the evaluation and quantitative determination of their intelligence in general. We shall determine their

intellectual level; and to give an idea of this level we shall compare it with that of normal children of the same age, or of an analogous level (quoted in Peterson 1925, p. 167).

The original Binet-Simon scale was comprised of thirty simple, rapid, and precise tasks or subtests "bearing principally on the faculty of judgment." Unlike the Galtonian tests, which they had criticized for being too sensory and too simple, the first scale of intelligence tapped essentially what the authors believed to be the fundaments of intelligence: that is, the ability to judge well, to comprehend well, and to reason well. Although Binet had borrowed and adopted the term "intelligence" as popularized by Galton and Spencer, he refuted and strongly opposed the widespread belief that it was "a fixed quantity." There is no doubt that Binet believed that intelligence could be improved by training, and to support his statement he cited the progress made by the children identified as mentally retarded during the first year of their enrollment in the special education classes. In the nature-nurture dichotomy Binet recognized the importance of nurture upon test performance and the necessity of controlling the cultural factors pervading his tests, which, it had been demonstrated, favored upper- and middle-class children while putting the children of the working classes at a disadvantage. These factors Binet identified as "home-training, attention, motivation, language, habit of looking at pictures and scholastic exercise." By the time the second edition of the intelligence scale was ready (1908), Binet and Simon had realized that their test did not measure just intellectual capacity. They remarked:

> It is something far more complex that we measure. The result depends first, on the intelligence pure and simple; second, on extra scholastic acquisition capable of being gained precociously; third, on scholastic acquisitions made at a fixed date; fourth, on acquisitions relative to language and vocabulary which are at once scholastic and extrascholastic, depending partly on the school and partly on the family circumstances (Binet and Simon 1916, p. 259).

James McKeen Cattell first introduced intelligence tests to the American scene. A self-proclaimed disciple of Galton, Cattell returned from Europe imbued with the belief that intelligence was hereditary, fixed, and determined by the genetic structure of the individual. Espousing Galton's view that in order to improve the human race "inefficient human stock" should be supplanted by "better strains," Cattell "offered each of his children $1000 if they would marry the child of a college professor" (Sokal 1971, p. 630). As the first professor of psychology to be appointed in the United States (a claim disputed by Sokal 1971), Cattell soon became extremely influential in spreading the testing movement. While teaching at the University of Pennsylvania, he published his classic article (1890) in which the term "mental test" appeared for the first time. And it was while directing the psychological laboratory of Columbia University in 1893 that he administered Galton's type of tests to 100 freshmen in order to show that mental ability could be evaluated and academic achievement predicted. However, once analyzed, the data collected over a period of four years failed to support Cattell's earlier promise. Equally instrumental in the field of testing was G. Stanley Hall, who, although he had never studied nor worked with Galton nor met Darwin, felt that the theory of evolution was, as he put it, "the thing for me" (Hunt 1967, p. 176). As the first president of Clark University, Hall's commitment to the notion of inherited and fixed intelligence was to leave its mark on the numerous students he taught, many of whom were to become the pillars of the testing movement in the United States—for example, Henry H. Goddard, F. Kuhlmann, Lewis Terman, and Arnold Gesell. The Binet-Simon scale made its first appearance in America in 1908, when Goddard translated it into English to use it with the feebleminded of the Vineland Training School in New Jersey. But it was another admirer of Galton, Lewis Terman of Stanford University, who revised the scale, tried out the items on an American population —modifying some, rejecting others, inserting new ones—and made it into the American instrument it still is today. Published in 1916, revised twice in 1937 and 1960, the Stanford-Binet soon became the most widely used scale of intelligence in the United States.

The purpose of this historical summary has been to show, succinctly, the way in which Galton's conception of intelligence and his attempts to measure it by means of simple tests traveled from Great Britain to the shores of America. The reason why Galton's notion of "hereditary genius" became incorporated into a seemingly more egalitarian society than that of Victorian England resides in the historical fact that the early American psychologists—Cattell, in particular —had studied and worked with Wundt and Galton and not with Binet (Hunt 1967). However, racist thinking in the interpretation of human differences predates Galton and the men of his time. Although its origins are difficult to establish, what is evident is that among the writings advocating the incontestable superiority of the white race (Aryans particularly) de Gobineau's *Essay on the Inequality of the Human Races* was most influential. Later, it provided Adolph Hitler with a base for justification for an otherwise unjustifiable policy of social and political actions. Taking "high reputation" as his criterion of "high ability," Galton came to the inescapable conclusion that the ablest race was the ancient Greek who surpassed all other races. When compared with the Anglo-Saxon race, blacks—in the judgment of Galton—were markedly intellectually inferior. Writing about Jews,

Galton found them to be "specialized for a parasitical existence upon other nations" and not "capable of fulfilling the varied duties of a civilized nation by themselves" (in Montagu 1974, p. 410). Pearson, in turn, strongly advocated that Jewish immigration into England be restricted. (See Pearson in Montagu 1974, p. 419.) Carl Brigham (1923), upon examining the army intelligence test results, was instrumental and successful in urging the U.S. government to open the door to immigrants from Northern European countries and to limit drastically the entry of Alpine and Mediterranean individuals, who he believed were responsible for the decline in "American intelligence." However, in due fairness to Brigham, it should be mentioned that he later deplored his earlier position. But, as a man of his age, Brigham's findings and interpretations were consistent with the doctrine of the superiority of the "Nordic race" as propounded in Schultz's *Race and Mongrel* (1908) and in Madison Grant's *The Passing of a Great Race* (1916).*

Using physics as his model, Galton set out to devise a scientific instrument that would help him accelerate nature's task of "supplanting inefficient human stock by better strains." As mentioned earlier, Quetelet's concept of the average man (nature's ideal) was based on his observations that human physical characteristics such as height tended to approximate the well-known bell-shaped probability curve. Thus Galton borrowed a concept related to physical traits and applied it to psychological traits. In order to explain why such characteristics tend to remain normally distributed throughout the population, Galton conceptualized the notion of regression to the mean, without which the stability of the bell-shaped curve would be impossible. The inevitable consequence of a theory that assumes that intelligence is and remains normally distributed is that it automatically dooms 50 percent of the people of most typical populations, at all times, to below-average IQs and thus to the permanent status of the unintelligent, dull, mentally retarded, or imbecile. In the eyes of the hereditarians this is an irreversible and inescapable condition about which nothing can be done. Therefore, attempts at raising the IQ level by corrective training (for instance, by compensatory education) are bound to fail. Not unlike Calvin's elect, Galton's eminent men are only those who will, of necessity, make it to the top of the ladder. Galton's Calvinistic approach to the psychology of human differences has been accepted for so many years that one tends to regard his theories as commandments, often forgetting that they are nothing more than artifacts.

* For more details, see Dorsey's "Race and Civilization" (1928) reprinted in Montagu (1974, pp. 437–462).

Introduction
The Hereditarian Argument
The Environmentalist Argument
Fallacies

NATURE AND NURTURE

3

INTRODUCTION

The nature-nurture issue is still prominent even today. Sir Percy Nunn reminds us that it was Shakespeare's Prospero, who, speaking of Caliban as "A devil, a born devil, on whose nature/Nurture can never stick" (*The Tempest*, IV, 1), first established the distinction—as we understand it now—between the two terms. Used by Sir Francis Galton in his *Inquiries into Human Faculty* (1883), it was to be accepted this way thereafter (Nunn 1945, p. 113).

Both sides of the heredity-environment controversy have supported their positions with a collection of evidence. The hereditarians undertook to demonstrate the facts of heredity by recounting the histories of twins who behaved predictably alike and by exhibiting the appalling record of the Jukes family, which "out of about 1,000 persons in five generations, 300 died in infancy; 310 spent 2,300 years in almhouses; 440 were wrecked by disease; 130 were convicted criminals (including 7 murderers); and only 20 learned a trade" (Nunn 1945, p. 115).

At the other extreme, the proponents of the environment side of the controversy accepted *in extenso* John Locke's doctrine of the tabula rasa—that is, the mind is likened to a clean slate, and all the ideas brought by way of the senses are imprinted on it. They believed that if a child was put in the right kind of environment, he would grow up to become the right kind of adult. Therefore, differences among people were deemed to be wholly related to education, both formal and informal. It was Helvetius' view that "enough is ascertained to prove, beyond a doubt, that if education does not perform everything, there is hardly anything that it does not perform" (Nunn 1945, p. 114). This is also the behaviorist position, summed up in the classic proclamation:

> Give me a dozen healthy infants, well-formed, and my own specified world to bring them up in and I'll guarantee to take any one at random and train him to become any type of specialist I might select—doctor, lawyer, artist, merchant-chief and, yes, even beggar-man and thief, regardless of his talents, penchants, tendencies, abilities, vocation and race of his ancestors (Watson 1963, p. 104).

The present trend seems to reflect a shift away from radical and global positions to an attitude of conciliation. As more and more is uncovered about the effects that nutrition, intrauterine conditions, maternal care, and so on, have on the fetus, the notion that the environment (in the broadest sense) or nurture can influence the nature of the individual is gaining momentum. Cynthia Deutsch refers to this interaction as interpenetration, which, in her opinion emphasizes the "modifiability of nature as well as nurture." She wrote:

> The interpenetration discussed involves the operation of environmental influences on the product of genic influences. However, modern genetics teaches that genic operation itself is responsive to environmental variation. Experiments show that incubating Drosophila larvae at one temperature will produce one color of adult fruit fly, while incubating larvae from the same genetic strain at a different temperature will result in adult individuals of a different color. The environment, then, affects the biological attributes of the organism by influencing the operation of the gene (1968, p. 61).

THE HEREDITARIAN ARGUMENT

The early hereditarians had seldom had the privilege of catching the public ear. Their theories of mental heredity, their studies of twins or foster children, their formulas, and their lengthy and esoteric debates, never moved beyond the pages of scientific journals or the floors of academic forums. Their more recent counterparts, on the other hand, have enjoyed much publicity and news through national and international newspapers, magazines, television networks, talk shows, and so on. With little disagreement the turning point can be identified as the year 1969; the man responsible was Arthur Jensen, and the cause was the persistence of differences in scores between blacks and whites on IQ tests.

Two successive aspects of the theory of mental heredity existed in the United States. At first, heredity and environment were considered to be not only antithetical but mutually exclusive. This was the either-or stage or what Burt (1958) labeled the "nothing-buttery" stage. It was also the stand taken by the early hereditarians—Galton in England and Goddard in the United States—who, from their respective examinations of prominent men and of the Kallikak family,[1] arrived at the conclusion that of the two—heredity and environment—the former had the more potent influence upon mental ability. In other words, intelligence, like eye color, was fixed at birth and immutable. The progeny of Galton's prominent men would, of necessity, become eminent ("few who possess these very high abilities can fail in achieving eminence," see Chapter 2).

As it became clear, however, that man inherits potential, the heredity-environment question became one of relative importance. In what proportion do genetic and nongenetic factors contribute to individual differences in measured intelligence? Or, in the more technical language of geneticists, what proportion of the variance among phenotypes (which will be explained shortly) is attributable to variance among genotypes? According to Jensen, studies conducted with whites in England and in the United States have shown that between 70 and 90 percent of the variation in the IQ can be accounted for by heredity. Jensen (1969) opts for 80 percent; Burt (1958) for 77 to 88 percent; Newman, Freeman, and Holzinger (1937) for 65 to 80 percent; Woodworth (1941) for 60 percent; Leahy (1935) for 78 percent; and Burks (1928) for 66 percent. More recently, Jencks dissented from a position that posits such high heritability estimates and argued instead that according to his own analysis, the correct figure is more like 45 percent (1972, p. 65). Regardless of the percentage, though, it seems essential to examine the evidence on which geneticists base their findings.

Genotype. Before proceeding further, it is necessary to define some technical terms. In order to understand the meaning of genotype, it is necessary to begin at the point at which the sperm unites with the ovum and mitosis begins. The fertilized egg, which represents the original single cell, is made up of a jellylike substance, the cytoplasm, and of a nucleus containing the chromosomes—stringlike structures composed of a vast number of minute particles called genes. Genes

---

[1] In order to show that heredity played a far more significant role than that of environment, Goddard proceeded to study the progeny of a revolutionary war officer fictitiously called Kallikak. From his marriage to a respectable middle-class woman and from his liaison with a barmaid, Kallikak fathered two sets of children. When Goddard compared the descendants of the legitimate branch of offspring with the descendants of the illegitimate branch, he found that there were many more feeble-minded, deviant, and criminal individuals among the progeny fathered by Kallikak and the barmaid.

exist as pairs; that is, one set of genes is given by the father and one set by the mother. The way genes are arranged and behave in the cells determines what the end product, the individual, will be. The ways in which genes combine are almost limitless. As Jennings remarked: "Different individuals are made as it were on diverse recipes; and the diverse recipes give different results. . . . No two individuals, in such an organism as man, are concocted on the same recipe (save in the rare cases known as identical twins)" (in Watson 1963, p. 51). It is the "unique recipe" that has been used for the making of a particular individual, his unique set of genes, that constitutes his genotype. Gottesman describes the genotype as "the totality of factors that make up the genetic complement of an individual" (1968, p. 29). It is received at the time of conception and is, therefore, fixed at birth. Hirsch (1970) estimated that there are over 70 trillion potential human genotypes.

Phenotype. Phenotype "refers to the totality of physically or chemically observable characteristics of an individual that result from the interaction of his genotype with his environment" (Gottesman 1968, p. 29). Dobzhansky describes it as follows: "The phenotype is the appearance of the individual—the structure and functions of his body. The concept of the phenotype subsumes, of course, not only the external appearance, but also the physiological, normal and pathological, psychological, socio-cultural, and all other characteristics of the individual" (1964, p. 58). Therefore the phenotype is not fixed, and it varies with time.

The interaction between genotype and phenotype, between unobservable and observable, can best be illustrated by the experiment of Cooper and Zubek (1958) as reported in Pettigrew (1964). After having bred two genetically distinct strains of rats (a bright strain and a dull strain) for thirteen successive generations, these investigators placed groups of both strains into three different environments: the natural habitat of the rat; a restricted environment (barren cage with food box and water pan only); and an enriched environment (bells, swings, tunnels, decorated wall, and so on). Results of the experiment (Pettigrew 1964, p. 106, Fig. 5) show that in their natural environment the learning ability of the bright rats is significantly higher than that of the dull rats (maze error scores of 117.0 for the bright rats and 164.0 for the dull rats; the lower the score, the higher the ability to solve maze problems). In the restricted environment both bright and dull rats performed equally poorly (scores of 169.7 for the bright strain and 169.5 for the dull strain). In the enriched environment the difference in scores is also negligible, and the performance of both strains is almost identical (scores of 111.2 for the bright rats and 119.7 for the dull rats). This experiment demonstrates that similar genotypes (bright rats) may have different phenotypes (their performance in the natural and in the restricted and enriched environments) and that different genotypes (bright rats and dull rats) may have similar phenotypes (their performance in the restricted and enriched environments). Gottesman (1968, p. 29) gives the account of a study conducted by Sinnott, Dunn, and Dobzhansky (1958) with similar implications. Genetically identical Himalayan rabbits (similar genotype) when reared in different environments present different phenotypes (white body and black extremities under natural conditions; completely white bodies when placed in a warm cage). Gottesman concluded that:

> Given uniformity of trait-relevant environment, almost all observed phenotypical variance in a trait must stem from variability in the genotypes. Given uniformity in that part of the genotype relevant to the trait under consideration, almost all the observed phenotypical trait variance must stem from variability in the environments. Given heterogeneity for both genotypes and environments—the situation which prevails for human populations—the observed trait variability must be attributed to some combination of genetic and environmental variances (1968, p. 32).

Heritability. The concept of "heritability" as described by Jensen is the "proportion of phenotypic variance due to variance in genotypes" (1969, p. 42). More clearly, heritability indicates, in the form of a number varying between 0 and 1.0, how large a role the genetic make‑up (genotype) plays in the total amount of the variation of a trait (for example, skin color, intelligence) of a particular group of people at a particular time. Heritability is not a property of the individual or of traits; it is the property of populations (Fuller and Thompson 1960). If the number is large, the trait concerned is highly heritable; that is, genes account for much of the variance. For *whites only* it was found that the heritability coefficient for intelligence was between 0.80 and 0.85 (Jensen 1969). Therefore, for the white population, as a whole, intelligence is a highly heritable trait, since 80 to 85 percent of the variation in IQs is due to heredity, and the environment accounts for only 15 to 20 percent. Hunt and Kirk defined and estimated heritability as follows:

> Thus, heritability is the correlation of the unobservable, theoretical, genotypic variance of a trait with the observed, and measured, phenotypic variance of the trait. . . . Since the genotype is a logical construct that is not observable, estimating heritability demands that investigators find ways to estimate the genotype variance of a trait from observables. The simplest index of heritability, originally invented by Francis Galton, estimates the genotypic variability through measures of the trait in parents, based on the average measure for the two parents, and correlates these measures with measures of the trait in the offspring of

these parents, based on the average measure for the children of each couple. The higher the correlation between such measures for parents and children, the greater the heritability (1971, p. 274).

The scientific basis for the existence of racial differences in intelligence rests on four premises. (1) The concept of intelligence is well understood. (2) Intelligence tests provide a true and reliable measure of intellectual functioning, and the differences in scores reflect differences in intellectual potential. Although Jensen (1969, p. 5) agreed that intelligence, like electricity, is difficult to define, he affirmed, however, that it can be easily measured. (3) Both whites and blacks represent separate but homogeneous groups racially distinct. (4) The effects of the variance in physiological, sociocultural, and economic conditions of both groups can be ignored.

In order to determine the respective influences of environment and heredity upon measured intelligence, it has been customary to look at studies involving related and unrelated persons within a family. Erlenmeyer-Kimling and Jarvik have summarized, in table form, and by means of correlation coefficients, the work done over the past 50 years on the relationship between mental functioning and genetic potentials. From the 52 studies collected in eight countries, the researchers concluded that "a marked trend is seen toward an increasing degree of intellectual resemblance in direct proportion to an increasing degree of genetic relationship, regardless of environmental communality" (1963, p. 1477). Although they do not reject the possible influence of the environment upon intelligence, the researchers remark, nonetheless, that the consistency of the data collected leads one to adopt a hereditarian stand in the nature-nurture controversy. Jensen's Table 2 (1969, p. 49), in which he lists the various correlations obtained among related and unrelated persons, is essentially based upon the table developed by Erlenmeyer-Kimling and Jarvik.

It is argued that monozygotic (identical) twins, who share the same genes and thus have the same heredity, should, if the environmentalist is correct, have significantly different IQs when reared in different environments. Jensen (1969) cites three major studies of monozygotic twins involving 232 white subjects (that is, 116 pairs) separated from six months to two years after birth and spread over the entire range of socioeconomic levels. The three studies, Jensen reports, revealed a high correlation between the IQs of the various pairs of twins. The correlation was 0.77 for the 14 pairs of twins in the study conducted by Newman, Freeman, and Holzinger (1937) and for the 44 pairs in Shields's (1962) study. It was 0.86 for the 53 pairs of twins investigated by Burt (1966). In other words, regardless of the environments in which those 116 pairs of twins lived from the times of their births, they obtained very similar IQ scores. Hence the claim that differences in IQs can be explained, in great part, by differences in environmental conditions is invalidated. Commenting upon the monozygotic twins data, Herrnstein remarked that "their IQs correlated by about 85 percent, which is more than usual between ordinary siblings or even fraternal twins growing up together with their own families" (1971, p. 55). To extend the point further, Jensen stresses the fact that in Burt's study the correlation for the twins' IQs was almost as high as that of their height and weight, which were 0.94 and 0.88, respectively. Can such findings be interpreted as meaning that intelligence is as heritable as height or weight?

On the other hand, studies of unrelated children from orphanages or adoption agencies, reared in the same environment, generally a foster home, have also been used extensively to illustrate the hereditarian position. In this case it is assumed that if the environment dominates, those children whose genes are different but whose environmental conditions are identical should make very close IQ scores. Erlenmeyer-Kimling and Jarvik's table of correlations shows that for these children the median correlation between their IQs is 0.23. Among the studies that Jensen believes illustrate this finding are Leahy's (1935) investigation, which yielded 0.20 correlation and Burks's (1928) data. Burks compared the average IQ of foster children and true children living in carefully matched environments. Comparisons favored the true children, who made higher scores than the foster children. Additionally, foster children tended not to resemble their foster parents in intelligence, a finding that did not occur in the case of the true children. A study involving 100 adopted children, conducted by Skodak and Skeels, also pointed to the fact that foster children, despite their improved environments, seemed to gravitate more toward the IQs of their natural parents than toward the IQs of their foster parents. Refraining from interpreting their findings in a hereditarian light, Skodak and Skeels, nonetheless, acknowledged the "increasing correlation between child IQ and true mother IQ with increasing age" (1949, p. 114).

There seems to be no consensual estimate of heritability. Figures vary from a high of 88 percent (Burt 1958) to a low of 60 percent (Woodworth 1941). Yet hereditarians still recognize the influence of the environment—diminished in importance as it may appear—on test results. Burt identified three ways in which the influence of environment is felt:

(a) [T]he cultural amenities of the home and the educational opportunities provided by the school can undoubtedly affect a child's performance in intelligence tests of the ordinary type since so often they demand an acquired facility with abstract and verbal modes of expression; (b) quite apart from what the child may learn, the constant presence of an intellectual background may stimulate (or seem to stimulate) his latent powers by inculcating a keener motivation, a stronger interest in intellectual things, and a habit of accurate, speedy, and diligent work; (c) in a few rare cases illness or malnutrition during the prenatal or postnatal stages may, and almost from the very start, permanently impair the development of the child's central nervous system. The adjusted assessments may do much towards eliminating the irrelevant effects of the first two conditions; but it is doubtful whether they can adequately allow for the last (1958, p. 9).

On the whole, except for physiological and nutritional handicaps, differences in the results of intelligence tests can be explained in terms of the genetic make-up; that is, the "innate amount of potential ability with which a child is endowed at birth sets an upper limit to what he can possibly achieve at school and in after life" (Burt 1968, p. 17). According to this view, endeavors to raise scores by modifying environmental conditions (by using compensatory education programs, for instance) are not only futile but inexorably doomed to failure (Jensen 1969). In fact, Herrnstein (1971) proceeds a step further and predicts the return of "aristocrats, privileged classes, unfair advantages and disadvantages of birth" if attempts are made at making the environment as good and as uniform as possible for everyone. Herrnstein contends that lowering the effects of the environment augments the heritability of intelligence, as well as the prospect of a society built on inborn differences:

> The higher the heritability, the closer will human society approach a virtual caste system with families sustaining their position on the social ladder from generation to generation as parents and children are more nearly alike in their essential features. . . . Greater wealth, health, freedom, fairness and educational opportunity are not going to give us the egalitarian society of our philosophical heritage. It will instead give us a society sharply graduated, with ever greater innate separation between the top and the bottom, and ever more uniformity within families as far as inherited abilities are concerned. . . . By removing arbitrary barriers between classes, society has encouraged the creation of biological barriers. When people can freely take their natural level in society, the upper classes will, virtually by definition, have greater capacity than the lower (1971, p. 64).

THE ENVIRONMENTALIST ARGUMENT

The environmentalist refutes the hereditarian's concept of a genetically determined intelligence and maintains, instead, that differences in intellectual performance can be explained in terms of environmental deprivation. Since it is generally agreed today that both nature and nurture interplay and elicit the observed differences between minority and majority IQ scores, most environmentalists and hereditarians disagree over the degrees of emphasis that should be placed on each factor.

Broadly stated, in the opinion of the environmentalist, the question of differences in intelligence scores becomes not one of race but one of class and caste. More specifically, the environmentalist studies those factors (physical or biological, psychological, and sociocultural) that membership in a lower class and caste entails and that cannot be disregarded when making racial comparisons. Because the environmental conditions, knowledge, and experiences of the lower classes, on the one hand, and those of the middle and upper classes, on the other hand, are so disparate, the environmentalist believes that the success of the lower classes in school, typically a middle-class-oriented institution, cannot be ensured without a vast program of remediation and compensation. One eminent psychometrician, in defending the virtues of the SAT, remarked to a skeptic: "What's wrong with being middle-class? Everybody wants to be middle-class." But what does it really mean to be of the upper class, middle class, or lower class?

Social Stratification Systems

Contrasting the three major types of stratification systems—caste, estate, and class—Mayer defines a class system as one that is:

> . . . based primarily upon differences in monetary wealth and income. Social classes are not sharply marked off from each other nor are they demarcated by tangible boundaries. Unlike estates, they have no legal standing, individuals of all classes being in principle equal before the law. Consequently, there are no legal restraints on the movement of individuals and families from one class to another. . . . Unlike caste, social classes are not organized, closed social groups. Rather, they are aggregates of persons with similar amounts of wealth and property, and similar sources of income (1959, p. 8).

Along the same line of thinking, Mueller and Mueller noted that "if 'social class' possesses any sociological meaning, it signifies a hierarchy in the distribution of the privileges of life. In fact, the measurement of the social distance between the respective classes is a measure of these differentials" (1953, p. 486).

A caste system is the most rigid type of social stratification and consists of closed social groups arranged in a fixed order of superiority and inferiority. An individual born into a particular caste cannot move easily into a higher social caste. Not unlike one's eye color or height, one's caste cannot be changed (Mayer 1959). Blacks in America have been in the unusual position of suffering from a class and color caste system. Because of their skin color blacks have been forced into a stratification system that holds that regardless of education, occupation, or wealth a white individual is, and remains, socially superior to any black individual. The sharply demarcated color line led the black community to develop a separate but parallel class structure trichotomized into upper, lower, and middle levels. Due to limited economic and educational opportunities, however, each level cannot be viewed as corresponding to its white counterpart; the black upper class, for instance, in terms of income and wealth does not rank beyond the white, upper middle class (Mayer 1959). In this caste-class system blacks emerge the victims and the losers. Drake believes that

> Negroes in America have been subject to "victimization" in the sense that a system of social relations operates in such a way as to deprive them of a chance to share in the more desirable material and non-material products of the society which is dependent, in part, upon their labor and loyalty. They are "victimized" also because they do not have the same degree of access which others have to the attributes needed for rising in the general class system—money, education, "contacts," "know-how." . . . The "victims," their autonomy curtailed, and their self-esteem weakened by the operation of the caste-class system, are confronted with "identity problems." Their social condition is essentially one of "powerlessness" (1966, pp. 4–5).

It was during the 1930s and 1940s that several investigators definitely put to rest the notion that equal opportunity in the "distribution of the privileges of life" prevailed in the United States. Extensive studies of geographically diverse communities (Lynd and Lynd 1929 and 1937; Warner and Lunt 1941; Davis, Gardner, and Gardner 1941; Warner, Havighurst and Loeb 1944; West 1945; Warner et al. 1949; Hollingshead 1949) documented the fact that social stratification exists; that success is not solely the result of individual effort and merit but greatly depends upon the individual's inherited position, wealth, social connections, formal education, and other advantages unrelated to personal qualities and achievements; and that a racial caste system denies large segments of the population equal participation in the distribution of opportunities and wealth (Mayer 1959). The Index of Status Characteristics (ISC) developed by Warner and his associates represents one way of dividing the population into social classes on the basis of occupation, income, type of house, and dwelling area. One needs no statistical evidence to support the observation that when these four criteria of class membership are adopted, minorities, in general, and blacks, in particular, are relegated to the lowest level of the social scale. The traditional black dwelling area is the overcrowded and spatially isolated ghetto, characterized by its run-down and vastly inferior housing, poor public services, inadequate medical facilities and health care, and low-quality schools and education. Despite some significant advances over the past few decades, blacks are still concentrated in the low-income sectors of the economy and still form the core of the blue-collar workers. Therefore, in proportion to whites they still receive significantly lower salaries, which are made even smaller by the fact that "non-white family heads in 1960 had a smaller median income than whites for every educational level . . . the average income for a non-white family with a male head who had finished high school was less than that of a white male head who had finished only the eighth grade" (Drake 1966, pp. 17–18). Moynihan (1965) also draws attention to the fact that the rate of unemployment for nonwhites, which more than three decades ago was lower than for whites, has now reached the point where it is more than twice as great.

Cultural Deprivation of Minorities

Both the hereditarian and the environmentalist agree that minorities generally score lower on tests of intellectual behavior, but they disagree as to the cause of the deficit. Whereas the former finds reason to believe that genes are at the root of the problem, the latter contends that those variables that relate the child's background to his performance must be identified. The home, cultural patterns, language, cognitive skills, and so on, must be explored, and a strategy of intervention must be devised in order to prevent, arrest, and reverse the effects of deprivation. This "cultural-deprivation" frame of reference in which some environmentalists view the minority child deserves closer attention.

An impressive number of studies dating from the early 1920s onward have amassed evidence supporting the claim for a theory of cultural deprivation and at least casting serious doubts upon, if not invalidating, the credibility of the genetic inferiority model. The pioneer work of Klineberg was of basic importance in bringing a new direction to the problem of racial differences in intelligence. For the first time the popular and widely accepted belief in the inherent inferiority of the "Negro" race was challenged, and the environment was offered as the causative agent. In *Race Differences* Klineberg categorically asserted that research had not yet revealed that there was any scientific proof of racial differences in intelligence (1935b, p. 345). As early as 1923, Gordon's study of canal-boat children and gypsy children living in England showed the effects of an intellectually deprived environment. In the case of the 76 canal-boat children and 82 gypsy children, poor school attendance coupled with parents' mobility and illiteracy conspired to relegate these children to the borderline of feeble-mindedness: means of 69.6 and 74.5, respectively, were obtained on measures of intelligence, and these dropped sharply with age. In the United States, mountain children, all of British descent and of Anglo-Saxon stock, were found to evince the same signs of retardation and the same age decrement in IQs as Gordon's subjects. The respective studies of Asher (1935) in Kentucky, Wheeler (1932) in Tennessee, and Sherman and Key (1932) in the Blue Ridge Mountains, conducted with subjects living in small, isolated, economically and culturally impoverished communities, proved that poor performance on the standard tests of intelligence could not be explained from a biological or genetic stance but had to be accounted for by the poverty and lack of stimulation of the environment. Along the same line Shimberg (1929), notably, has shown that there exists a discrepancy in test scores between urban and rural white children, which is not confined to this country but can also be found with European groups whenever city and country people are compared (Klineberg 1931). As an additional proof that race can hardly be viewed as the cause of the difference, the army test results collected during World War I revealed that blacks from the states of Pennsylvania, New York, Illinois, and Ohio attained higher scores than whites from Mississippi, Kentucky, Arkansas, and Georgia (Klineberg 1935b). Furthermore, ample evidence exists to suggest that there is a large supply of gifted black children in America. Jenkins (1948) found that "there was at least sixteen published studies that give an account of Negro children possessing IQs above 130; twelve of these report cases above IQ 140" (in Wilcox 1971, p. 103). Of 18 black children who tested above IQ 160, Jenkins continues, 7 were above IQ 170; 4 were above IQ 180; and 1 was at IQ 200. It is interesting to note that no trace of white ancestry could be found in the child, a girl, who made such a high IQ score. Although some researchers are of the opinion that light-skinned blacks tend to perform better than dark-skinned blacks, the preceding finding departs notably from a theory such as William Shockley's that for every 1 percent of white mixture, there is a gain of 1 IQ point.

Additionally, there has been a series of studies that have demonstrated that a richer environment can actually raise the test scores of blacks. Klineberg undertook to test 3000 Harlem school children matched by sex, age, schools attended, socioeconomic status, and birthplace (all Southern-born) but differing in the number of years they had lived in New York City. Results indicated that, without exception, blacks who had most recently arrived from the South had made the lowest scores and that there seemed to be a definite trend toward a relationship between test score and length of residence in New York City. The longer the stay, the higher the score obtained (1935a). Lee (1951) replicated Klineberg's study with Philadelphia-born and Southern migrant black students and arrived at the same conclusion. On this basis, the theory of selective migration (brighter persons migrate to the cities and to the North), which was used to explain the superior scores of urban and Northern black children, gave way to the more adequate explanation that improved environment means improved test scores (Freeman, Holzinger, and Mitchell 1928). A 15-year study of 100 adopted children of inferior socioeconomic backgrounds placed in foster homes of above-average economic, educational, and cultural status, under the direction of Skodak and Skeels (1949), also revealed a similar trend. As in similar studies (for example, Burks 1928), it was found that the children's IQs tended to resemble the biological parents' IQs more closely than the foster parents' IQs. However, when one considers that the true mothers' mean IQ was 85.7 and the children's was 106, the difference of over 20 points is too great not to reflect the influence of a rich environment. Skodak and Skeels (1949, Table 12, p. 110) show that out of the 63 children and their mothers who took the 1916 version of the Stanford-Binet 52 children and only 19 mothers made above-average scores (IQs of 95 to 134). Such findings seem to be inconsistent with a position that gives preponderance to the influence of the genetic make-up. Therefore, the authors concluded: "It is inferred that maximum security, an environment rich in intellectual stimulation, a well balanced emotional relationship, intellectual agility on the part of the foster parents—all these and other factors contributed to the growth of the child" (Skodak and Skeels 1949, p. 116). Deutsch and Brown (1967) studied 543 urban black and white first and fifth graders from three different socioeconomic levels. Results of the Lorge-Thorndike intelligence test corroborated the general conclusion that as the quality of the environment improves, so does the IQ score, regardless of race. Decroly and Degand (1910) and the army test results attested to the fact that members of the middle and upper classes, without regard to race, perform on intelligence tasks significantly better than those of the lower classes. In a study involving 1800 black elementary schoolchildren of the Southeast (Florida), Kennedy, Van de Riet, and White (1963) found that the higher the socioeconomic level, the higher the IQ score on the Stanford-Binet. They observed a difference of over 20 points between the mean IQ (79) of the lower-status children and that (105) of the higher-status children.

Moreover, many other investigations (Collins 1928; Haggerty and Nash 1924; Havighurst and Breese 1947; Pressey and Ralston 1919;

Standiford 1926) have established the existence of a relationship between parental occupation and a child's intellectual level. Apparently, the higher the father's occupation on the social scale, the higher his child's IQ score. Traditionally, children whose parents are professionals or involved in managerial activities make higher intelligence test scores than children whose parents are skilled and unskilled laborers. Terman and Merrill (1937), Seashore, Wesman, and Doppelt (1950), and others have found that there exists a difference of approximately 20 IQ points between the upper and lower ends of the social scale. The mean IQs of children living with parents in the low occupational categories is 95 compared with a mean IQ of 115 for the children of professional and managerial parents.

Must such consistent results be interpreted as meaning that the higher the socioeconomic level, the higher the intelligence level? Are people poor because they are dull or dull because they are poor? This is a perennial question, and whereas proponents of a genetically determined level of intelligence elect the first alternative, environmentalists choose the second. But when socioeconomic factors are considered, the problem of racial differences in intelligence becomes difficult to explain in terms of the superiority or inferiority of one race or another. As Klineberg wrote:

> Intelligence may be regarded as the cause of economic status if opportunities are equal and competition is entirely free. Even within a relatively homogeneous native born White American population, this is not altogether true; the handicaps are not evenly distributed. In the case of the Negro, however, the difficulties in his way are so great that any inference from industrial status to intelligence is completely unwarranted. . . . Until we can be certain that the same opportunities have been given to the Negro as to the native-born White, any direct comparison of average test scores will be meaningless (1935b, pp. 163–164).

Simply stated, the cultural deprivation theorists have formulated the following basic assumptions: (1) the environment plays a major role in the development of cognitive skills and in the learning process—that is, learning how to learn; (2) some types of environments are more stimulating to cognitive development than others; (3) the proper task for early childhood educators of disadvantaged children is to identify stimulation lacks in the environment (Deutsch and Deutsch 1967). Basically, the assumption is made that the minority lower-class environment lacks those attributes that are essential to future success in school and that the traditional white, middle-class milieu already possesses. Thus the deprivation theorists have painted a picture of deficiencies and failures.

Contrasting privileged and disadvantaged environments, investigators have identified the following characteristics. The typical dwelling area of most minority children is the urban ghetto, a spatially isolated, overcrowded community lacking in the fundamental amenities. The typical minority household is noisy, disorganized, and contains more siblings—often illegitimate—and more relatives than the households of typical white families (Keller 1963). There is a greater incidence of unstable and broken homes due to the father's desertion or absence; consequently, boys lack experience with a male model, particularly a successful male model, and are raised in a predominantly matriarchal home atmosphere (Deutsch 1967; Ausubel and Ausubel 1963). Surrounding buildings and housing are substandard and located in areas where there is usually "little opportunity to observe natural beauty, clean landscapes or other pleasant and aesthetically pleasing surroundings" (Deutsch 1967, p. 44). Inside the home the few pictures, books, objects to manipulate, toys, and furniture offer the child a restricted range of tactile, visual, and aural stimuli. Furthermore, children of lower socioeconomic levels receive more physical punishment than children of the higher levels (Milner 1951).

Child-Rearing Practices

According to Davis and Havighurst (1946), considerable social-class differences exist in child-rearing practices. Except for the two areas of feeding and cleanliness training, in which blacks, regardless of class, are more permissive in the former and stricter in the latter, Davis and Havighurst indicated no color differences in child-rearing practices. They observed:

> Middle-class families are more rigorous than lower-class families in their training of children for feeding and cleanliness habits. They generally begin earlier . . . place more emphasis on the early assumption of responsibility for the self and on individual achievement . . . are less permissive . . . in their regimen . . . they require their children to take naps at a later age, to be in the house at night earlier, and, in general, permit less free play of the impulses of their children . . . middle-class children are subjected earlier and more consistently to the influences which make a child an orderly, conscientious, responsible and tame person . . . middle-class people train their children early for achievement and responsibility (1946, pp. 707–708).

In general, the environment of the lower-class child is described as being less verbally and visually stimulating than that of the middle- or upper-class child. Deutsch claims that while the lower-class environment is a noisy one (continuously running television sets, cry-ing babies, and screaming children), the noise is not meaningfully related to the child himself. As a result, his auditory discrimination —which Deutsch (1967) found to be related to reading ability—his attention span and memory span, as well as responsiveness, are diminished markedly. Furthermore, the lower-class child's concept of time is different, his concentration is poor, and he is less able to handle abstract concepts. Hess et al. related the child's poor ability to conceptualize abstractly to maternal language style. They found a significant correlation between the mother's language abstraction and the child's performance and concluded that "there is an abstraction factor in the middle-class mother's language which may have far-reaching implications for the subsequent intellectual development of the child" (1968, p. 168). They described the lower-class working mother's language as being more restricted, less linguistically subtle and elaborate, less complex syntactically, less abstract, and less imaginative. That Hess and his associates agree with Bernstein's (1960) notion of formal (middle-class) and public (lower-class) language dichotomy is obvious. Handicapped by these early deficits, the minority child enters into the school situation with a marked disadvantage and falls victim to the cumulative-deficit phenomenon as described by Deutsch (1967). Unlike the middle-class child whose home, with its "hidden curriculum," provides him with the basic school-related skills, the lower-class student sees the school as a strange and discontinuous environment. Unable to catch up with an intellectually nurtured, school-oriented, and achievement-motivated group, the typical disadvantaged child falls further behind as time passes.

FALLACIES

Interracial comparisons of intellectual ability have been the long-standing subject of national and international attention. In the United States, especially, there is ample documentation of the respective performance of whites and blacks on intellectual tasks and of the poor test standing of the latter group. Theories espousing a racist or an egalitarian approach to the question of racial differences have been advanced on the belief in the inherent intellectual superiority of whites, on the one hand, and on the cultural disadvantage of blacks, on the other hand. However, both the hereditarian and environmentalist positions seem to rest on certain fallacies.

The Concept of Race

Before any inference of so-called racial differences in test performance can be made, one must first understand the meaning of race and then establish whether black Americans constitute a racial group distinct and separate from that of white Americans.

In the United States the concept of race has bartered its purely scientific meaning for a more social and popular one; that is, the term has been defined within a cultural or sociological frame of reference. Biologically, a race is a subspecies, a variety of the single species to which all people belong—*homo sapiens*. Whatever diversity existed among the subspecies could be attributed to the diversity of the environments in which these different groups lived.

Natural selection is the process through which most changes within the genetic constitution of a population occur. Briefly stated, only those genotypes that are best suited to the environment adapt and survive and thus contribute more to the next generation of individuals. Gottesman remarks that "many of the characteristics observed in current races are the results of adaptation to ancient environments" (1968, p. 23). As an illustration, he cites the reduction in the frequency of the sickling trait among black Americans, due, in large part, to the malaria-free environment in which they have lived for so long. The dark skin color of the African, for instance, can be explained in terms of his prolonged exposure to intense sunlight, for what was adaptive for him was not so for the Nordic, who, on the contrary, developed a light pigmentation in order to capture the faintest ray of sun necessary for the manufacture of vitamin D (Pettigrew 1964).

Genetically speaking, all human beings are alike, for the genes of one group can also be found in another group. It is the way in which genes cluster and organize, however, that differentiates people. Thus race becomes invariably associated not with the types of genes present in a population but with the frequency with which a particular genetic composition is found in a particular population. In the words of Boyd a race is "a population which differs significantly from other human populations in regard to the frequency of one or more of the genes it possesses" (1950, p. 201).

There exist about as many race taxonomies as there are investigators interested in the task of compiling them. Gottesman (1968, pp. 12–13) lists the works of Boyd (1950), Coon, Garn, and Birdsell (1950), Garn (1961), and Dobzhansky (1962), who describe from 6 to 34 different races. On the other hand, Montagu opposes the classification of races on the basis that it runs counter to the process of evolution, but he favors the position that represents races as "different kinds of temporary mixtures of genetic materials common to all mankind" (1952, p. 46). Serological experiments have permitted the organization of races along the lines of blood types. Africans, Caucasians, and Orientals differ, for instance, in frequency of the genes for blood types A, B, and

O. Bodmer found that "in Oriental populations, for instance, the frequency of the gene for the blood type B is 17 percent, while it is only 6 percent in Caucasians. This means that type B individuals are generally three times as common in most of Asia than they are in Europe" (1972, see Fig. 1, p. 89).

As Mayr pointed out, "biologically, it is immaterial how many subspecies and races of man one wants to recognize" (1963, p. 644). What is more important, however, within the context of the present discussion, is the fact that today there is no such thing as a pure race. The possibility that a racially distinct group of people has not been interbred with the rest of mankind seems to be remote, and, as Dunn and Dobzhansky (1952) emphasized, "nothing can be more certain than that pure races in man never existed and cannot exist" (in Pettigrew 1964, p. 62).

Where, then, does the black American stand biologically? In the gene pool of the "Negro," or "colored man," of the past and the black American of today are the genes of two of the major races, African and Caucasian. (Conversely, the white American must also claim some Negro ancestry, though quantitatively less.) Pettigrew gives the following account of the relative percentage of Caucasian blood to be found in the black American:

> A series of investigations over the years provide comparable estimates of the genetic influence of cross-racial mating upon Negro Americans. Early studies lacked modern blood system genetic methods and relied upon morphology and the reconstruction of ancestral lines. This research estimated that the percentage of Negroes with at least one known white forebear ranged between 72 and 83 percent (Wirth and Goldhamer 1944). With a large sample of fifteen hundred Negroes, Herskovits in 1930 arrived at more detailed figures. He calculated from the reports of his subjects that roughly a seventh (14.8 percent) had more white than Negro ancestors, a fourth (25.2 percent) had about the same number of white and Negro ancestors, almost a third (31.7 percent) had more Negro than white ancestors, and the remainder (28.3 percent) had no known white ancestor. In addition, a quarter of the sample's Negroes (27.2 percent) claimed one or more known Indian forebears (1964, p. 68).

Glass and Li (1953) estimated that the total amount of white genes in the present black American reached 30.56 percent; Roberts (1955), upon reexamining their data, arrived at the lower figure of 25 percent. Pollitzer (1958) calculated the "genetical distance" between whites and West Africans, whites and Charleston blacks (Gullah), and whites and blacks from other parts of the United States. From this and other studies it can be concluded that, genetically, the average American black is about as far removed from the pure Negroid type as he is from the pure Caucasian type.

If the black American cannot be said to belong truly to the Negro race, it seems incongruous to call any black having the remotest trace of Negro ancestry, black and to proceed to make "racial" comparisons in test performances, as though both black and white subjects belonged to scientifically determined, separate and distinct races. As Gottesman concluded, "if you choose to call the white individual with a Negro grandfather, a Negro, then logic would require you to call the 'average' Negro in New York or Baltimore, white" (1968, p. 22).

The fallacy behind the hereditarian position is to ignore the facts as biology presents them today and to perpetuate a socially and culturally diminishing labeling based entirely on skin color and external features such as hair, nose, and lips. If the distinctive physical aspects of the black man were removed, it would be impossible to determine his race with certainty. Therefore, to associate mental qualities with such superficial physical qualities seems rather nonsensical for, "no one asks whether there are mental and temperamental differences between white, black or brown horses" (Montagu 1952). Furthermore, if proof can be obtained that brain size correlates with intelligence and that, as a consequence, the white man (whose brain is 50 cubic centimeters larger than that of the black man) is more intelligent, then logic would require that the Neanderthal man (whose brain was 75 cubic centimeters larger than that of the modern white man) be considered mentally superior to him (Montagu 1952, pp. 60–61).

Difficulties in Equating Black and White Groups

If one assumes that it is possible to draw a clear line of demarcation between black and white groups and to separate them into two distinct racial entities, then the failure to control adequately certain environmental, cultural, and sociopsychological variables still invalidates any interpretation of intellectual superiority or inferiority of one group or the other. More specifically, a procedure that attempts to equate the two racial groups in order to see which one is "better" is doomed from the very start for the following reasons.

It is standard procedure for investigators interested in comparing the intellectual performance of black and white subjects to choose, as their representative sample, groups matched on a variety of factors such as sex, age, amount of schooling, parental education, socioeconomic status, parental occupation, family size, social status, and so on. By controlling such variables, they believe, differences in test results will reflect differences in intellectual attainment and ability. The a priori assumption underlying such a belief is that the historical and cultural circumstances of the black people can be ignored and that blacks and whites have shared in the same history and culture and in similar educational, professional, and economic opportunities.

Several investigators have drawn attention to the scarcity of adequate instruments for measuring environments. Anastasi remarks that the "*Mental Measurements Yearbooks* contain a section on socioeconomic scales, but few entries are included. Moreover, most of the available measures are crude and superficial. It is only since the late 1950s that serious efforts have been made to develop sophisticated indices of environmental variables for specific purposes" (1958, p. 579). Bloom concurs with the preceding view and also notes that "our catalog of tests of individual differences is enormous, whereas our instruments for measuring environmental differences consist of a few techniques for measuring social class status and socioeconomic status" (1958, p. 185). Furthermore, the tendency of the existing scales has been to classify environments globally in terms of good or bad, desirable or undesirable, favorable or unfavorable. More recently, Wolf (1964) has opposed and rejected this one-dimensional view of environments and devised a procedure stressing not so much the physical characteristics of the home and the parental occupational status, but rather the interactions between parents and children insofar as the development of intelligence is concerned (see Bloom 1964, pp. 78–79). Although there exist several techniques to identify an individual's social-class status (Warner's method of Evaluated Participation and Index of Status Characteristics; Sims's SCI Occupational Rating Scale), the occupational level of the major breadwinner has proved to be a simple and fair approximation of social status.

Occupational Factors. The fact that blacks and whites have not been granted equal occupational opportunities is well documented. Demographic studies have repeatedly shown that, in proportion to whites, black workers have been and still are grossly underrepresented in the professional, managerial, sales, and crafts occupations, despite a substantial gain in better-paying, white-collar jobs since 1960 (Bouvier and Lee 1974). Hauser (1966) estimated that such an advance in obtaining white-collar and skilled jobs represented only half that of the white population. Wide discrepancies between the two groups still exist as evidenced by the unemployment rates. The recent figures released by the U.S. Bureau of the Census (U.S. Department of Commerce 1973) show that, in 1972, 10 percent of the black labor force, compared to 5 percent of the white labor force, remained unemployed. Figures for previous years indicate that there has existed an almost constant 2-to-1 ratio of black-to-white unemployment. Along with higher unemployment rates, blacks face more frequent and longer periods of unemployment as well as more part-time than full-time work (Fein 1966).

Wages are, naturally, commensurate with occupations. The heavy concentration of blacks in blue-collar jobs has created an income gap that is further aggravated by the fact that minority wage earners are consistently underpaid in regard to their educational attainment. If the census data are to be interpreted literally, the median income of black families has, indeed, increased remarkably in the past two decades from $2,807 in 1950 to $4,236 in 1960 to about $6,700 in 1970 (Bouvier and Lee 1974). But during the same year—1970—the median income of whites reached the figure of $10,236. Further investigations into the census data reveal, however, that "part of the explanation for the narrowing of the gap in income between whites and blacks is attributable to the working wife. . . . Many more black than white wives work" (Bouvier and Lee 1974, p. 3). Furthermore, blacks do not receive the same remunerations as whites for performing the same jobs (Drake 1966). For instance, a black teacher with four years of college education or a black carpenter, fireman, or truck driver, all with four years of high school education, receive substantially smaller salaries than their white counterparts (Bouvier and Lee 1974, p. 7). Hauser (1966) reported Siegel's monetary estimate of being a black American:

> The difference between nonwhite and white earnings in 1959 of males 25 to 64 years old was $2,852.00 as reported in the Census. Of this difference, $1,755.00, or 62 percent, is attributable to the differences in the regional occupational, and educational distribution of whites and nonwhites. Thus, even if nonwhites had achieved the same regional, educational, and occupational distribution as whites, nonwhites would still have earned only $1,097.00 or 38 percent below the level of whites. The average cost of being a Negro in the United States in 1960, then, was about $1,000.00 in earnings (in Parsons and Clark 1966, p. 84).

Educational Factors. Blacks, especially in the South, have had a long history of limited educational opportunities. Hauser (1966) provides pertinent data in this respect. Although illiteracy among blacks declined from 30.4 percent in 1910 to 23 percent in 1960, it was still three times as great as that of whites (7 percent). Until 1960 white children of elementary- and secondary-school age not only attended school in greater proportion but spent more years in school than black children of the same age. By 1971 and 1972, however, the proportion of blacks attending school had doubled, and the number of years of school completed had increased vastly (Bouvier and Lee 1974). But here, too, despite the apparent gargantuan gains of blacks in the field of education, whites—over the same period of time—also progressed steadily, thus reducing the hope of narrowing the racial gap substantially. As a consequence of wider illiteracy, lower enrollment, and fewer years of schooling, black family heads find themselves in a situation in which the quantity of education received is dangerously under par. As Edwards observed, "the low level of educational achievement for such a large proportion of nonwhite family heads has obvious implications for the cultural life to which the Negro child is exposed in the home and doubtless for the type of motivation the child receives for achievement in school" (1966, p. 289).

Differences between the educational attainment of blacks and whites are not only quantitative but qualitative as well. That is, in proportion to the number of years that both ethnic groups spend at school, the black child is very likely to receive a lesser amount and a lower level of instruction. It was the observation of Deutsch (1967) that the typical black school generally devotes an inordinate amount of classroom time (80 percent) to matters of discipline, disruption, and organizational details, thus seriously reducing the amount of time assigned to actual subject teaching. Deutsch estimated that students in these schools receive one-half to one-third the exposure to learning that their white counterparts receive (1967, p. 117). Teachers, especially white teachers, regard slum schools as having low prestige and, therefore, consider a teaching assignment to one of them as only temporary pending the availability of a better vacancy (Green 1971; Haubrich 1963). Predominantly black schools are characterized by unusually high turnover rates of teachers as Becker's study of the career patterns of Chicago public school teachers illustrated (Cloward and Jones 1963, p. 191). The recruitment of qualified staff for these schools poses a serious challenge to administrators, who are left with no alternative but to hire the young, inexperienced, and mobile teacher whose choice is limited by the available openings. Indeed, it is difficult to convince anyone that creative, effective, satisfying, and remunerative teaching can be done in typically overcrowded, inadequately furnished, and poorly financed schools. Jencks estimates that 15 to 20 percent more is spent, per year, on the average white than the average black schoolchild (1972, p. 28).

If, as Canady (1943) outlined, "the sine qua non of comparison must be first, a dependable measurement of each 'race,' second, a representative sample of each 'race,' and third, identical or not significantly different environmental conditions—especially educational opportunity" (in Wilcox 1971, p. 94), then it is clear that lacking the first, failing to obtain the second, and wanting the third, no meaningful interracial comparison can be made.

Cultural Factors. A common misconception among white Americans lies in the belief that the slaves arrived culturally naked. Consequently, they fail to realize that, although both blacks and whites have lived as compatriots for over 300 years, they do not, however, share in the same culture (Canady, 1943 in Wilcox, 1971). The diversity of folkways that such a wide assortment of slaves (from West Africa, Angola, Madagascar, and so on) brought to the shores of America has, despite the constant attempts to annihilate it (by the separation of fellow tribesmen and of families, loss of dialects, acceptance of a new language and customs, and so on), resisted these assaults and deeply influenced the lifestyle and life patterns of blacks. Canady reported that:

> [A]lthough the American Negro's accommodation to European custom has been far-reaching, nevertheless, Herskovits finds that many forms of his present-day behavior are readily recognizable as of African origin, that is, manifestations of the carry-over of aboriginal customs. For example, Africanisms in religious beliefs and practices, music, dance, folklore, attitudes and certain aspects of motor behavior are generally observable in the United States (in Wilcox, 1971, pp. 95–96).

Notwithstanding its African origin and its European veneer, the culture of the black man is a sequela of slavery. The high concentration of ex-slaves and their descendants in the "black belts" of this country led to what St. Clair Drake has called the ghettoization of the black man:

> The "ghettoization" of the Negro has resulted in the emergence of a ghetto subculture with a distinctive ethos, most pronounced, perhaps, in Harlem, but recognizable in all Negro neighborhoods. For the average Negro who walks the streets of any American Black Ghetto, the smell of barbecued ribs, fried shrimps, and chicken emanating from numerous restaurants gives olfactory reinforcement to a feeling of "at-homeness." The beat of "gut music" spilling into the street from ubiquitous tavern juke boxes and the sound of tambourines and rich harmony behind the crude folk art on the windows of store-front churches give auditory confirmation to the universal belief that "We Negroes have 'soul.' " The bedlam of an occasional brawl, the shouted obscenities of street corner "foul mouths," and the whine of police sirens break the monotony of waiting for the number that never "falls," the horses that neither win, place, nor show, and the "good job" that never materializes. The insouciant swagger of teenage drop-outs (the "cats") masks the hurt of their aimless existence and contrasts sharply with the ragged clothing and dejected demeanor of "skid-row" types who have long since stopped

trying to keep up appearances and who escape it all by becoming "winoes." The spontaneous vigor of the children who crowd streets and playgrounds (with Cassius Clay, Ernie Banks, the Harlem Globe Trotters, and black stars of stage, screen, and television as their role models) and the cheerful rushing about of adults, free from the occupational pressures of the "white world" in which they work, create an atmosphere of warmth and superficial intimacy which obscures the unpleasant facts of life in the overcrowded rooms behind the doors, the lack of adequate maintenance standards, and the too prevalent vermin and rats (1966, pp. 9–10).

To assume that the black lower-class culture is identical to that of the white middle class is to lack historical judgment. It is simply impossible to equate black and white cultural differences. Eells and his co-workers (1951), notably, recognized the influence of cultural differences upon the test performance of minority groups. Their culture-free test, though an avowed failure, represented, nonetheless, an effort to eliminate or attenuate the disadvantage encountered by minority groups on tasks foreign to them. Klineberg (1935b) gives several accounts of how different modes and ways of living can affect test results. He cites his experiences with the Dakota Indians, whose custom it is not to answer a question in the presence of someone who does not know the answer. Or an individual may answer only when he is absolutely certain of the response (Klineberg 1935b, p. 155).

Even in a hypothetical case in which all other variables could be controlled, the psychological effects of prolonged membership in a lower caste would still corrupt and hence nullify any comparisons between minority and majority groups. Those effects have been explored extensively: poor self-concept, identity conflicts, submission to white dominance, fear of white competition, high anxiety level, sensitivity to the race of the examiner, poor motivation to achieve, low aspirational levels, fatalistic attitude, and so on (see Chapter 4). There is an indelible stigma attached to being black. Unlike immigrants who could melt more easily into the mass of people, blacks have always been too conspicuous as a group to vanish into their respective niches. No matter whether he is a successful businessman, lawyer, professor, or senator, a black man is first and foremost a *black man*. American public opinion, despite a recent favorable trend, has always been reluctant to admit that a black man is as intelligent as a white man. Pettigrew reports that "in 1942, only 42 percent of white Americans believed the two groups to be equally intelligent; by 1944, the figure was 44 percent; by 1946, 53 percent; by 1956, 78 percent" (1964, p. 195).

In conclusion, there seems to be, at the moment, hardly any basis for attempting to make any valid interracial comparisons of test performance. Rebutting Eysenck's argument that experimental evidence of nurture's influence be brought forth, Rex summarized his position as follows:

> Since, however, the crucial variable is the difference between white and Negro history and the fact that Negro history involves the fact of slavery, experiment would mean subjecting the group of Negroes to white experience. The empirical study which holds constant, size of income, type of neighborhood and length of schooling in the United States of the present day, therefore, should in theory be supplemented for an experiment in which the peoples of Africa conquer, capture and enslave some millions of European and American whites under conditions in which a very large proportion of the white population dies and in which the white culture is systematically destroyed and in which finally a group of emancipated whites living in "good neighborhoods" are then compared to their Negro masters. It is not sufficient to brush aside this assertion, merely by saying that we should not draw conclusions from "hypothetical experiments." The fact is that the differences in the history of Negroes and whites are a factor of immense significance and that any statistical reasoning which leaves them out can reach no conclusions of any value whatever (1972, pp. 170–171).

The Theory of Cultural Deprivation or Disadvantage

Frank Riessman's widely read book, *The Culturally Deprived Child* (1962), has been credited with having popularized—if not launched —the label "cultural deprivation." Although Riessman refutes the notion that lower socioeconomic groups have no culture of their own, nonetheless, he uses such a term to describe those groups that "lack many of the advantages (and disadvantages) of middle-class culture" (1962, p. 3). By cultural deprivation Riessman means "those aspects of middle-class culture—such as, education, books, formal language —from which these groups have not benefited" (p. 3). Though the term was accepted in everyday parlance, it was opposed from the very beginning by several educators and writers, among them Clark (1963a) and Mackler and Giddings (1965). Various labels have been suggested for characterizing the child who does not fit into the mainstream culture. He has been alternatively called disadvantaged, underprivileged, socially deprived, socially disadvantaged, educationally deprived, and socially rejected. Clark and Plotkin reiterated the need for a moratorium on the usage of euphemisms like cultural deprivation. "Serious adverse effects in social planning, educational policy and research follow from its wide acceptance. Conceptual and theoretical confusion is generated by the loose definition of the term. The deficiencies of the concept far outweigh whatever advantages are gained by its continued use" (1972, p. 69).

Actually, to be culturally deprived means either to lack a cultural background—a contradiction in itself, for no individual is devoid of culture—or to partake in a culture that is deemed deficient and constitutes a handicap for its members. In other words, the black culture is not regarded as being conducive to the kinds of attitudes, skills, and knowledge required by the schools and by society at large. Mackler and Giddings state that whenever the words "culture" and "deprivation" are used together, "they suggest very incorrectly that a culture can of itself be deprived or that a culture can somehow deprive its members who depend upon it of the goods, skills, and behaviors, which are necessary for survival and adjustment" (1965, p. 609). Cultural deprivation, in the opinion of the authors, represents one of those tags or labels that "do not help to banish the myth of Negro inferiority" but maintain and entrench it.

Not surprisingly, a culture can only be found wanting whenever the yardstick that is applied to measure it is basically ethnocentric in its gradations. More specifically, advocates of the cultural-deprivation thesis have posited that "the customs and values and the language of one's group are superior to those of other groups and are the 'right' and 'good' standards by which the behavior of all persons ought to be measured" (Mercer 1971, p. 317). Therefore, they have concentrated on "describing Negro behavior not as it is, but rather as it deviates from the normative system defined by the middle-class" (Baratz and Baratz 1970, p. 32). They have stressed its negative and pathological aspects and confused equality with sameness (Baratz and Baratz 1970).

The philosophical basis of a theory that postulates cultural deprivation is that of the "average child" who is subject to the same laws and principles as Quetelet's "average man" so that any departure from the mean becomes expressed in terms of deviance. The mean or norm is, naturally, embodied in the values, standards, experiences, and knowledge of the white middle class, of which the school is a mirror. Any failure to measure up to so-called normal behavior and any failure to meet success as prescribed are attributed, not to genetic factors in this case, but to the familial, social, and cultural milieu in which the child lives. It is his culture and his heritage that are failing him, not his genes! As Baratz and Baratz remarked: "Both the genetic model and the social pathology model postulate that something is wrong with the black American. For the traditional racists, that something is transmitted by the genetic code; for the ethnocentric social pathologists, that something is transmitted by the family" (1970, p. 32).

If, as Hunt (1967) succinctly stated, "the difference between the culturally deprived and the culturally privileged is, for children, analogous to the difference between cage-reared and pet-reared rats and dogs" (in Passow et al. 1967, p. 202), it follows that in order to protect the child from the invidious influences of his environment, measures must be taken to alter and radically change the ways and patterns of thinking, communicating, and behaving of a group whose orientations, life style, and language differ so markedly from those of the middle class. Since middle-class children do well at school partly because it is simply an extension of their home (Cloward and Jones 1963), intensive remedial and compensatory programs must be devised so as to bring the "substandard" children up to the level of the "normal" children. Such an enterprise, however, can only be successfully carried out if, and only if, intervention is begun before school, at the earliest possible stage of the child's life. What is being advocated, in fact, is that underprivileged families and mothers abandon their child-rearing practices for "better" ones and relinquish their maternal duties to the care of social scientists, linguists, psychologists .d so on. As the originators of the Early-Training Project remarked, "the general strategy of our research is based upon the fact that, short of a complete change of milieu for children in infancy, we have yet to demonstrate that it is possible to offset in any major way the progressive retardation that concerns us" (Gray and Klaus 1965, pp. 887–888). Ideally then, the infant should be taken away and brought up in the kind of environment conducive to academic performance and success. Ideally then, ethnic groups should barter those customs, patterns, mores, and attitudes that keep them culturally distinct for those of the middle class. The futility of the attempt to turn ghetto children into middle-class children has been well expressed by Gordon and Wilkerson:

> [T]he unexpressed purpose of most compensatory programs is to make disadvantaged children as much as possible like the kinds with whom the school has been successful, and our standard of educational success is how well they approximate middle-class children in school performance. It is not at all clear that the concept of compensatory education is the one that will most appropriately meet the problems of the disadvantaged. These children are *not* middle-class, many of them never *will* be, and they can never be anything but second rate as long as they are thought of as potentially middle-class children. . . . At best, they are different, and an approach which views this difference as something to be overcome is probably doomed to failure (1966, pp. 158–159).

There is an impressive amount of evidence that has found the black mother inadequate and responsible for producing "linguistically and cognitively impaired children who cannot learn" (Baratz and Baratz 1970, p. 36). Hess et al. (1968), for example, have related the lower-class child's poor ability to conceptualize abstractly to maternal language style. Hunt also adopted the view that parents themselves are poor linguistic models for their young children (1968, p. 31). But Baratz and Baratz have denounced what they call the "inadequate mother hypothesis" and claimed that:

> One of the chief complaints leveled against the black mother is that she is not a teacher. Thus one finds programs such as Caldwell's (1968) which call for the "professionalization of motherhood" or Gordon's (1968) which attempts to teach the mother how to talk to her child and how to teach him to think (1970, p. 37).

The apparent failure—irrefutable proof of failure has not yet been established—of the compensatory or enrichment enterprises used as antidotes to cultural deprivation has been viewed in very different lights. Hereditarians, for example, find in it an additional proof that genes play a much more significant role than is generally conceded. On the other hand, opponents of the social pathology model attribute the failure of Head Start and similar types of programs to the dehumanizing implications of a theory that rejects the concept of cultural pluralism and postulates the "white, middle-class way" as the only viable way of life. Moreover, they denounce such a position as a theory of distortion and "a built-in rationalization for the educator who fails to teach minority children effectively" (Clark and Plotkin 1972, p. 65). Educational institutions and society in general, not parents, must answer for school retardation. "There is no question," Clark and Plotkin continue, "that the uncritical attitude towards deprivation in the child relieves school administrators and teachers from their primary function of education" (1972, p. 65). They further contend that: "The possibility that the failure may stem from budgetary deficiencies and other more direct educational inadequacies such as teacher attitudes and training, inadequate supervision, bureaucratic rigidity, and outmoded curricula and materials is short circuited by the prevailing concept of cultural deprivation" (1972, p. 56).

Introduction
Nutrition
Self-Concept
Motivation
Anxiety
Test Environment
Language

ENVIRONMENTAL FACTORS
INFLUENCING TEST PERFORMANCE

4

INTRODUCTION

From all accounts the early test developers believed that it was possible to assess intelligence independently of the environment and that measures of IQ were true expressions of intellectual potential. Although Binet and Simon were aware that their scale tended to favor certain groups, they did not, however, pursue the matter systematically. Klineberg (1935b) departed from a position that disregarded environmental factors and affirmed that, when making racial comparisons, no valid interpretation of test results can be made without accounting for motivation, examiner race, test content, speed, socioeconomic status, amount of schooling, and language as possible influences on test performance.

Environment can be defined as the "conditions, forces, and external stimuli which impinge upon the individual. These may be physical, social, as well as intellectual forces and conditions" (Bloom 1964, p. 187); or, "the sum total of the stimulation the individual receives from conception until death" (Anastasi 1958, p. 64). Thus attention must be given to those physiological, psychological, and sociocultural factors that shape the character and personality of the individual. The purpose of this chapter, then, is to examine more specifically the influence of such factors as nutrition, self-concept, motivation, anxiety, examiner race, test sophistication, and language upon the performance of minority and lower-class subjects on tests purporting to measure intelligence.

NUTRITION

In 1931 McGraw made public the results of an experiment that seemed to confirm the belief that blacks are innately inferior to whites. The purpose of the study was to evaluate the performance of 128 black and white infants from Tallahassee, Florida, ranging from the ages of eleven months to two years on the Buhler Baby Tests. Examination of the mean scores revealed a distinct superiority in the performance of the white sample. McGraw concluded, therefore, that "in general, the developmental level achieved by the Negro babies appears to be 80 percent as mature as that of the white babies" (in Pasamanick 1946, p. 5).

Successively, in 1935 and 1944, Klineberg called attention to the fact that McGraw had failed to consider the gross body size differences between the black and white infants and that, as a consequence, differences in scores might not have reflected differences in maturational levels but differences in nutritional conditions. The precocity of the white babies as observed by McGraw could be attributable, in the opinion of Klineberg, to the fact that at birth they were markedly heavier and taller than the black infants. He wrote: "The important problem in this study is that of the comparability of the two groups studied. The investigation does not point out that the colored babies, both boys and girls, fall noticeably below their norms in weight, and that the divergence from the standard increases with age" (in Pasamanick 1946, p. 5).

Since then, several investigators have brought evidence contradicting McGraw's conclusions, and McGraw herself later felt the need to deny the implications of her earlier thesis on the basis that "the number of infants studied was too small to justify any such generalization. The Buhler tests in no way presage mental endowment, and in the twentieth century it would be impossible to find pure genetic strains of Negroes" (1964, p. 56).

In 1946 Pasamanick compared the behavioral development of 53 New Haven, Connecticut, black babies, whose weights and heights approached the white norms, with three groups of white infants: illegitimate infants living in foster homes, infants residing in a child-care institution, and infants from superior homes. Both ethnic groups were tested twice, at approximately six-month intervals, by means of the Yale Development Schedules of Gesell. Results of this investigation clearly indicated that "the average New Haven Negro infant of this study is fully equal in behavioral development to the average New Haven white baby" (Pasamanick 1946, p. 41). That is, the black sample performed just as well as the white sample in the areas of fine motor skills, language, personal-social behavior, and significantly better in gross motor development. A third examination of 44 of the original 53 black infants yielded similar results, thus confirming the general conclusion that, at least in the first two years of life, blacks present no sign of retardation when compared with their white contemporaries (Knobloch and Pasamanick 1953).

Repeatedly, in 1946 and in the follow-up study published in 1953, Pasamanick emphasized the importance of maternal prenatal diet and infant postnatal nutrition. He attributed the increase in birth weight and height of the black babies of his original study over that of previously tested babies (see Pasamanick 1946, p. 13, Tables 4, 5, and 6) to the effects of the improved black mothers' diets which, for the first time, approached those enjoyed by the New Haven white mothers. He explained that the normal developmental progress displayed by the black infants was the consequence of a sustained good postnatal nutrition.

Emphasis on the importance of nutrition at the prenatal, in utero, and postnatal stage is relatively recent, as the Committee on Maternal Nutrition has demonstrated:

> The 1940's, a decade of enthusiasm about the importance of nutrition in bringing about improvements in pregnancy outcome, were followed by a period of disillusionment and disinterest after the publication of a series of reports during the 1950's whose chief conclusions appeared to contradict earlier concepts. It was not until the late 1960's that interest was reawakened and a period of reappraisal began. Attention is now being given not only to the immediate effects of nutritional deficits on the outcome of pregnancy but also to the long-term effects on the subsequent physical and mental development of the child (1970, p. 2).

The concern over malnutrition as a possible factor in the educational achievement level of disadvantaged children emanated, according to Gussow (1974), from three sources: (1) the rediscovery of hungry poor in the United States, which led to the publication of well-circulated reports (Hungry Children 1967; Hunger, U.S.A. 1968); to the establishment of a special Senate Select Committee on Nutrition and Human Needs, which released its final report in January 1974; to the convocation of a White House Conference on Food, Nutrition and

Health (1969); and to the undertaking of a nutrition survey (*The Ten State Nutrition Survey, 1968–1970, Highlights*); (2) the world-wide concern for the mental aftereffects of severe early malnutrition as outlined by the reports of the National Academy of Science (1966) and the Conference on Deprivation in Psychological Development (1966); (3) the apparent failure of programs of compensatory education designed to help poor and disadvantaged children learn.

Such enterprises succeeded in awakening public and governmental interest to the dimensions of poverty and hunger in the United States and to the conditions of an estimated 30 million poor, 6 million of who were of school age (*Hunger, U.S.A.*). Summarizing the plight of the poor of this country, Frost and Payne observed:

> A frightening paradox in the country with the world's greatest surplus of food is that in the past two decades the poor suffering from hunger and malnutrition have increased in number. The multiplicity of causes revolve around three central ones: (1) the increasing mechanization of farming and industry calls for less and less unskilled labor: (2) the mobility of the major portion of a fluid American population makes it possible for the poor to exist unnoticed; (3) the educational system of America is failing to help the poor defeat the vicious cycle of ignorance, listlessness, defeat, despair and hunger (p. 14).

The link between malnutrition and impaired physical development has been well documented. It is the conclusion of researchers that normal growth cannot take place without the indispensable presence in the diet of protein and calorie nutrients. Numerous animal studies and a few human studies limited to necropsies performed on dead children have demonstrated that calories affect cell multiplication and protein affects the ability of cells to enlarge, so that the "failure of cells to receive sufficient proteins and calories during certain periods of body growth may lead to slowing down and ultimately to cessation of the ability of the cells to enlarge, divide and develop specialized functions" (U.S. Department of Health, Education and Welfare 1973, p. 22). Whenever malnutrition occurs before and persists beyond eight months of age, the number and size of body cells are reduced and physical growth is retarded (Winick 1972). Frost and Payne cite the example of the average twelve-year-old undernourished child whose physical stature matches the average European or Anglo-American eight-year-old.

The suggestion of a link between malnutrition and mental functioning has generated recent criticisms. The threat of a possible relationship believed to exist between malnutrition in children and their subsequent irremediable intellectual deficit has been, today, considerably attenuated. Ricciuti (1973), among others, questioned the validity of such a conclusion:

> Rather prematurely, research findings indicating an association between malnutrition and impaired intellectual functioning (were translated into) somewhat oversimplified and, in some instances, rather exaggerated conclusions concerning a direct causal relationship between nutritional deprivation and mental retardation (quoted in Gussow 1974, p. 6).

Similarly, Gussow observed:

> Children whose mothers were ill-fed, or who were themselves ill-fed in early childhood might—we were warned—suffer a permanent reduction in the number of brain cells or in the critical interconnections between them. If we did not remedy these children's hunger in time, it was argued, they might come to school permanently and severely retarded. As the intervention data suggest, such a concern may not even be justified in countries where near-starvation among children is common; in this country such concern is a distraction (1974, pp. 29–30).

However, no study has yet proved the unquestionable impossibility of such a concern. The observation that brain size is affected, that more premature and low birth-weight infants are born as a result of malnutrition, gave the problem of nutrition a new sense of urgency. Although brain studies of humans are very limited, the existing data suggest that the earlier malnutrition occurs, the greater the danger of permanent brain damage and the poorer the recovery, since the brain reaches 80 percent of its growth during the first three years of life. Whenever malnutrition occurs before and persists beyond one year of age, certain changes that are functionally significant may happen within the brain and cause faulty intellectual development. Actually, much of what is known about the effects of malnutrition upon the brain has been extrapolated from studies performed on animals, particularly on rats, thereby limiting drastically the meaning and usefulness of such findings when applied to man (Coursin 1965; Dobbing 1973). Roeder and Chow (1972) have reviewed several such studies and reported that, in general, the learning ability of the offspring of rats fed on a low-protein diet during pregnancy is reduced. Similarly, the work of Maurer and Tsai (1929) and of Maurer (1930, 1935) has demonstrated that:

> In rats, a rapidly growing system deprived of adequate quantities of vitamin B (B_1) is injured to the degree that, judging from several criteria of learning ability, it requires about twice as many trials and errors to learn a maze as do rats whose nervous systems have been fed normally during this early period of growth. Our experiments show that vitamin B (B_1) must be present in liberal quantities for the normal functional develop-

ment of a rapidly growing nervous system (in Harrell, Woodyard, and Gates 1955, p. 3).

Summarizing the available animal data, Birch and Gussow (1970) reached the following conclusions:

> (1) [B]oth brain size and composition, and performance on a variety of behavioral measures appeared to be affected by "various kinds and degrees of nutritional deprivation in young animals"; (2) the growth deficits as well as some of the behavioral and learning difficulties might persist even after refeeding and rehabilitation; and (3) intergenerational deprivation could lead to learning handicaps which "might persist even after a generation of refeeding—mimicking a hereditary condition" (quoted in Gussow 1974, p. 14).

Fewer studies relating early life nutritional status to learning ability have been conducted at the human level. Harrell, Woodyard, and Gates (1955) attempted to investigate the effects of maternal prenatal diets on the intelligence of offspring. The study consisted of a sample of 2400 women registered in two maternity clinics located respectively in the eastern part of Kentucky and in Norfolk, Virginia. Racially, the Kentucky subjects were, without exception, all white and from Anglo-Saxon ancestry, while 80 percent of the Norfolk sample consisted of black women. Economically, both groups belonged to the low-income bracket, although the Kentucky women were slightly better off. From a nutritional point of view, diets were plain, the Kentucky women again having a slight advantage. The purpose of the study was to distribute to each subject, over a period of three years, and during pregnancy and lactation, a supplemented diet in the form of daily tablets containing either a placebo, ascorbic acid, thiamine, or a combination of thiamine, riboflavin, niacinamide, and iron.

The second phase of the investigation consisted of testing the offspring on their third and fourth birthdays, on the Form L and Form M of the Terman-Merrill Revised Stanford-Binet. Results of the tests show that contrary to the Kentucky sample, which failed to evince any relation between intellectual performance and enriched diet (presumably because the mothers were not as deprived as the Norfolk women), the children of the Virginia subjects who were given a supplemented diet made higher mean IQ scores than the children of the mothers who received a placebo. The authors drew this conclusion: "This study demonstrates, beyond a reasonable doubt, that vitamin supplementation supplied to pregnant and lactating women under certain circumstances such as those prevailing in the Norfolk group described in this report, does increase the intelligence of their offspring, at least for the first four years of their lives" (Harrell, Woodyard, and Gates 1955, p. 62).

However, their conclusion was seriously questioned on the basis that "the outcome variable—the intellectual status of the child—is so far removed from the input variable—the changed nutritional status of the mother—that the possibility of drawing convincing conclusions is nil" (Gussow 1974, p. 9).

Birth weight has been traditionally considered to be a good indicator of the status of the newborn baby. And as the birth weight declines (below 5½ pounds), the frequency of neuropsychiatric disabilities, hence of retarded mental development, increases. Investigating such a relationship, Knobloch and associates (1956) observed a greater incidence of neurological defects ranging from minimal damage to overt abnormality among their sample of 500 premature Baltimore infants. When the intellectual potential of the babies was assessed, the premature group scored significantly more within the dull range than the group of full-term babies.

The fact that undernourished mothers give birth to lighter-weight children is well established. Birth-weight data collected by Meredith (1970) show that there are twice as many black babies under 5½ pounds as white babies. In the Baltimore sample Knobloch and his associates also observed that there was a significantly higher percentage of nonwhite infants (51.7 percent) than white infants (48.7 percent) among the lower-weight groups. But Malina (1969) found that whenever adequate diets and infant medical care and supervision are supplied, the tendency for black babies to be somewhat shorter and of lighter weight disappears and the growth patterns of both black and white babies are essentially similar.

Premature babies (5½ pounds or less) have been shown to happen more frequently among the lower socioeconomic levels of the population and thus among the nonwhite elements of society. Rider, Taback, and Knobloch (1955) have found prematurity to be determined by and inversely related to socioeconomic status. That is, as the socioeconomic level of the Baltimore mothers under consideration by the authors for the period of 1950–1951 declined, the frequency of prematurity augmented. Moreover, a similar trend was observed in regard to ethnicity; nonwhite mothers had almost twice as many premature babies than white mothers (Pasamanick and Knobloch 1958). Summarizing their Baltimore study, Rider, Taback, and Knobloch estimated that:

> The frequency of prematurity among liveborn white single babies was 6.8 percent and varied from 7.3 percent in the lowest socioeconomic tenth of the city to 5.1 percent in the highest tenth. . . . The premature ratio for the total nonwhite population was 11.3 percent, which was considerably above the ratio for the lowest socioeconomic tenth of the white group (1955, p. 1027).

The Committee on Maternal Nutrition affirmed that there is "a strong positive association between the total weight gain of the mother and the birth weight of the infant" as well as "a strong positive association between the prepregnancy weight of the mother and the birth weight of the infant" (1970, p. 8). As early as 1943, Burke and associates had also formulated such a relationship (Burke et al. 1943). Of the 216 mothers involved in the experiment, those who had a diet rated as good or excellent during pregnancy gave birth to more infants diagnosed as being in excellent condition. In contrast, mothers with poor or very poor diets had a much lower percentage of infants whose conditions were good or superior but a significantly greater percentage of infants who were stillborn or premature, who died shortly after birth, or who were afflicted by congenital defects. The study showed that the average birth weight and birth length of infants born of properly nourished mothers surpassed that of infants born of poorly fed mothers. At birth, the "superior" infants averaged 8 pounds, 8 ounces in weight and 20.4 inches in length, while the average weight and length of the "poor" babies was 5 pounds, 13 ounces and 18.6 inches respectively. The logical conclusion of similar studies made in the United States and abroad is that the risk of intellectual dysfunction is reduced as birth weight is increased. However, intervention must begin early because "it is estimated that it takes three well nourished generations to eradicate the effects of severe malnutrition" (Grambs 1972, p. 179).

It is the contention of writers like Gussow that "if malnutrition is to cause what can be described as mental retardation, it must be early, prolonged, and relatively severe" (1974, p. 30). It is true that today in the United States few children starve to death; yet many *are* hungry. The impact of hunger upon school achievement is practically unknown, but whatever it is, it must be differentiated from those effects that are the result of long-term protein calorie malnutrition (Ricciuti 1973).

Nutritional surveys (Armes 1968; Owen and Kram 1969; Hutcheson 1968; Schaefer 1969) have revealed the existence of large numbers of undernourished children, particularly black children, in the United States (especially in Tennessee, Mississippi, and Texas). Zee, Walters, and Mitchell, when they investigated the nutritional status of an almost entirely black population in south Memphis, Tennessee, reported the same general characteristics of anemia, stunted growth, and nutritional shortcomings as those described in the previously mentioned surveys. Inability to obtain a sufficient quantity of food of adequate quality was found to have contributed significantly to the growth retardation and anemia of the children tested (1970, p. 742). Although poverty is not confined to blacks only, Fein has shown that they are more likely than whites to be born in poverty (the likelihood being almost three times greater).

> In 1964, the relative situation was only slightly better: 7.7 percent of Negro families had incomes below $1,000 (measured in 1964 dollars) but this was true for only 2.7 percent of whites. Our child had a twenty-two in one hundred chance (unadjusted for differential birth rates by income) of being born to a family with an income below $2,000. A white child would have an eight in one hundred chance (1966, p. 119).

Along with low median incomes, fertility rates have conspired to create an untenable situation for the black family. Birth rates for blacks are, indeed, well above those for whites. Hauser estimated that "by 1960, nonwhite natural increase at 22.0 was about two-thirds greater than that of whites at 13.2" (1966, p. 73). He further remarked that while it would take well over 50 years for the white population to double itself, blacks would do so in less than 30 years, if the 1960 rate of population growth for both ethnic groups is sustained. Not only do black women have more children than white women, but they generally have them at a much younger age. Rainwater's six-year study of a federal slum housing project has revealed that premarital pregnancy is very frequent and generally occurs for the first time at about the age of fourteen (1970, p. 58). Moynihan found the same trend among married women:

> Thus in 1960, there were 1,247 children ever born per thousand ever-married nonwhite women fifteen to nineteen years of age, as against only 725 for white women, a ratio of 1.7. The effect of the burgeoning population in family life is accentuated by its concentration among the poor. In 1960 nonwhite mothers age thirty-five to thirty-nine with family incomes over $10,000 had 2.9 children; those with less than $2,000 had 5.3 (1965, pp. 758–759).

The Summary Report of the Committee on Maternal Nutrition has stated that pregnancies occurring during adolescence impose additional demands for calories and nutrients, so that an especially enriched diet becomes indispensable. The report stated that "the course and outcome of pregnancy of girls 17 to 20 years of age resemble those of mature young women (20 to 24 years of age) whereas there is a sharp increase in infant mortality for each year of age under 17" (1970, p. 9). Along with increased rates of neonatal, postnatal, and infant mortality, the report also stressed that the median birth weight for infants born of young mothers is much lower and the incidence of prematurity much greater.

Based upon the findings of the foregoing discussions, it can be said, beyond doubt, that:

1. The percentage of black liveborn babies who have managed to survive the complications of pregnancy and the trauma of childbirth is, compared to that of whites, very limited. Fein estimated that in 1962 the rate of nonwhite infant mortality was still 90 percent greater than that of whites (1966, p. 103).
2. There are twice as many premature black babies, therefore, twice as much chance for them to suffer from a host of neurological impairments ranging from severe brain damage to minor abnormalities.
3. It is more likely for black than white children to be deprived of nutrients indispensable for normal growth, and hence to evince the signs of retardation in physical, motor, and intellectual development.
4. The chances of black children, as a whole, to reach school age physically, psychologically, and behaviorally equal to white children are drastically reduced.

How can a hungry child compete? Frost and Payne have emphasized the fact that the apparent apathy, lethargy, lack of initiative, and interest, traditionally attributed to "laziness, indolence, and other so-called ethnic traits" (p. 9), represent, in fact, the way in which the weak body protects itself; by reducing its expenditure of energy, it decreases its productivity.

The fact that nutritional factors may seriously and permanently retard intellectual functioning has generated increased interest on the part of those who have attempted to explain the differential performance of black and white, lower-class and middle-class subjects on tasks of mental ability in particular. At the same time, it has generated increased attacks on the part of those who feel that such a concern is misplaced because (1) mental retardation seems to occur only when malnutrition is early, severe, and prolonged; (2) rehabilitation appears to be possible; (3) the American poor are not so much severely malnourished as they are chronically hungry (Gussow 1974). No clear-cut resolution of the problem has been forthcoming so far. Nutrition, as it affects mental functioning, still remains a debatable factor. However, what is certain is that hunger, which is a sign of poverty, is stigmatizing and "may be debilitating to the school performance of a child in the affluent United States as more severe malnutrition is to a child in a society in which malnutrition of some degree is the social norm" (Gussow 1974, pp. 1–2).

SELF-CONCEPT

So much has been written about the negative aspects of black identity that "the reader is sometimes left with the image of an entire race of psychologically crippled people reduced to a level of minimal functioning and a state of precarious mental health" (Proshansky and Newton 1968, p. 212). Although it is true that centuries of slavery and poverty and the apparent lack of cultural heritage have played havoc with the way in which blacks perceive themselves, there are, nonetheless, stable, strong, self-respecting black families that strive to provide their children with the necessary conditions conducive to the development of a healthy personality. *The Strengths of Black Families*—a National Urban League research study conducted by Robert Hill —represents an attempt to contradict the deeply rooted view that black families are characterized by instability, disintegration, weakness, or pathology. According to Hill's findings, black families evidence strength in five respects: (1) adaptability of family roles—neither spouse dominates, but both share in decision making and the performance of expected tasks (1972, p. 38); (2) strong kinship bonds—most black illegitimate babies are kept by parents or relatives, and most black families tend to absorb other related children (p. 5); (3) strong work orientation—strong emphasis is placed on work and ambition; the husband remains the main provider of the family (pp. 9–13); (4) strong religious orientation (pp. 33–35); (5) strong achievement orientation —the number of low-income black students attending college often equals or surpasses the number of middle-income blacks attending college (p. 30). Writing about the middle-class black, Ginzberg warns against the tendency to overemphasize the negative aspects of the black family:

> In the current struggle over Civil Rights, the sympathetic supporter as well as the recalcitrant opponent has tended to stress the negatives in the situation, and this has obscured the existence of the large and growing numbers of Negro families who are no longer poor or ignorant. Such oversimplifications can lead to serious errors in the design and implementation of policies aimed at eliminating segregation and discrimination (1967, pp. 1–2).

In the wake of the civil rights movement, the slogans "Black Power" and "Black is beautiful," the feeling of partaking in the emerging Third World, and the resurgence of the black American as the Afro-American rejecting the white man's game and rediscovering his ancestry and traditions have, undoubtedly, conspired to create in the eyes of blacks and of whites a very different image. As a case of successful identity change, Clinard (1970) cites the Black Muslim group, whose movement attempts to effect a mass identity change by stressing the positive, worthy, and noble aspects of blackness.

Although it is still too early to assess the full impact that the black revolution has had upon blacks' self-evaluations, it seems reasonable to conclude that whatever effects it has produced have been positive. A number of recent studies have all rejected the negativism syndrome and affirmed the fact that black children do not have the poor self-concept attributed to them by many writers prior to the 1960s. Arnez (1972) reported four studies that adopt such conclusions. Larson et al. (1966) found that, contrary to previous research (by Clark and Clark), black kindergarten children showed no significant preference for either race when assigning roles to black dolls. Georgeoff (1967) and Roth (1969) emphasized the fact that black-studies programs favorably improved the self-concept of black fourth and fifth graders, respectively. Roth further demonstrated the positive effects of attendance in integrated classes. Finally, Hodgkins and Stakenas (1969) showed that a sample of 142 black students attending segregated high schools and colleges tended to score higher than the white counterpart sample of 100 students in self-adjustment and self-assurance. As early as 1927, some investigators had also found that not only were blacks' perceptions of themselves as good as those of whites but, in many instances, much higher (Hurlock 1927; Geisel 1962; Levin 1964).

It is undeniable that since the works of Kenneth and Mamie Clark the way in which blacks perceive themselves has evolved along the positive lines described by the foregoing studies and by the more recent summaries of the available research on self-concept (Goldschmid 1970; Baughman 1971). However, the achievement of dignity and self-respect is too recent and the scars of long servitude and discrimination too old to have vanished entirely. It may very well take three psychologically "well-nourished generations" in order to eradicate such effects.[1] As the editors of *Black Self-Concept* noted in the introductory chapter of their book:

> More research and standardized definitions of *self-concept* are needed before we can make conclusive statements about black self-esteem. However, the current research on a *global* type of self-concept and our own observations and analyses force us (the editors) to conclude that the positive impact of the black revolt of the last decade has been exaggerated by many writers, and that the perceptions and attitudes which many black children have toward themselves are still negative despite the profoundly positive effects of the black revolt on the black psyche. A vocal black minority shouts Black Power and Black is Beautiful, but most black children still live within a world where to be black produces feelings of shame, despair and anger. These children find it difficult to believe that they are beautiful when so many of the conditions within their home,

---

[1] Reference to a statement made about nutrition by Grambs (1972, p. 179).

school and community do not support such a belief (Banks and Grambs 1972, xiv).

Developing a Self-Concept

Notwithstanding its assortment of terms (self-image, self-esteem, self-perception, and so on) and definitions, *self-concept* is generally recognized as being that composite of attitudes, beliefs, and thoughts one has of oneself. In the succinct words of Wylie (1961), the self-concept can be defined as "the individual who is known to himself." Although it is the nature of the self-concept to be stable and orderly, it does not follow that it must be fixed, rigid, or unchanging in order to be healthy. The infant is not born with a ready-made, predetermined, and static self-concept. Ausubel (1950) asserts that it is "the product of an orderly process of growth which evolves out of the life experiences of the child" (quoted in Seidman 1963, p. 477). One's self-perception is, therefore, a social product, for it is shaped and modified through the constant interaction with one's environment. It is obvious, then, that parent-child relationships will play a role of paramount importance in the development of an individual's self-concept. Such an influence will tend to diminish as the child grows up and be replaced by that of the significant others, that is, other members of the family, peers, teachers, and the like.

It is a matter of agreement that the most crucial period in the expansion of the self-concept lies between the ages of three and seven. Researchers report that the development of self-consciousness and racial awareness occurs between ages three and four (Clark and Clark 1939). Pasamanick and Knobloch (1955) have compiled evidence supporting the hypothesis that as early as age two black children are aware of the presence of racial differences. Landreth and Johnson assert that by age three black children have learned that "skin color is important, that white is to be desired, dark to be rejected" (1953, p. 78). Goodman states that "four-year-olds see and hear and sense much more about race than one would suppose after watching them at school or even at home" (1964, p. 45). As an illustration, Goodman cites the striking remark made by a child of less than four-and-a-half years of age about black and white people: "The people that are white they can go up. The people that are brown, they have to go down" (p. 45). Experiments with dolls clearly indicate that young children group dolls, hence people, first in terms of their physical traits: skin color, hair type, and so on. They begin to sort people into color kinds, they also begin to value them differently. Thus it is reasonable to assume that, primarily, it is the way in which the family behaves toward and reacts to the reality of color differences that significantly determines the child's perception of himself and of others. Seward emphasized that "before the child is conscious of being a Negro himself, he is affected by the tensions in his parents over their being Negro" (1956, p. 130).

It has already been mentioned that the child's first social learning occurs at home, particularly through his contact and experiences with his mother. According to Erikson, the way in which the mother interacts with her infant either favors or inhibits the child's sense of trust for her and, by extension, for others.

> Experiences connected with feeding are a prime source for the development of trust. At around four months of age, a hungry baby will grow quiet and show signs of pleasure at the sound of an approaching footstep, anticipating (trusting) that he will be held and fed. This repeated experience of being hungry, seeing food and feeling relieved and comforted assures the baby that the world is a dependable place (quoted in Mussen 1963, p. 67).

Research workers have found enough evidence to prove that the slum or ghetto home contributes very little in the way of helping the child acquire a sense of trust for the outside world, or for equipping him with the indispensable arm of competition, a sense of his own dignity and worth as a human being. Typically, the minority child has been described as living in an overcrowded home in which the recurrence of illegitimate or frequent pregnancies may result in the rejection of the unwanted baby; in which the prospect of unemployment, the shortage of money, and/or the desertion of the father, compel the mother to seek work and thus relinquish her maternal duties to a grandmother or older siblings. Furthermore, it is not long before the black child learns that his mere physical appearance (dark skin, kinky hair, negroid features) automatically relegates him to an inferior, stigmatized, humiliated, and powerless group. Hence he promptly and deeply internalizes his parents' feelings of anger, resentment, and shame. Except for Hispanic children (Puerto Rican and Mexican), whose ties with the family are stronger and longer lasting (Ausubel and Ausubel 1963), the black child assumes an early independence from a home that fails to provide him with the sense of importance and self-esteem he needs and will seek among his peers (Ausubel and Ausubel 1963). In contrast to the middle-class child, who typically derives status and a feeling of worth and dignity from his parents' place and achievements in society, the black child cannot find pride, hope, or encouragement in the diminishing and degrading role his parents, particularly his father, usually play in the white man's world (Proshansky and Newton 1968). Unable to achieve economic and occupational respectability, failing to provide adequate support for his family in order to fulfill his duties as head of the household, the black man's image is belittled further, within his own milieu, by the inevitably authoritarian and derogatory attitude of the black female who takes over and dominates the home. The reversal of sex roles, the decidedly matriarchal atmosphere of the home, hence the preference accorded to girls over boys, the greater occurrence of negative self-images among black boys (Ausubel and Ausubel 1963), and the absence of a father figure or strong male model—all these factors explain, in large part, the identity conflicts that the black male must face. It is no wonder that the research findings up until the mid-1960s were unanimous in revealing that the black child tended to hate himself, was reluctant to identify with, yet ready to reject, his own racial group, favored members of the white groups or strove to "pass as white"—in the case of light-skinned blacks—or wished to be white (Clark and Clark 1947; Morland 1963).

Using a variety of techniques (dolls, line drawings, coloring tests) the Clarks (1947, 1950) have explored extensively black children's racial awareness, identification, and preference. The 1950 experiment—in which five-, six-, and seven-year-olds were asked to color a little boy or girl (depending on their own sex) the same color as theirs and then the color that they would like that boy or girl to be —yielded results that further confirmed evidence gleaned from previous studies (Clark and Clark 1947). In the case of the first task (identification) results indicated that (1) the subjects tended to color themselves with a lighter color than their own; (2) such a tendency decreased with age; (3) 97 percent of the seven-year-old children as compared with 80 percent of the five-year-olds made correct racial identification in terms of their own skin color (Clark and Clark 1950, p. 343). The second task (preference) revealed that (1) 52 percent of the total group of testees rejected the color brown; (2) 59 percent of the dark-skinned children rejected the color brown; (3) by age seven 65 percent of the children expressed their preference for the color brown; (4) when geographical differences were considered, 70 percent of the Southern children preferred the color brown as opposed to 36 percent of the Northern children (pp. 344–346). Summarizing their study, the Clarks pointed to the fact that:

> The discrepancy between identifying one's own color and indicating one's color preference is too great to be ignored. The negation of the color brown exists in the same complexity of attitudes in which there also exists knowledge of the fact that the child himself must be identified with that which he rejects. This apparently introduces a fundamental conflict at the very foundations of the ego structure. Many of these children attempt to resolve this profound conflict either through wishful thinking or

phantasy—expressing itself in a desire to escape a situation which focuses the conflict on them. By the seven-year level the Negro child seems to be developing some stabilizing ideas which might help to resolve the basic conflict between his social self-image and the negative social evaluation of his skin color (Clark and Clark 1950, p. 350).

The study conducted by Radke, Sutherland, and Rosenberg (1950) further substantiates the Clarks' findings regarding children's racial preferences. Drawn from a predominantly black school located in a low socioeconomic area of Pittsburgh, the subjects (475 black and 48 white children between ages seven and thirteen) were administered a picture test and a picture sociometric test. Both tests used a series of photographs of black and white children of both sexes projected on a screen. For the picture test subjects were asked to identify the child best fitting the behavioral description given orally with each slide. This technique utilized the most common stereotypes used to describe black people. The second test demanded that the subjects reveal their preference or antipathy for the children projected on the screen. Information on the subjects' real-life friends was obtained a week before the testing session. Examination of the data clearly indicated that (1) white children preferred their own racial group and expressed unfavorable attitudes toward the black children; (2) black children showed a much less positive attitude toward their own race than their white counterparts showed for theirs; (3) both groups expressed the wish to have white children as friends (Radke, Sutherland, and Rosenberg 1950, pp. 170–171).

The Role of the School

The predominantly negative self-image that the minority child develops during his preschool years is further consolidated by his experiences with the school, which makes little or no attempt to recognize his history, heritage, and place in the world. Although the 1954 Supreme Court decision legally desegregated the public schools, it is very doubtful that it cured the ills or halted the devastating effects of segregation. In reality, there is reason to believe that attendance at racially mixed schools might even aggravate and further entrench the belief in blacks' inferiority. Green (1971) pertinently draws a distinction between an interracial school, "one in which students of varying racial backgrounds are found," and, an integrated school, "one in which students of varying racial backgrounds are found *and* a mutual interaction between them occurs" (1971, p. 28). It is only in the latter type of school, he contends, that meaningful social and academic learning can take place. Observers of schools and colleges across the country are prone to admit that the integrated school is not yet a reality. The reciprocal distrust that black and white students reflect and manifest by means of "group voluntary segregation" or deplorably, but not infrequently, by violent encounters cannot be alleviated by mere physical exposure, for "increased physical contact per se between white and Negro children does little to reduce prejudice" (Ausubel and Ausubel 1963), and prejudice against blacks is one of the pillars of the American culture. Even though equal legal status of blacks and whites has now been obtained, it is unlikely that prejudice will die of its own accord. And while it is true that desegregation is a necessary condition for the amelioration of race relations in America, it is not, however, a sufficient condition. The way in which schools are integrated may actually cause greater injustice to blacks, for no provisions are made for facilitating the psychological and academic passage from a low-quality segregated education to an intellectually nurtured and highly motivated classroom. Reports on the academic achievement of blacks in desegregated schools have tended to present a favorable picture of score gains (Coleman et al. 1966). But many questions have been raised about the purity of some of the data. On the other hand, Katz (1968b) contends that desegregation has created conditions that can be detrimental to the performance of blacks, conditions such as social rejection, social isolation, fear of competing with better-prepared white classmates, and feelings of inferiority. As an illustration, an experiment conducted by Katz and Benjamin (1960) at a Northern university showed that despite comparable scores on intellectual tasks, the black sample underestimated its performance and rated it as inferior to that of the white sample. Katz further presents a collection of studies pointing to the fact that, rather than closing the gap between majority and minority achievement, desegregation conditions may have helped to expose it and even widen it. Experts agree that the slum or ghetto home lacks the adequate educational stimulation (how can such homes have it?) conducive to academic success and that second- and third-rate schooling has denied blacks the opportunity to compete with white students; but the experts forget to stress that it is primarily the task of the school and the teacher to elicit and foster the interest for academic pursuit and to grant the student the opportunity to be successful, for "success begets success" and repeated failure discourages the student from even attending school, which becomes the symbol of his inferiority.

The Role of Teachers. Next to parents, teachers are, among the significant others, those who play an important role in the formation of children's attitudes toward themselves and others. Investigations have clearly demonstrated the relationship that exists between students' self-concepts and their teachers' perceptions of them. Clark (1963b)

summarized the plight of the poor and minority child and the consequent responsibility of his teachers.

> The children in these schools come generally from homes and com-
> munities which were so lacking in educational stimulation and other
> determinants of self-respect that they seemed even more dependent
> upon their teachers for self-esteem, encouragement and stimulation.
> These children like most deprived human beings were hypersensitive
> and desperate in their desire for acceptance (in Passow 1963, p. 148).

Unfortunately, Clark continued, "the overwhelming majority of these
teachers and their supervisors rejected these children and looked upon
them as inherently inferior" (1963b, p. 148). Research data indicate that
the typical white classroom teacher perceives lower-class and deprived
children in accordance with the stereotypes traditionally ascribed to
these groups: poor intellectual ability, lazy, disruptive, and so on.
Gottlieb (1964) found that black children who had been described by
their black teachers as "fun-loving, happy, co-operative, energetic, and
ambitious" were viewed negatively by their white teachers, who found
them "talkative, lazy, fun-loving, highstrung, and rebellious."

In a study conducted with 89 male and 114 female fourth, fifth,
and sixth graders, Davidson and Lang (1960) verified the hypothesis
that children's perceptions of their teachers' feelings toward them
were correlated with self-concept, academic achievement, and social
class. They found that children with positive self-concepts were those
who had rated their teachers' perceptions of them as favorable, who
achieved better, evinced desirable classroom behavior, and belonged
to the upper or middle social classes. Aware of the self-fulfilling
prophecy at work in the classroom, they wrote:

> The teacher's feelings of acceptance and approval are communicated to
> the child and perceived by him as positive appraisals. It is likely that
> these appraisals encourage the child to seek further teacher approval by
> achieving well and behaving in a manner acceptable to his
> teacher. . . . The child who achieves well and behaves satisfactorily is
> bound to please his teacher. She in turn communicates positive feelings
> toward the child, thus, reinforcing his desire to be a good pupil (Davidson
> and Lang 1960, p. 112).

In conclusion, Davidson and Lang warned against the vicious entan-
glement that traps the lower-class child into a world of negative rein-
forcers and urged teachers to "communicate positive feeling to their
children and thus not only strengthen their positive self-appraisals but
stimulate their growth academically as well as interpersonally" (p.
112).

Proshansky and Newton report a study conducted by Brown (1967) that pointed to the fact that "the Negro children, more often than the White children, tended to believe that their teachers perceived them negatively" (Proshansky and Newton 1968, p. 210). Rosenthal and Jacobson (1968) have provided evidence to illustrate the fact that whenever a child, particularly a minority child, is believed to be and is looked upon as being intellectually inferior, unable to learn or function at the same academic level as other children, he will indeed become intellectually inferior and uneducable, behave as such, and thereby confirm his teachers' original opinions. Unless white teachers are cognizant of the fact that they approach minority children with stereotyped preconceived ideas, mainly based on IQ scores, social-class status, and simple prejudice, the minority child will remain a prisoner of a vicious educational self-fulfilling prophecy. The significance of the role played by the school and by its teachers upon the development of the minority child's self-concept was well expressed by Deutsch:

> School experiences can either reinforce invidious self-concepts acquired from the environment, or help to develop or even induce—a negative self-concept. Conversely, they can effect positive self-feelings by providing for concrete achievements and opportunities to function with competence, although initially these experiences must be in the most limited and restricted areas. The evidence leads us to the inescapable conclusion that, by the time they enter school, many disadvantaged children have developed negative self-images, which the school does little to mitigate (1967, p. 35).

Contrary to some studies (Coleman et al. 1966) that do not find that the self-concept influences the ability to achieve, the bulk of the available research tends to confirm the existence of a relationship between self-concept and school performance. Although it cannot be said conclusively that low self-esteem inevitably forecasts a lowered level of achievement, Brookover and Erikson (1969) have, however, shown that students with low self-concepts of ability practically never achieve at a high level. Several other studies such as that of Davidson and Greenberg (1967) and Whiteman and Deutsch (1967) have pointed to the fact that the lower the level of self-esteem, the lower the level of performance. The latter study, particularly, demonstrated the relation between negative self-concept and poor test scores on ability and reading tests with a sample of fifth-grade children. It further showed that deprived children view themselves significantly more negatively, and hence perform significantly less well than advantaged children. A series of experiments conducted by Katz and his associates have revealed that blacks' fear of competing with whites, especially on tasks of intellectual ability (Katz, Roberts, and Robertson 1965), their unrealistic inferiority feelings and performance ratings (Katz and Benjamin 1960), their marked subordination to white partners (Katz, Goldstein, and Benjamin 1958) and passive submission to white companions (Katz and Cohen 1962), all reflect "an emotional accommodation to the demeaning role in American culture that has been imposed upon his racial group by the dominant white majority" (Katz 1968b, in Deutsch, Katz, and Jensen 1968, p. 267).

MOTIVATION

A person who is being tested usually tries to do his best. Therefore, motivation is one of the a priori assumptions upon which tests are built. The great majority of the available data leads to the observation that motivation has a determining effect upon the level of performance. Thus differences in performance may be attributed, in part, to differences in motivation.

It is generally contended that almost all behavior is motivated. Although simple reflex behavior such as heartbeat and digestion may escape motivational control, learned behavior does not (Hilgard and Atkinson 1967). Motivation researchers or the "hidden persuaders" who manipulate us (Packard 1957) have based their efforts on the premise that motivation *is* the sole determinant of behavior. The search for motives—why an individual does what he does (why, for instance, people choose or reject a car or select a particular brand of cigarettes or gasoline)—has been the primary concern of motivation research. Not unlike public relations or advertising agents, teachers also find themselves in the position in which they must present their materials and conduct their classes in a way that will stimulate their "audience," their students. They must motivate students to learn and help them to maximize their intellectual potential. However, no matter how ingenious a teacher may be, no matter how extraordinary a student's intellectual potential or environment may be, "no matter how many teachers, friends, computing machines and relatives surround a student, he himself finally has to learn to spell and memorize the multiplication tables" (Mosteller and Moynihan 1972, p. 54). In other words, if a student lacks the motivation to learn, then teachers' help, innate potential, and favorable environmental circumstances will not pull him up the ladder. Notwithstanding individual considerations, students from the lower class seem to evince a lower motivation level and, therefore, perform less well than upper-class students (Rosen 1959).

Testing Motivation

It is not the purpose of this section to engage in a theoretical discussion of the concept of motivation. McClelland and his associates have dealt with it extensively. Rather, the focus here will be on motivation as one of the factors affecting test performance and accounting for some of the variance between majority and minority test scores. One of the most comprehensive books concerned with the theoretical aspects of motivation, *Motivation: Theory and Research* (1964), offers a variety of definitions that the term has been given over the years. Here *motivation* refers to the need to excel in the pursuit of academic endeavors. Measures of achievement motivation (nAch) are obtained by means of the Thematic Apperception Test (TAT), which consists of a series of pictures depicting various social situations about which subjects are requested to make up short stories within a given time period. The TAT represents a method of investigating fantasies and imagery based on the assumption that "when a person interprets an ambiguous social situation he is apt to expose his own personality as much as the phenomenon to which he is attending. . . . To one with double hearing, however, he is disclosing certain inner tendencies and cathexes: wishes, fears and traces of past experiences" (Murray 1938, quoted in Weiner 1972, p. 172). The Murray TAT has been praised as a well-proved technique having demonstrated value both clinically and experimentally. McClelland and Atkinson adapted it and so did Thompson. Dreger and Miller (1960) report that in 1949 Thompson published a black version (T-TAT) using black characters exclusively, in order to facilitate identification. Despite his laudable efforts, Thompson apparently failed to show that black subjects identify better with pictured characters of their own race. More recently, the Themes Concerning Blacks (TCB), often referred to as the black TAT, was designed by Robert Williams in order to elicit from black subjects themes of achievement, black pride, awareness, aspiration, and so on. It is administered in the same way as the TAT and requires the subjects to tell a story for each of the fifteen different situations, which relate to the black experience only.

If, as Lowell's data (1952) strongly suggest, highly motivated subjects perform significantly better than subjects with a relatively low level of achievement motivation, one must seek the factors that facilitate or inhibit one's drive to achieve. As many studies attest, a person's need to excel academically is itself a function of ethnicity, social class, and test-taking experiences. In other words, a person's level of motivation seems to depend upon parental and cultural attitudes toward education, in general, and tests, in particular, as well as upon one's racial- and social-class membership. Generally, white, middle-class students are more motivated than white, lower-class students, who, in turn, show a stronger need to achieve than their black counterparts (Rosen 1959).

Motivation in the Home

Attitudes toward achievement begin and develop principally within the home. Parents set the standards of excellence for the child; they communicate to the child the feeling that he is expected to direct his energy toward the attainment of the goals, or standards, set by them. That rewards will recompense his efforts and punishment his failures is also made explicit to the child. Achievement training refers to that particular process whereby parents are concerned with "getting the child to do things well" (Rosen 1959). The teaching of self-reliance and autonomy in decision making, frequently referred to as independence training, is also taught by the parents. Rosen indicated that both achievement training and independence training are indispensable to the development of achievement motivation, the former being the more important of the two. In a study investigating the orientation toward achievement and social mobility of six ethnic groups—white Protestants, Jews, Greeks, Italians, French Canadians, and blacks —Rosen (1959) found that the children of white Protestants and Jews are expected to do things on their own, as are black children. However, unlike the first two groups, blacks show few or no signs of much achievement training. Hypothesizing that the parents of high achievers are more authoritarian and more restrictive in the treatment of their children than the parents of low achievers, Drews and Teahan (1957) conducted a study with the mothers of straight-A and B-minus groups of students of both gifted and average intelligence. Examination of the results of the Parental Attitude Scale (PAS) verified the hypothesis; that is, the high achiever tends to come from a home in which he occupies a rigidly defined place, is expected to meet the standards set by the parents, and is required to obey (or he incurs punishment).

The Impact of Cultural Differences on Motivation

As exemplified previously, parental intervention and demands considerably influence the development of achievement motivation (McClelland 1953). Yet parents are only mirrors of the culture in which they partake, and cultural differences in motivation cannot be ignored.

Anastasi (1958) recognized the importance that differential sets of values and attitudes have upon an individual's drive to excel. She wrote:

> Thus, for the middle-class white American child the usual intelligence test bears a close resemblance to his everyday school work, which is probably the most serious business of his life at the time. He is therefore easily spurred on to exert his best efforts and to try to excel his fellows. For an American Indian child, on the other hand, the same test cannot have such significance. This type of activity has no place in the traditional behavior of his family or tribe. Similarly, many investigators have noted that among Negro children interest in intelligence tests is not as keen as among white children, and that the former seem not to be so strongly motivated as the latter (1958, p. 552).

Among the six groups identified earlier by Rosen, both the Jewish and white Protestant cultures have had a long tradition of heavy emphasis upon achievement. Dating back to the early beginnings of America, there has existed an endemic Puritan ethic with its concept of individualism, hard work, competitiveness, and manifest destiny. White Americans have been nurtured in the belief that education is the means to a career and hence to social advancement. It is the "American belief that children should be encouraged to develop their talents and to set high goals, possibly a bit beyond their reach" (Rosen 1959, p. 51). Along with the Jewish and Greek cultures, Rosen identified that of the white Protestant as being more individualistic, activistic, and future oriented than those of the other three groups. If one accepts Rosen's classification of values (activistic-passivistic, individualistic-collectivistic, present-future), blacks stand diametrically opposed to whites in their cultural orientations. In no way and at no time did the life situation of blacks in this country permit them to believe that they could effectively manipulate their environment and control their destinies or ameliorate their condition by working hard and sacrificing immediate rewards. Delayed gratification—one of the tenets of the school—has little meaning for a group that, for want of academic training, does not stress its pursuit, that has little or no tradition of scholarship, and that has seen its educational aspirations consistently curtailed. Investigating the contents of the TAT stories of 100 lower-class white and black boys, matched in age and of normal intelligence, Mussen (1953) observed that, unlike the white sample, the minority children perceived the general environment as hostile and themselves as being less respected, followed, or obeyed by others. Summarizing his study, Mussen concludes that:

> [T]here are major differences in the fantasy productions of the two sociocultural groups studied. In addition to personal dynamic factors, the

historical, economic and social forces impinging on the group are reflected in the stories told by the group members. Apparently, a certain amount of variation in these projective responses may be attributed to the individual's cultural background (1953, p. 376).

The previously mentioned study, in which the subjects were matched in age, socioeconomic status, and intelligence, could suggest that ethnicity accounts for the relative paucity of responses indicating striving for accomplishment and success (nAch). Yet it appears that social class is responsible for a sizable proportion of the variance between the two groups. In contrast to the more privileged classes, lower-class individuals typically display an anti-intellectual attitude toward education, live in surroundings that lack cultural tradition and stimulation, experience unsuccessful learning efforts at school and greater failure on tests. Distinguishing between middle-class and lower-class parental attitudes toward education, Eells et al. suggest that:

> The characteristic middle-class attitude toward education is taught by middle-class parents to their children. School is important for future success. One must do one's very best in school. Report cards are studied by the parents carefully and the parents give rewards for good grades, warning and penalties for poor grades. Lower-class parents, on the other hand, seldom push the children that are in school and do not show by example or by precept that they believe education is highly important. In fact, they usually show the opposite attitude. With the exception of a minority who urgently desire mobility for their children, lower-class parents tend to place little value on high achievement in school or on school attendance beyond the minimum age (1951, p. 21).

Katz noted that "in white middle-class children, on the other hand, internalization of the achievement motive presumably is relatively well advanced at the time of entering school" (1968a, p. 58). Most studies show that lower-class individuals obtain significantly lower nAch scores than middle-class individuals (Veroff et al. 1960; Rosen 1959), regardless of ethnic membership. Although ethnicity remains a contributing factor, social class appears to be a better predictor. Rosen's study attested to the fact that mean scores were low for all ethnic groups of low SES and that the mean score of the black middle-class individual was significantly higher than that of the white Protestant lower-class person. Generally, Rosen concluded, "a high status person from an ethnic group with a low mean achievement motivation score is more likely to have a high score than a low status person from a group with a high mean score" (1959, p. 53).

Test Taking

An abundance of observations lead to the conclusion that practice on tests and with test-taking situations have negatively reinforced the low-socioeconomic group members and the minority group members, in particular. Inappropriate curricula and repeated failures at school and on tests have resulted in discouragement, anxiety, fear, and diminished motivation to learn and work hard. As Eells et al. noted, "to the average lower-class child . . . a test is just another place to be punished, to have one's weaknesses shown up, to be reminded that one is at the tail end of the procession" (1951, p. 21). The minority child has long ago learned that his chances of succeeding when competing with whites are low. As a consequence, as Atkinson has postulated and Katz has demonstrated, the minority child's motivation to achieve declines significantly. According to Atkinson, a given individual performs at his maximum when he perceives that his probability of success is slightly better than even. But when the expectancy of success is seen as being too remote or too easy, motivation diminishes.

Katz (1968b) tested such a hypothesis with a group of Southern black male students in their freshman year. Katz manipulated the experiment by giving each subject a letter from the fictitious "Southern Educational Testing Service" bearing what was perceived by the subject as his chance of succeeding on the actual test. Such a probability had been established, the subject was led to believe, on the basis of his score on the trial test. The recorded percentages were either 10, 60, or 90. Results of the experiment confirmed the preceding hypothesis as expressed by Atkinson. That is, it clearly demonstrated that "the best motivation and performance occurred, regardless of racial conditions, when the subject was told that he had a slightly better-than-even chance of succeeding. If his chances seemed very low or very high he apparently lost interest" (Katz 1968b, in Deutsch, Katz, and Jensen 1968, p. 279).

ANXIETY

Very few individuals approach examinations or test situations devoid of anxiety, no matter how bright, confident, or well prepared they may be. Research findings seem to agree that, as a consequence, performance on tests is affected by the individual's ability or inability to withstand debilitating conditions. Thus individuals whose anxiety threshold is low (high anxious) consistently perform less well than low-anxious individuals, for whom anxiety acts as an energizer. The effects of anxiety on test performance, both at the grade school and college levels, have been investigated extensively, notably by Sarason and his collaborators.

Anxiety Scales

Because anxiety represents an emotional state that cannot be measured directly, the most straightforward way of finding how anxious a person feels is to ask him. Many techniques for assessing anxiety have been developed. In his extensive survey of available techniques McReynolds (1968) identified 88 formal anxiety-measurement procedures. Here, however, mention will be made only of the most widely used. Among anxiety scales, one distinguishes between those that attempt to measure a subject's overall, or general, level of anxiety and those that indicate a subject's degree of specific anxiety, such as test anxiety.

Starting with the premise that there exists within each individual a relatively constant "level of anxiety or internal emotionality," Taylor (1953) devised her Manifest Anxiety Scale (MAS) to measure levels of general anxiety. Made up of 50 items, such as, "I cry easily" or "I am a high-strung person," the MAS is considered to be one of the most, if not the most, popular of all anxiety tests. In 1956 Castaneda, McCandless, and Palmero published the Children's Manifest Anxiety Scale (CMAS), which they adapted from Taylor's adult form for use with fourth, fifth, and sixth graders. The IPAT Anxiety Scale developed by Cattell and Scheier (1961) is a 40-item questionnaire that consists of two 20-item subscales to measure overt anxiety and covert anxiety, respectively. On the other hand, Mandler and Sarason (1952) and Alpert and Haber (1960) have concerned themselves with the construction of scales specifically designed to measure subjects' proneness to anxiety when taking tests.

The Test Anxiety Questionnaire (TAQ) of Sarason explores the extent to which individuals, before and during a test, worry, perspire, experience discomfort or heart palpitations, and so on. The questionnaire comprises 39 items, such as: "If you know that you are going to take a group intelligence test, how do you feel beforehand?" "While taking a group intelligence test, to what extent do you perspire?" "In comparison to other students, how often do you (would you) think of ways of avoiding an individual intelligence test?" (Sarason and Mandler 1952, p. 810.) A children's version of the questionnaire was developed by S. B. Sarason, Davidson, Lighthall, and Waite in 1958 and published as the Test Anxiety Scale for Children (TASC).

Unlike the TAQ, which surveys the adverse effects of anxiety, Alpert and Haber constructed the Achievement Anxiety Test (AAT) to indicate "not only the presence or absence of anxiety but also whether the anxiety facilitates or debilitates the test performance" (1960, p. 207). Thus they included two independent scales: a facilitating scale that explores anxiety as a possible stimulating force ("nervousness while taking a test helps me do better") and a debilitating scale that describes anxiety as an inhibitor of performance ("nervousness while taking an exam or test hinders me from doing well").

Factors That Heighten Anxiety

Acting singly or in combination, various factors have been recognized to heighten test anxiety. They are: a strong achievement need, fear of failure or punishment, deflated self-concept and inferiority feelings, negatively reinforcing experiences with school examinations and tests, hostile test-center environment, and unfamiliarity with testing procedures and test-taking skills. Because minority members, in particular, seem to evidence such characteristics, they are more prone to anxiety than white individuals of higher socioeconomic levels (Hawkes and Furst 1971). Therefore, "it is questionable whether intelligence test scores adequately describe the underlying abilities of individuals who have high anxiety drive in the testing situation" (Mandler and Sarason 1952, p. 172; Sarason and Mandler 1952, p. 817). From the numerous investigations conducted over a number of years, S. B. Sarason and his collaborators were able to formulate certain conclusions about the performance of high-anxious students (those who score high on the anxiety scale) and low-anxious students (those who score low on the anxiety scale).

First, it has been their repeated observation that high-anxious students perform less well than low-anxious students; that is, students who succumb to anxiety make more task-irrelevant responses than those whose tolerance for stress is high. Wrightstone (1963) observed that, very frequently, minority and low SES members, especially when taking tests involving speed, work rapidly, randomly, disorderly, and without the necessary application for securing good grades in an attempt to rid themselves of the unpleasant task that the test represents. Atkinson (1960) also noted a strong tendency among highly anxious students to leave the site of the examination or to go for the all-or-nothing type of rewards in an effort to reduce anxiety. Because they become the victims of "feelings of inadequacy, helplessness, heightened somatic reaction, anticipations of punishment or loss of status and esteem, and implicit attempts at leaving the test situation" (Mandler and Sarason 1952, p. 166), high-anxious individuals are distracted from their tasks and thus tend to make random responses, which, in turn, decrease their test performance. Experiments using stress-producing conditions illustrate this last point (Sarason, Mandler, and Craighill 1952). Both high- and low-anxious groups were split into two subgroups to which differential sets of instructions were given. Whereas one subgroup was told that the test was easy enough to be completed within the allotted time, the other believed that the test could not be finished within the time limit. The experiment was replicated with ego-involving and nonego-involving instructions. In both instances, results showed that the high-anxiety group that was given the expected-to-finish and ego-involving instructions performed much worse than the high-anxiety group that was given the not-expected-to-finish and nonego-involving instructions. For the low-anxiety group, on the other hand, results indicated that stress (time limit and ego involvement) produced opposite effects, for it enhanced performance.

Second, it would appear that anxiety is a function of social class; that is, a higher percentage of middle-class individuals than upper- or lower-class members is found in the high-anxiety group (Sarason and Mandler 1952). Sarason suggests that such an overrepresentation can be explained by the fact that middle-class individuals for whom intellectual achievement is not only important but vital for career and social mobility are overly eager to achieve and afraid of failing. Spielberger and Katzenmeyer (1959) found that anxiety is felt mostly by the mass of students whose intellectual ability is average. Both extremes of the distribution are insignificantly affected, for very bright children not only overcome but seem to need the challenge of pressure, whereas dull children perform poorly under all conditions. Feldhausen and Klausmeier (1962) also observed that among fifth graders of both sexes, children with low IQs are more prone to anxiety than very bright children, for whom anxiety acts as a stimulating agent.

Studies investigating the relationship between anxiety and performance among elementary schoolchildren are numerous (Waite et al. 1958; Castaneda, McCandless, and Palmero 1956). Basically, findings for school-grade children are similar to those for college students; that is, low-anxiety children perform better than high-anxiety children. Waite et al. in a study conducted with 747 children in grades two through five concluded that "as expected, the direction of the results coincides with that obtained in similar studies with college students" (1958, p. 269). Furthermore, several studies have pointed to the presence of sex differences in anxiety. Castaneda, McCandless, and Palmero (1956) observed that girls scored higher than boys on the CMAS, indicating that fourth-, fifth-, and sixth-grade girls evince a higher degree of anxiety than boys of the same age. Loughlin et al. investigated further the preceding observation and suggested that for girls anxiety manifests itself at an early age, reaches a peak in the fifth and sixth grades, and then diminishes by the time they enter the eighth grade (1965, p. 144).

In a series of experiments McKeachie, Pollie, and Speisman (1963) attempted by means of "feel-free-to-comment" instructions to reduce or dissipate anxiety. The authors' original thesis was that when given the opportunity to comment about the test, "to blow off steam about items that caused them difficulty," students will discharge their frustration and tension and thus improve their performance. Many techniques that attempt to reduce test anxiety have been employed. It was believed that if high-anxious students were trained to use more efficient study methods, the debilitating effects of anxiety would be drastically eliminated (Spielberger 1966). However, several recent studies have gathered evidence to support findings that systematic desensitization proves far superior to both study-skills counseling and implosive therapy in the treatment of test anxiety (Osterhouse 1972; Cornish and Dilley 1973).

TEST ENVIRONMENT

As stated previously, test anxiety is produced by a variety of factors. There exists a host of anxiety-producing, thus performance-inhibiting, environmental features that the minority test taker must also face. More specifically, these are the test center itself, its location, organization, and supervisors; other features are the familiarity, or lack of it, with test-information procedures, test format, test instructions, and test-taking skills.

Constituted in April 1971, the Committee on Hostile Test Center Environment, under the auspices of the CEEB, has conducted investigations and offered recommendations in three principal areas —namely, test-center management, test administration, and joint publications of the Educational Testing Service and the CEEB. The preliminary report of the committee made available data concerning the SAT, gathered from a sample of 3038 minority and nonminority students enrolled in 100 city schools. Pertinent to the present topic, the report demonstrates, unequivocally, that:

1. Almost twice as many minority (12 percent) as nonminority candidates (6.8 percent) indicated having encountered problems in obtaining test information, and more than double (3.7 percent) the percentage of whites (1.2 percent) revealed having received none at all.

2. Only 53 percent of the minority sample knew about the possibility of obtaining fee waivers when test fees cannot be afforded.

3. A majority (65 percent) of the minority students surveyed indicated their preference for a familiar test center conveniently located (for example a predominantly minority school rather than all-white facility).

4. A significantly greater percentage of minority (7 percent) than white students mentioned the failure to understand the instructions or to get satisfactory answers to their questions (13 percent).

5. Three times as many minority (45 percent) as white candidates considered test content biased against them and irrelevant to their studies and life experiences.

6. Minority and nonminority students were unanimous in stating that there was no minority person performing the role of supervisor, proctor, or examiner.

More and more, investigators are calling attention to the possible effects that examiners have on the results they elicit from test takers (Gibby, Miller, and Walker 1953; Sacks 1952). Bernstein (1956) suggests that whenever examinees are presented with strongly emotional material such as on the TAT, the presence of an examiner acts as an inhibiting factor. In testing the hypothesis that examiners' behavior during a testing session significantly influences examinees' test results, Wickes (1956) found that verbal comments such as "good," "fine," and "all right," and nonverbal actions such as nodding the head, smiling, and leaning forward in the chair can modify responses on tests.

Although Shuey dismissed the possibility that the presence of a white examiner adversely affects the intelligence scores of black test takers (1966, p. 507), many studies (Canady 1936; Vega 1964) have cast doubts upon such a conclusion. In a longitudinal study conducted with a group of 40 black children whose physical growth and behavioral development progressed at the same rate as that of white children of comparable age, Pasamanick and Knobloch reported a significantly lower language behavior for the black children at age two. As an explanation for the discrepant scores between black and white infants, the two investigators advanced the theory that "awareness of the examiner's different skin color caused sufficient inhibition to decrease verbal responsiveness by the children" (1955, p. 401). In an experiment with a group of black students enrolled at a Southern black college, Katz, Roberts, and Robinson (1965) found that the sample performed better when tested by a white examiner on a relatively simple digit-symbol code disguised as an eye-hand coordination instrument but that the sample scored more poorly when the same task was presented as an intelligence test by the white examiner instead of by the black examiner. Katz concluded:

> Negro students performed better with a white adult than with a Negro adult when the task was supposed to assess an ability which Negroes are not stereotyped as lacking (eye-hand coordination). . . . On the intellectual task the Negro subject saw very little likelihood of meeting the white experimenter's standard of excellence (1968b, p. 277).

In another study investigating the influence of differential test instructions (IQ test versus research instrument) and examiner race upon the arousal and expression of hostility of junior high and high school black male students, Katz et al. (1964) reported no significant effects with either race of examiners under neutral instructions when the questionnaire was presented as a research instrument. When the sample perceived the test as a measure of intellectual ability, hostility scores increased with the black examiner but significantly decreased when the experimenter was white. Katz interpreted the findings as follows:

> Both task administrators instigated hostility in subjects when they announced that they were testing intelligence; when the experimenter was Negro, students revealed their annoyance by forming aggressive concepts, but when he was white, the need to control hostile feelings resulted in avoidance of aggressive words (Katz 1968b, p. 282).

A good many studies, cited by Katz (1968b, p. 281), have suggested that blacks usually, strongly inhibit their feelings of hostility toward whites, and that, as a result, the blocking of aggressive impulses has a detrimental effect upon their intellectual performance.

LANGUAGE

It is an established fact that intelligence tests, with the exception of the so-called performance or nonverbal tests, are heavily verbally loaded and that, therefore, familiarity with the language of the test becomes paramount. Immigrants and Hispanic children face an evident language obstacle when taking tests. Many studies investigating the effects of bilingualism on intelligence-test performance have demonstrated its adverse consequences on test results; children who are in the process of learning English score consistently lower than those who have already mastered the language (Anastasi and Cordova 1953; Klineberg 1935b). The solution for these "atypical" children does not lie simply in translating the Stanford-Binet into Spanish, for instance, for the language these minority children speak is an adulterated Spanish resulting from the constant interaction with an English-speaking school and a Spanish-speaking home. In this particular case, the handicap arises from the lack of mastery of either language.

Black English

On the other hand, the black American finds himself in a completely different situation, for he is and has been anglophone all his life. English is his native tongue; yet the black child seems to suffer from the same deficiency as the foreign speaker in his ability to comprehend and use the language of the test, that is, standard English. What the black ghetto or slum child speaks is, if not altogether foreign, often highly unintelligible to the white, middle-class ear and entirely unacceptable to the school and society in general. How does saying "Where Charlie?" differ then from saying "Where is Charlie?" That is, in what respect does black English differ from standard English?

It would not seem too much of an exaggeration to state that black English, when compared to the language of the middle class, has been found wanting in a manner not too foreign from that of primitive languages in respect to Western languages. Cole et al. (1971) provide two good illustrations of the way in which many early travelers and certain anthropologists thought and still think of the "primitive mind." The following excerpts (p. 176) represent the reflections of the explorer Bentley (1929) and of the eminent anthropologist Tylor (1965), respectively.

> The African Negro, or Bantu, does not think, reflect, or reason if he can help it. He has a wonderful memory, has great powers of observation and imitation . . . and very many good qualities . . . but the reasoning and inventive faculties remain dormant. He readily grasps the present circumstances, adapts himself to them, and provides for them but a carefully thought out plan or a clever piece of induction is beyond him (Bentley 1929).

> [B]etween our clearness of separation of what is in the mind from what is out of it, and the mental confusion of the lowest savage of our own day, there is a vast interval (Tylor 1965).

In both instances, emphasis is placed on the lack of logic and rationality and on the inability to carry on abstract thinking. To infer nonlogical thinking because a particular language does not reflect the "model of logic put forth by Aristotle and his successors" (Cole et al. 1971, p. 177) is to display an "ignorance of language" (Labov 1971). Such ignorance is, in the opinion of Labov, at the very center of the present dichotomy between standard English and black English. Reminiscent of Bentley's and Tylor's reflections is Bereiter and Engelman's evaluation of the language of the black children enrolled in their intervention program:

From our earlier work in teaching concrete logical operations it became evident that culturally deprived children do not just think at an immature level: many of them do not think at all. That is, they do not show any of the mediating processes which we ordinarily identify with thinking. They cannot hold on to questions while searching for an answer. They cannot compare perceptions in any reliable fashion. They are oblivious of even the most extreme discrepancies between their actions and statements as they follow one another in a series. They do not just give bad explanations. They cannot give explanations at all, nor do they seem to have any idea of what it is to explain an event. The question and answer process which is the core of orderly thinking is completely foreign to them (Bereiter et al. 1966, p. 107).

These authors maintain that the language of culturally deprived children is not only an underdeveloped form of standard English but "basically a nonlogical mode of expressive behavior" (Bereiter et al. 1966, p. 112).

The distinction between standard English and black English seems to parallel Bernstein's distinction between elaborated code and restricted code. In 1960 the *British Journal of Sociology* published Bernstein's "Language and Social Class," which, as the name indicates, deals with the language behavior of British lower-class and middle-class children. His findings and conclusions were not only accepted immediately but transposed to the American milieu, where they became the integral rationalization for the differential scholastic achievement of black and white children. The basis of Bernstein's thesis rests on the concept of linguistic deprivation. In other words, because of their distinct social backgrounds lower-class children have "learned two different forms of spoken language; the only thing they have in common is that the words are English" (in Passow et al. 1967, p. 232). Of these two forms of language, the one spoken by the middle class is the only one spoken and accepted by the school, whereas the lower-class speaker finds himself in the situation in which he must, make responses "to which he is neither oriented nor sensitized," and where "his natural responses are unacceptable" (in Passow et al. 1967, p. 239). The backwardness presented by the lower-class child, Bernstein continues, is "culturally induced backwardness transmitted and sustained through the effects of linguistic processing" (in Passow et al. 1967, p. 240). The linguistic forms characteristic of the middle class, on the one hand, and of the lower-class, on the other, Bernstein called formal language or elaborated code and public language or restricted code, respectively. This is not to be taken as meaning that lower-class or middle-class members speak one form of language exclusive of the other; instead, the probability that the middle class will use a formal code and the lower class a restricted code is very high.

Contrasting the two forms of language, it appears that the differences reside in the syntactical flexibilities and possibilities, repertoire of vocabulary, level of conceptualization and abstraction, and orientation. More specifically, Bernstein (1961) identified the following characteristics. A public language utilizes the following:

1. Short, grammatically simple, often unfinished sentences with a poor syntactical form stressing the active voice.
2. Simple and repetitive use of conjunctions (so, then, because).
3. Little use of subordinate clauses to break down the initial categories of the dominant subject.
4. Inability to hold a formal subject through a speech sequence; thus a dislocated informational content is facilitated.
5. Rigid and limited use of adjectives and adverbs.
6. Infrequent use of impersonal pronouns as subjects of conditional clauses.
7. Frequent use of statements where the reason and conclusion are confounded to produce a categoric statement.
8. A large number of statements/phrases which signal a requirement for the previous speech sequence to be reinforced: "Wouldn't it? You see? You know?" etc. This process is termed "sympathetic circularity."
9. Individual selection from a group of idiomatic phrases or sequences will frequently occur.
10. The individual qualification is implicit in the sentence organization: it is a language of implicit meaning. (Quoted in Passow et al., 1967, p. 233.)

A public language is characterized by redundancy or repetition and by dislocation or disjunction. In the words of Bernstein (1961), "the thoughts are strung together somewhat like passing beads on a frame rather than following a planned sequence" (in Passow et al. 1967, p. 235). It is also more oriented toward the expression of the immediate present. In contrast, a formal language presents the following:

1. Accurate grammatical order and syntax regulate what is said.
2. Logical modifications and stress are mediated through a grammatically complex sentence construction, especially through the use of a range of conjunctions and subordinate clauses.
3. Frequent use of prepositions which indicate logical relationships as well as prepositions which indicate temporal and spatial contiguity.
4. Frequent use of the personal pronoun "I."
5. A discriminative selection from a range of adjectives and adverbs.
6. Individual qualification is verbally mediated through the structure and relationships within and between sentences.

7. Expressive symbolism discriminates between meanings within speech sequences rather than reinforcing dominant words or phrases or accompanying the sequence in a diffuse, generalized manner.
8. It is a language use which points to the possibilities inherent in a complex conceptual hierarchy for the organizing of experience. (Quoted in Passow et al., 1967, pp. 233–234.)

Unlike lower-class children, middle-class speakers are not confined to formal language only; they have access to both forms.

Verbal Deprivation Theory

As noted earlier, Bernstein's findings on the verbal behavior of socially different groups have been considered to be valid for the lower and middle classes of the United States and, by extension, for black and white groups. Briefly stated, blacks have been found to be verbally destitute and linguistically underdeveloped when placed within an educational context (Baratz and Baratz 1970). And the native tongue of the ghetto or slum has been shown to possess more of the features of the restricted code. By what process, then, do black children become verbally handicapped?

Generally, it is agreed that what differentiates a lower-class home from a middle-class home is a paucity of verbal stimulation and interaction. Unlike privileged children who learn "by feedback: by being heard, corrected, and modified" (John and Goldstein 1967), the poor child's early vocalizations are rarely, if at all, reinforced, and the corrective feedback he receives, if any, tends to be very poor and faulty. His parents are usually busy and "preoccupied with the problems associated with poverty and their crowded living conditions leaves them with little capacity to be concerned with what they conceive to be the senseless questions of a prattling infant" (Hunt 1967, p. 203). Thus the lower-class child's early attempts and questions are more likely to go unanswered or to be answered in a fragmented and brief manner (a yes, no, or a nod), encouraging no further exchange. In addition, more often than not, the child lacks the variety of objects that serve as references for language acquisition (Ausubel 1964); he is not read to aloud; he does not see books, newspapers, or magazines around the house, nor does he see his parents reading; he does not engage in verbal exchanges of any great length with adults, notably with his parents; mealtime, which the middle class generally considers as the opportune moment for conversational interaction, is practically nonexistent. Whiteman and Deutsch (1967), for example, found that although the father's or mother's mere presence at mealtimes does not correlate with reading ability, conversation with parents during dinner does affect reading ability in a significant way. Deutsch observed that:

> Strong evidence can be adduced to support the assumption that it is the active verbal engagement of people who surround him which is the operative influence in the child's language development. . . . In the cognitive style of the lower-class family . . . The feedback is not such that it gives the child the articulated verbal parameters that allow him to start and fully develop normative labelling and identification of the environment. Family interaction data which we have gathered in both lower class socially deprived and middle class groups indicate that, as compared with middle class homes, there is a paucity of organized family activities in a large number of lower class homes. As a result, there is less conversation, for example, at meals, as meals are less likely to be regularly scheduled family affairs (1967, pp. 358–359).

Lower-class parents and lower-class mothers, in particular, have been judged to be very poor linguistic models for their young children. Hunt, for example, stated that "the variety of linguistic patterns available for imitation in the models provided by lower class adults is both highly limited and wrong for the standard of later schooling" (1967, p. 203). Ausubel also believes that "the syntactical model provided him by his parents is typically faulty" (in Passow et al. 1967, p. 314). Begun in 1962, the Hess and Shipman study represents an extensive investigation of "the specific elements of maternal behavior and home environments which are related to the cognitive performance of children" (1968, p. 3). Focusing on mother-preschool child interaction patterns, the study involved 163 black mothers of different socioeconomic status and their four-year-old children (Hess and Shipman 1965). Summarizing their findings, the authors observed the following characteristic language behaviors of lower-class and middle-class mothers:

> [L]arge, sometimes dramatic, differences exist among social class groups, with a clear social class level trend. The middle-class mothers were consistently the highest on all scales and tasks. . . . The skilled-working-class mothers generally coming next, and the two unskilled groups usually scoring the lowest. The middle-class mothers spoke in longer sentences, exhibited a wider range of adverbs, manifested a larger repertoire of complex verb types, used more complex syntactic structures, exhibited greater perceptual discrimination as shown by their attending more of the stimuli in test pictures, displayed more abstract concepts in their language usage, and in the case of the fanciful story told to the child, showed more imaginative thought elaboration by going beyond the information given and introducing characters and objects not manifest in the lion-mouse picture . . . the working-class mothers showed a general picture of language restriction—a restriction that became greater with lowered social class level. The working-class groups consistently spoke in shorter sentences; demonstrated a narrow range of

linguistic subtlety and elaboration, as evidenced by their smaller reper-
toires of adverbs and complex verb types and their tendency to use
simpler syntactic structures; exhibited a more constricted perceptual
system, as shown by their lowered attention to the stimuli in test pictures;
displayed a marked inability to use abstract concepts; and evidenced a
deficit in the area of imaginative thought elaboration when asked to
fabricate a fanciful story (Hess et al. 1968, pp. 168–169).

Critics of the verbal-deprivation theory contend that such a notion
is "unrealistic in terms of current linguistic and anthropological data,
and, at worst, ethnocentric and racist" (Baratz and Baratz 1970, p. 30), as
well as the result of "the work of educational psychologists who know
very little about language and even less about black children" (Labov
1971, p. 59). This school of thought centers on workers like Stewart,
Labov, and the Baratzes, who oppose and challenge the views advanced by Deutsch, Bereiter, Engelman, Hunt, Bernstein, and others
for explaining the poor test performance of lower-class children, in
general, and of black children, in particular. What is essentially questioned and rejected is the notion of deficit in lieu of difference and the
model of the black man as a "sick white man" (Baratz and Baratz 1970).

Labov, for example, refutes the theory of verbal deprivation on the
ground that it has

no basis in social reality; in fact, black children in the urban ghettos
receive a great deal of verbal stimulation, hear more well-formed sentences than middle-class children, and participate fully in a highly verbal
culture; they have the same basic vocabulary, possess the same capacity
for conceptual learning and use the same logic as anyone else who learns
to speak and understand English (1971, pp. 59–60).

Black children do not speak an underdeveloped form of standard English or a nonlogical mode of expressive behavior, as has been claimed.
Black English, when it is considered as separate and distinct from
standard English, represents a well-ordered, highly structured, fully
developed language system that is more than adequate for aiding in
abstract thinking (Baratz and Baratz 1970, p. 36). Labov demonstrates
that when black children say "They mine," for instance, they are not
merely expressing "a series of badly connected words," as Bereiter
might assume, but a statement that "follows the same regular rules as
standard English contraction" (1971, p. 65).

Wherever standard English can contract, black children use either the
contracted form or (more commonly) the deleted zero form. Thus "They
mine" corresponds to standard English "they're mine," not to the full
form "They are mine." On the other hand, no such deletion is possible in
positions where standard English cannot contract: just as one cannot say
"That's what they're" in standard English, "That's what they" is equally
impossible in the vernacular we are considering (Labov 1971, p. 65).

Moreover, replying "In the tree" to the question "Where is the squirrel?" is not an illogical or badly formed answer as Bereiter or Hess and Shipman (1965) contend but a perfectly acceptable elliptical form used by everyone—speakers of standard English or not—a form that demonstrates that the syntactical structure of the question has been well understood and assimilated (Labov 1971). Analyzing a conversation exchanged with a fifteen-year-old Harlem speaker, Labov proceeds to show the logic and the grammatical richness contained in the young man's statements, which were expressed in the black English vernacular (1971, p. 63).

Another point advanced by the advocates of the difference model is the impact that situations perceived as threatening have on the verbal output of the interviewee. Labov again demonstrates in his research report (1971) that the ineptitude, bashfulness, ignorance, and monosyllabic behavior of the black child in school disappears when the same child is at ease and operating within his own frame of reference. He then becomes extremely verbal, assertive, and capable of dealing with complex and abstract formulations expressed in a different idiom from that of standard English. Labov and his associates have been accused of romanticizing black English, for many educators feel that such a position is unrealistic in terms of the essential needs of education in the society at large. However, the main point of Labov's argument is that the education of the black ghetto child can only proceed from a proper understanding of the individual within his own linguistic and cultural milieu, so that emphasis is placed on a bicultural and bilingual perspective rather than on one that stresses the rightness of standard English and standard middle-class norms. Labov admits that there do exist black English speakers who are developmentally immature in the thinking process, but, on the other hand, he points to the multitude of nonstandard English speakers who can and do express themselves in a black idiom and at a level of abstraction that connotes a high capacity for logical thought. In sum, there is an urgent need to distinguish between these two kinds of speakers in order to prescribe the right kind of education matched to the individual needs of the individual child. Baratz and Baratz call for the teaching of standard English to black ghetto children in a manner similar to the teaching of English to nonnative speakers—English as a foreign language:

> Education for culturally different children should not attempt to destroy functionally viable processes of the subculture, but rather should use these processes to teach additional cultural forms. The goal of such education should be to produce a bicultural child who is capable of functioning both in his subculture and in the mainstream (Baratz and Baratz 1970, pp. 42–43).

Introduction
A Brief Review of the Research
Consequences of Ability Grouping
    for Blacks and Other Minorities
Testing and College Admission
    of Minority Students

EDUCATIONAL AND SOCIAL CONSEQUENCES

5

INTRODUCTION

There seems to have been a widespread belief among teachers, and the general public, that the learning situation is improved when classes have pupils of more or less the same level of ability. It is no wonder that grouping in education has been one of the most popular topics of study in the entire field of pedagogical research. What is remarkable, however, is that despite hundreds of studies conducted since the 1920s, there appears to be a consistent inconclusiveness in the findings (Findley and Bryan 1971); no clear-cut positive or negative effect on average scholastic achievement seems to have emerged. While the earlier studies, as a whole, indicate slight gains by low groups, more recent studies show that the advantage of homogeneous ability grouping usually accrues to the brighter or high groups. What is even more remarkable is that entire systems of education, at the local, regional, and national levels in the United States and in several other countries, have continued to embrace homogeneous ability grouping as the basic method for curricular organization within schools and among different schools. Such groupings are of vital significance in maintaining and supporting the social cleavages existing in any population. But the effect becomes even more marked when such educational practices, despite dubious pedagogical advantage, tend to divide groups of children in terms of class and caste.

Homogeneous grouping, which has been practiced for centuries, refers to the division of students according to any common characteristic. The grouping characteristics most frequently used are: sex, religious affiliation, or estimated level of achievement or ability. Such grouping can be overt or covert. Eton, Harrow, and Shrewsbury in England and Lawrenceville, Phillips Andover, and Choate in the United States are examples of schools that cater almost exclusively to boys of the upper and upper-middle classes. Selection is based on the ability to pay the high cost of tuition and on admission criteria that inevitably exclude the vast majority of school-aged children. In practice, if not wholly in theory, such schools are organized to train the children of aristocrats, to cater to a specific homogeneous population, and, consequently, they subscribe to certain customs and practices that flow from a prescribed set of values and educational philosophy. Each of these schools has a statement of standards, and they all practice the kind of social separation endemic in their view of society and education. They are, essentially, private institutions committed to a definite code.

Homogeneous ability grouping is widely practiced in public schools as well as private schools. It is based on the principle of classification according to estimated level of achievement or native potential. Whatever social stratification it incurs is covert rather than overt. Paradoxically, ability grouping was heralded as the means by which educational opportunity for the mass of citizens in many countries might be achieved in a democratic society. Yet in the past decade ability grouping is increasingly seen as one of the most divisive factors in retarding the integration of classes and castes and in relegating the poor and the ethnic minorities to inferior educational opportunity. For it is only recently that the findings of research studies have directed the attention of educators and political leaders to the fact that, aside from having no conclusive pedagogical advantage per se, homogeneous ability grouping can and often does operate to the detriment of the disadvantaged, the poor, and the ethnic minorities. Its most damaging effect is in separating students along socioeconomic and ethnic lines.

Homogeneous ability grouping, when applied to a total school system is called tracking in the United States or streaming in the United Kingdom. Generally speaking, such classifications of pupils are accomplished by means of standardized tests. The more recent British system of education, established by the Butler Act of 1944, was essentially geared to a critical selection process of pupils at age eleven plus. In that year the school population from the primary schools were required to take a series of tests (in mental ability, arithmetic, and English), which, in addition to previous records and recommendations of teachers, became the criteria for admission into one of three types of secondary schools—grammar, technical, or modern. Each type of school was organized to match the expectations of ability and achievement levels of the students, and each comprised a curriculum related to certain career and vocational goals. With few exceptions, those students attending a secondary modern school could rarely hope to attend a university, and, therefore, the attainment of professional status for such an individual would be highly unlikely. In addition, separation into ability groups was widely practiced within schools; those students who showed evidence of learning at a faster pace were sorted into the "A" stream, while those at the lower end of the ability scale were placed in "B" or "C" streams according to demonstrated performance on tests.

Severely criticized during the 1950s, the British system of streaming became the subject of a series of research studies that culminated in the Plowden Committee Primary School Report (1967). As the undesirable effects of streaming were recognized, its practice at the infant-school level was abandoned "with the hope that it would spread to primary and junior schools" (Findley and Bryan 1971, p. 37). However, streaming at the secondary-school level, particularly, still forms an essential part of the programming of the educational system of Great Britain despite studies indicating the negative effects of a sense of failure, lowered morale, and attainment on the lower streams of the school population (Ogletree 1969). Later studies conducted on the effects of streaming corroborate the position that children of average and below-average ability fare better in nonstreamed schools (Lunn 1970). In reviewing and summarizing the findings related to the British style of ability grouping, Findley states:

> On the current scene, then, the impact of ability grouping on the affective development of children is to build (inflate?) the egos of the high groups and reduce the self-esteem of average and low groups in the total school population. A new dimension of interpretation has been emphasized chiefly in the British studies of "streaming" where teacher attitude toward achievement is shown to have marked effect. In particular, teachers who bear attitudes of almost exclusive emphasis on academic achievement to the neglect of personal development exercise an especially pernicious influence on low-achieving children in heterogeneous classes where the differences are widest (Findley and Bryan 1971, p. 40).

Moreover, Yates concluded that the means employed in both interschool and intraschool grouping were simply educationally indefensible, since they were based on the assumption that intellectual capacity was a relatively fixed hereditary trait that could be accurately assessed. Indeed, placement of students in homogeneous groups for all instructional purposes cannot be successful.

In the United States the prototype of the secondary school is what the British call the comprehensive school. Ability grouping in this country exists at the primary levels within schools. At the secondary level the school also admits pupils of all ability levels, and its curricular programs cater to a wide spectrum of achievement levels and career goals. Like the intraschool streaming of England, the typical American secondary school is organized in terms of ability groups. Such a grouping system comprises vocational, commercial, general, technical, or college-preparatory tracks. Consequently, the effect of the grouping system is such that students attending the same school may have entirely different subjects, schedules, or levels of instruction, and those who perform well on IQ tests and on objective tests of the basic skills are, as a rule, taught separately from those at the lower end of the ability scale. Moreover, ability grouping is frequently practiced in the primary grades, and as early as kindergarten, with certain devastating results for lower-achieving pupils (Rist 1970).

A BRIEF REVIEW OF THE RESEARCH

There have been hundreds of studies over the past 50 years purporting to examine the effects of grouping in the United States. The vast majority of such studies have been severely criticized in terms of overall conceptualization and methodological inadequacy (Goldberg, Passow, and Justman 1966). Fortunately, the research studies on ability grouping have been well summarized by three recent surveys—the NEA Research Summary (1968) covered the period from 1960 to 1968; a study by Heathers (1969) covered the period from 1932 to 1968 but focused mainly on the research since 1960; and the most recent survey was prepared by Warren Findley and Miriam Bryan and published in 1971 as the culmination of the work of a task force established in December 1969.

In addition to the excellent and most recent survey of Findley and Bryan, two significant pieces of research were published in 1966—one by Borg and the other by Goldberg, Passow, and Justman. These two relatively recent longitudinal studies contrast markedly with many other research reports on ability grouping in which findings were questionable because of methodological inadequacies. Borg's study covered a period of four years and compared the effects of ability grouping (plus specially adapted curriculum and instruction) with that of random grouping (plus enrichment to account for individual differences within classes). The ability-group sample was drawn from a school district in Utah, and the heterogeneous-group sample was taken from an adjacent and comparable district in the same state. Placement into ability groups, in the case of the first sample, was accomplished on the basis of results from the California Achievement Tests in the first year and from the Sequential Tests of Educational Progress in the final three years; data were collected for all grades from four through twelve.

On the whole, despite the slight advantage of ability grouping for superior pupils and of random grouping for slow pupils, Borg concluded that neither ability grouping with acceleration nor random grouping with enrichment is superior for all ability levels of elementary school pupils. In general, while the poorer students tended to do better in randomly selected heterogeneous groups, homogeneous ability grouping tended to have modest advantages for superior groups.

In contrast to the Borg study, Goldberg, Passow, and Justman (1966) focused on grades five and six in 86 classes within 45 New York City elementary schools. Ability groups were established on the basis of standardized group tests of intelligence. The study showed that the narrowing of the ability range per se produced negligible positive effects on the attainment of students, and, in fact, for all the variables studied, the effects of grouping per se were, at best, minimal. Despite the belief of many teachers that it is easier to teach all subjects to a class of narrow ability range than to teach one subject to a class of a broad spread of ability, the study shows that the facts are just the reverse. In addition, the findings lend support to the evidence provided by an English study (Douglas 1964) demonstrating the significance of teacher expectations on the actual performance of pupils. Thus the Goldberg investigation provides evidence to support the conclusion that ability grouping, in itself, far from having a beneficial or facilitating effect on the achievement of pupils, or on the administrative organization of the school, can be harmful in leading the teacher to underestimate the learning potential of students in the low end of the scale. Goldberg and associates concluded that:

> At least until such time as procedures for more completely individualized instruction become incorporated into school policy and teacher preparation, schools will continue to rely on various kinds of grouping in their attempt to differentiate instruction. It is, therefore, essential to recognize that no matter how precise the selection of pupils becomes or how varied and flexible the student deployment may be, grouping arrangements, by themselves, serve little educational purpose. Real differences in academic growth result from what is taught and learned in the classroom. It is, therefore, on the differentiation and appropriate selection of content and method of teaching that the emphasis must be placed. Grouping procedures can then become effective servants of the curriculum (1966, p. 169).

The NEA Research Summary (1968) based on 50 studies on ability grouping since 1960 found that the inferences were generally inconclusive and that factors other than ability grouping were responsible for whatever gains in attainment occurred in homogeneous groups. What made the difference was not the fact of grouping but the changes that were made in curriculum, teaching methodology, and instructional materials. Similarly, Heathers (1969), having surveyed 84 studies, found that especially those conducted subsequent to 1960 tended to support the view that ability grouping does exercise a harmful and pernicious influence on the attainment and the self-concept of those students placed in the lower-ability classes. The most evident and damaging result was a drop in achievement level. The lowered expectations of teachers, often coupled with reduced quality of instruction, lead inevitably to the phenomenon of the self-fulfilling prophecy. The use of tests to label the child also helps the teacher to rationalize the failure of the poor-achieving students, so that the blame for failure is shifted from the teacher to the child, from the need for a teacher to be creative and effective to an acceptance of what is perceived as an irremediable condition in the student. Heathers further questioned the validity of the widely held belief that the achievement level of brighter pupils is enhanced by reducing the ability range. Similarly, in summing up the evidence from all possible sources, Findley and Bryan (1971) found that ability grouping on the basis of standardized tests shows no consistent positive effect for helping any particular group of students, or students in general, to learn better. Analyzing the gist of the total number of studies up to the end of the 1960s, the team concluded that "the slight preponderance of evidence showing the practice favorable for the learning of high ability students is more than offset by evidence of unfavorable effects on the learning of average and low ability groups, particularly the latter" (Findley and Bryan 1971, p. 54). There would seem to be a general consensus of opinion that when instances of special benefit accrue, the results could be traced to modifications of materials and more effective teaching and learning methods rather than to the fact of the beneficial results of homogeneous ability grouping. Moreover, from the affective point of view, such a system of grouping tends to stigmatize the average and low groups as inferior, to deflate the self-concept, and to affect motivation adversely.

CONSEQUENCES OF ABILITY GROUPING
FOR BLACKS AND OTHER MINORITIES

The cardinal and most salient point of this present section is that ability grouping inevitably leads to ethnic and socioeconomic separation. The second point, which follows logically from the first, flows from the unequivocal and clear demonstration of research studies which indicate that socioeconomic status is correlated positively with both the scores on intelligence tests and the level of scholastic achievement. Third, since blacks and other minorities are, as a whole, in the lower socioeconomic bracket, then it follows that ability grouping will have its most potent effect on the learning situations of minority children.

The consequences of ability grouping are not merely confined to the cognitive domain. The most pernicious influence of such a strategy is found in forming, reinforcing, and maintaining myths and stereotypes which themselves become part of the value systems of teachers and the public at large; thus the vicious cycle is formed. Tests, especially standardized group tests of intellectual ability, are used to "prove" the "inherent intellectual inferiority" of blacks, which leads to stratification in terms of estimated potential, which leads to lowered self-concept and the perceived lowered expectations of teachers, which, in turn, leads to poor learning conditions and, inevitably, to inferior performance on tests of achievement. In other words, the application of standardized tests and the general organization of classes in terms of ability groups (together with the assumed relationship of IQ scores with potential achievement level) subscribe to the celebrated predictive validity of the IQ and other tests of intellectual aptitude. In these circumstances it is not so much that x (IQ) is related positively to y (achievement), but that xz is related to yz where z (the moderator variable) produces the positive correlation between aptitude and achievement. This means simply that minorities, in particular, and poor people, generally, bear the brunt of those stereotypes and practices that assume the appearance of scientific objectivity but have dire consequences that are educationally unsound, socially divisive, dehumanizing for minorities, and politically indefensible within a democratic society.

The only proper responsible and valid reason for adopting any educational device or strategy should be that it serves to enhance the learning of students in general. In the following pages the consequences and empirical evidence concerning ability grouping will be examined in terms of (1) segregating of citizens ethnically and socioeconomically within school systems, (2) resegregating of students within schools, (3) mislabeling of minority children in classes for the mentally retarded, (4) perpetuating racial discrimination and unfair educational practices, and (5) denying minorities and the poor the right to equality of educational opportunity.

Racial Segregation

Racial segregation, until fairly recently, was an established and institutionalized fact in the social, political, and educational structure of the United States. The Court's decision in *Plessy* v. *Ferguson* (1896) formally and legally sanctioned the establishment of parallel systems of education and the separation of students in different schools. Segregation was enforced in the Southern states as a way of life while in the North the races intermingled to a slight degree in the schools of New York, Chicago, Detroit, and elsewhere.

But whether or not segregation existed by law, the clustering of whites in certain more affluent, and often exclusively white, neighborhoods tended to ensure de facto segregation. In reality, then, blacks were isolated by economic limitations and by residential restrictions. The consequences of both de jure and de facto segregation were that blacks were either isolated within low-income neighborhoods and excluded from white school districts or attended schools within mixed neighborhoods where the majority of students were black.

The principle of "separate but equal" facilities was challenged in the case of *Brown* v. *Board of Education of Topeka* (1954), when it became illegal to bar any student from attending a school on the basis of his ethnicity only. However, passing a law cannot guarantee changes in the ingrained attitudes and stereotypes born of centuries of racial discrimination. Nor did the militancy of the civil rights movement and the aggressive desegregationist postures of the Kennedy and Johnson administrations serve to eradicate, or even substantially reduce, the fact of segregation. For, as the U.S. Commission on Civil Rights (1967) reported, racial isolation in the schools was perpetuated and compounded by policies and practices within school districts, by the influx and concentration of blacks within urban centers of Northern cities, and by the exodus of whites to the suburban neighborhoods where the purchase of homes by even those few blacks who could afford them was made almost impossible by real-estate manipulation.

In 1965 it was reported that 75 percent of black students lived in areas where the elementary schools contained 90 percent or more black children; 83 percent of the white elementary school population was living in areas 91 percent or more white. One may well ask: Why should schools be integrated? What is the educational advantage ensuing from desegregation?

As we have seen in earlier sections, it is a well-documented fact that lower socioeconomic classes and minority ethnic membership are highly correlated with lower levels of performance on tests of intellectual ability and achievement. Thus ability grouping, especially when practiced by whole educational systems, results in racial isolation. The deleterious effects of ethnic isolation and de facto socioeconomic separation operates to the detriment of children of black, Puerto Rican, Indian, and Mexican-American ethnicity, since they are denied the opportunity of an optimum learning situation. For whether isolation of ethnic minorities and lower socioeconomic groups is accomplished through overt or covert strategies of discrimination, or whether the separation of class and caste is the result of ability grouping, the effect is to isolate students of one level from those of another to the detriment of the ethnic minority individuals and the less fortunate white students. As Findley and Bryan put it, "the impact of school upon individual students is a function of peer interactions—that is, students tend to learn as much from other students as they do from teachers" (1971, p. 45). Moreover, the basic issue and the consequences of segregation were nicely articulated in the judgment prepared and presented by the late Chief Justice Earl Warren on behalf of a unanimous court. The central theme of the judgment might very well apply equally to ability grouping as it does to the separation of the races and the concomitant isolation on the basis of ethnicity:

> Does segregation of children in public schools solely on the basis of race, even though the physical facilities and other "tangible" factors may be equal, deprive the children of the minority group of equal educational opportunities? We believe it does.
>   . . . To separate children in grade and high schools from others of similar age and qualifications solely because of their race generates a feeling of inferiority as to their status in the community that may affect their hearts and minds in a way unlikely ever to be undone. The effect of this separation on their educational opportunities was well stated by a finding in the Kansas cases by a [lower] court which nevertheless felt compelled to rule against the Negro plaintiffs.
>   Segregation of white and colored children in public schools has a detrimental effect upon the colored children. The impact is greater when it has the sanction of the law; for the policy of separating the races is usually interpreted as denoting the inferiority of the Negro group. A sense of inferiority affects the motivation of a child to learn. Segregation with the sanction of law, therefore, has a tendency to retard the educational and mental development of Negro children and to deprive them of

some of the benefits they would receive in a racial[ly] integrated school system.

We conclude that in the field of public education the doctrine of "separate but equal" has no place. Separate educational facilities are inherently unequal. . . . Such segregation is a denial of the equal protection of the laws (*Brown v. Board of Education of Topeka*, 347 U.S. 483, 1954).

The decision of the Supreme Court, aside from recognizing that racial segregation is incompatible with the basic tenets of democracy, also forced many teachers, social scientists, and the general public to reexamine their values. Though the "separate but equal" doctrine died legally on May 17, 1954, it triggered a sociopolitical conflict that has not yet been resolved, for integration in education is part of the larger context of integration and equality of opportunity in employment, housing, and political representation. Until there exists unfettered participation in the political and economic arenas, until there is the possibility for true social mobility with free access to residence, there can be no equality of educational opportunity.

Impact of the Exodus from the Cities

The judgment of the Warren Court outlawed overt segregation. However, the crucial issue of the 1970s is found in the more or less covert separation of the races in urban and suburban neighborhoods. It represents, indeed, de facto segregation, for although integration within the local political boundaries of the district may have been accomplished, the city-suburban boundary and the ability to purchase a home in a suburban neighborhood have now become the deciding factors of segregation and racial isolation. The special problems of urban areas, in particular, and the critical issues in American education, generally, find eloquent expression in Peter Schrag's (1967) words:

> In city after city the exodus continues. A few years ago urban planners spoke hopefully of the return to the center, of a migration back to the core city by people who had had enough of car pools and commuting, of mowing lawns and compulsory neighborliness. But although some came back—most of them people whose children had grown and moved away—the tide never turned. Nevertheless the planners continued to produce their schemes, each of them calling for more ambitious programs in transportation, housing, and general redevelopment. Yet none ever focused on the single public service that must constitute the very essence of urban life and renewal—public education. . . .
> . . . The resources exist, but they still flow in overwhelming abundance to the private sector and to the communities that least need

them. They flow to the suburbs and to the great establishments of private wealth; and every year, despite the apparently increasing programs of public welfare, the inequities become greater. If we really mean to have effective public education, then urban and suburban systems can no longer operate as independent enterprises each with its separate and unequal local financial capabilities, its own special, and often limited facilities, its own little circumscribed area of concern. . . . There is, moreover, no academic rationale for the maintenance of clusters of hundreds of independent little school districts in a single metropolitan region; what they can do separately in integrating schools, and in financing them, in planning and operating programs, they can do far more effectively together. The only educational reason for their separation is the perpetuation of segregation and inequity (in Ehlers 1969, pp. 75–76).

The migration of white, middle- and upper-class citizens from the cities can only help to compound the problem inevitably making of the city a place for the very rich, the poor, the old, and the minorities. At the heart of the issue lies social injustice and racial prejudice. The differential migration of whites to the suburbs and blacks to the inner city can only ensure a return to separate, but unequal, facilities, for it is not possible to establish separate and equal facilities while this trend continues. Segregation stamps an inferior status on the persons who are barred from full participation in society—with it go inescapable and concomitant feelings of rejection and lowered self-esteem, which in turn affect performance in school and elsewhere. As the president of Morgan State College, Martin Jenkins, has stated, "the best education for all students, from the elementary through the graduate level, can be achieved only under conditions of racial integration in our society" (in Wilcox 1971, p. 49).

Resegregation Through Ability Grouping

Ability grouping operates as a kind of fail-safe mechanism to ensure that when children of mixed ethnicity attend the same school, they are once more resegregated along essentially ethnic and socioeconomic lines under the guise of grouping by standardized objective-test results. As was stated previously, there is no lack of evidence to support the fact that black students score, on the average, one standard deviation below the level of white students on standardized tests of intellectual ability and also on standardized achievement measures (Shuey 1966; Dreger and Miller 1960; Heathers 1969; Findley and Bryan 1971).

Therefore, it stands to reason that placement into classes on the basis of standardized tests—must result in a preponderance of minorities in those tracks comprising lower-achieving students. Ability grouping, it has been pointed out, results in socioeconomic and ethnic stratification and consequently, drastically affects the learning of the poor and minority students through the negative attitudes of teachers, the lowered expectations held by teachers and students themselves, the loss of self-esteem of the minority students, the watered-down curriculum within the class, the impediment to ego development for students labeled inferior, the feelings of rejection, and the overt and covert attitudes of superiority and dominance on the part of students in high-ability groups. When the facts of the student's color and ethnic origin are coupled with lowered performance, lowered self-concept, and, as is frequently the case, with the conditions of poverty and insufficient facilities within the home, the minority child sooner or later comes to accept his role and to act in accordance with the social stereotype. As Heathers (1969) remarked: "Ability grouping may thus be, in effect, an agency for maintaining and enhancing caste and class stratification in a society."

The issues and consequences of ability grouping were dramatically surveyed and presented in the critical court decision of *Hobson* v. *Hansen* (1967). Once again, as in the *Brown* case concerning racial segregation, it was the courts that determined educational policy and pinpointed the injustice of ability grouping as another form of racial isolation through resegregation within the school itself. The case dealt with the use of standardized tests to establish the tracking system of homogeneous ability groups throughout the entire school system of Washington, D.C. Both elementary and secondary school levels were stratified on the basis of test results into homogeneous ability groups ranging from "basic" for the lowest achievers to "honors" for gifted students. The curricular content of each track, or ability level, was geared accordingly. The elementary and junior secondary schools were organized into three tracks: basic or special academic (for "retarded" students), general (for the average or above-average students), and honors (for gifted students). At the senior high school level, a fourth track, called regular, was added for college preparatory study for above-average students.

Data presented by the defendants clearly demonstrated that: (1) track placement was directly and almost perfectly correlated with income levels of the students' homes; (2) those schools within the income bracket of $6,000 or below enrolled over 90 percent black students; (3) the predominantly white high school served a community of average income equivalent to $10,374 and had all but 8 percent of students enrolled in honors or regular tracks in 1964 and 1965; (4) while 16 percent of blacks in elementary and junior secondary schools were enrolled in honors programs in 1965, 70 percent of their white peers were enrolled in the advanced curriculum; (5) black students were substantially overrepresented in special academic tracks for the "retarded." Thus the court was compelled to recognize the separation of students along socioeconomic and, to a lesser degree, ethnic lines. As Judge Wright put it:

> The evidence shows that the method by which track assignments are made depends essentially on standardized aptitude tests which, although given on a system-wide basis are completely inappropriate for use with a large segment of the student body. Because the tests are primarily standardized on and are relevant to a white middle-class group of students, they produce inaccurate and misleading test scores when given to lower class and Negro students. As a result, rather than being classified according to ability to learn, these students are in reality being classified according to their socio-economic or racial status, or—more precisely —according to environmental and psychological factors which have nothing to do with innate ability.

Mislabeling of Minority Students

The overrepresentation of minority students in the lowest-ability classes of elementary and secondary schools is an observable and easily documented fact. The classes for slow learners, the educable mentally retarded (EMR), and the mentally retarded (MR) house significantly greater proportions of black and Hispanic students than white students. The study by Coleman et al. (1966) showed that at the elementary and secondary levels the school attended by the average black child contained a significantly greater proportion of children in the lower tracks. Dunn (1968) noted that at the national level, minorities comprised more than 50 percent of the mentally retarded. The figures issued by the Bureau of Intergroup Relations of the State Department of Education for the State of California in the fall of 1970 reveal that whereas blacks, who represent 9.1 percent of the total student population of the state, account for 27.5 percent of the educable mentally retarded, they constitute only 2.5 percent of the mentally gifted. Although these statistics have been publicly recorded and announced, it took two major "studies" to point up in clear and dramatic detail the pernicious effects of standardized tests of intelligence and their use for mislabeling minority children. The first was a study conducted over an eight-year period by Jane Mercer, a sociologist and researcher at the University of California at Riverside; the second consisted of the presentations and judgment of a case (supported by the ABP of the Bay Area) tried in the city of San Francisco on behalf of black students against Wilson Riles, the superintendent of education for the State of California.

Mercer's study (1971), since it was confined to the southern region of California, is of particular significance for children of Chicano Hispanic-American ethnicity, but it dealt also with the mislabeling of black children and their placement in mentally retarded classes on the basis of tests of intelligence. Her contention is that so-called intelligence tests, as presently used, are, to a large extent, "Anglocentric"; that is, they mirror the standards, values, and experiences of the white, Anglo-Saxon middle-class person. Inevitably, the results of such tests affect, to a greater degree, persons from a different cultural background and those from lower socioeconomic status. The eight-year study documented the fact that public schools had been sending more children to MR classes than any of the 241 organizations contacted by Mercer and her co-workers (law enforcement agencies, private organizations for the MR, medical facilities, religious organizations, public welfare centers, and so on). Criteria for selection and placement in such classes were based on (1) the almost exclusive reliance on IQ test scores and the almost total absence of medical diagnosis; (2) the utilization of a high cutoff score (IQ of 79 or below as compared to a recommended IQ of 69 or below) in order to draw the border line between mental retardates and normal students; (3) the failure to take into account sociocultural factors when interpreting IQ test results. The study found that over four times as many Mexicans and twice as many blacks were enrolled in the classes for the mentally retarded, a disproportionate number for their population in the state. However, when a "two-dimensional" definition of mental retardation is used (a definition that not only takes into consideration intellectual performance but also assesses adaptive behavior) and when IQ scores are interpreted with the knowledge that sociocultural factors contaminate them, then, Mercer showed that racial imbalance in classes for the MR disappeared. Consequently, she argued, approximately 75 percent of the children enrolled in MR classes were mislabeled, incorrectly placed, and suffered from stigmatization and lowered self-esteem as well as a learning environment that was far from optimum.

In the Case of *Larry P. et al.* v. *Wilson Riles et al.* (1972), the plaintiffs, six black San Francisco elementary schoolchildren, charged the defendants, namely, the California State Department of Education and the San Francisco School District, with having placed them in EMR classes on the basis of IQ tests alone. When the plaintiffs were retested by certified black psychologists using techniques that took account of the cultural and experiential backgrounds of the students, all achieved scores above the cutoff point of 75. Accordingly, the U.S. District Court judge Robert Peckham ordered that:

> [D]efendants be restrained from placing black students in classes for the educable mentally retarded on the basis of criteria which place primary reliance on the results of IQ tests as they are currently administered, if the consequence of the use of such criteria is racial imbalance in the composition of such classes.

In an unprecedented decision, the court recognized the pervading cultural bias of the present tests and the misplacement of and ensuing harm done to black children when tested by such measures. The court order was aimed at preventing future wrongful placement of black children in special classes, but it did not provide for the elimination of the effects of past discrimination, nor did it rule that the use of intelligence tests be suspended or that the EMR black children should be released and retested for fairer placement. However, it cited the efforts of the New York City school system, which banned group IQ tests, and the Massachusetts school system, which attempted to minimize the importance of IQ tests, as alternative plans to be used pending the development of appropriate tests.

Summary

In the studies and court judgments cited in this section on ability grouping, evidence has been brought to bear upon the harmful effects of the use of standardized tests to establish homogeneous ability groups in schools. As Mayeske (1970) in his interpretation of the Coleman Report has indicated, the environment of the school reflects, in large part, the underlying problems of American society—that of racial prejudice and ethnic separation, which permeate almost all institutions. Standardized tests, inasmuch as they are used to rationalize such cleavages, are injurious to minorities and adversely affect the well-being of the entire nation.

Ability grouping seems to have no positive value for helping students in general. Its major and hence most undesirable effect is to isolate the poor and minority students in lower-achieving classes. As Findley and Bryan (1971) concluded, removal of ability grouping does not affect racial discrimination in areas where the exodus from the city has left the urban areas ethnically isolated. Finally, ability grouping per se without drastic changes in curriculum, teaching methods, and materials does more harm than good.

TESTING AND COLLEGE ADMISSION
OF MINORITY STUDENTS

The Problem of Low Minority Enrollment

The basic issue of this section concerns the relationship of test scores to the selection of minority students for admission to colleges and universities. The problem of the relatively low proportion of minority enrollment in higher education can only be properly appreciated by viewing it within the context of the postsecondary academic and professional preparation of the total population of students. What is primarily significant is the disproportionately small numbers of black, Spanish-speaking, and other minority students attending college. More important for the purposes of this review and summary are the causes of this discrepancy and the role played by testing to create, maintain, and/or ameliorate the access of minority students to the institutions of higher education in the country as a whole.

Among the more radical critics of testing, there are those who claim that tests were created and are used by a racist society to bar minorities from enjoying parity in the goods of the society and from sharing on equal terms in the socioeconomic, educational, and cultural advantages offered to the more privileged white population. Such claims, even when they seem intuitively obvious, do not, in fact, provide the proper perspective. To accept them one would have to believe that something like a Machiavellian power group or organized intrigue exists to humiliate, retard, and dehumanize blacks and other minorities in the United States. The operation of social and educational inequity is certainly more subtle and more complicated than this. Yet facing the realities of unfair conditions could lead to a sort of paranoiac belief that an academic establishment governs the paraphernalia of admission to higher education so as to keep blacks "in their place," to ensure the relative inferiority of minorities, and to prove, in the final analysis, their inherent intellectual deficiencies and the natural superiority of the white race. Given the facts as they exist, this may very well appear to be the case.

If we accept the proposition that there is no high command of university presidents, no coterie of willing admissions officers plotting to guarantee the intellectual genocide of nonwhites, then it follows that the disproportionately small numbers of minority students in higher education are a result of the system—a result as pervasive, invidious, and just as effective as if there were a conspiracy. The system of higher education is inextricably interwoven with the total fabric of American society. Poverty, place of residence, the history of racial discrimination and segregation, the social stereotypes of race, the predominance of minorities within the lower stratum of the society, and the concomitant denial of educational opportunities—all these conspire to create and to perpetuate the imbalance and to entrench ethnic cleavages in the areas of higher education. The system, not a deliberate intrigue, perpetuates the boundaries that bar minorities from higher education, and standardized testing plays a part (indeed, quite a significant one). Therefore, it is only by viewing testing and college admission within the whole social fabric that the contribution of testing to the inequality of the status quo can be brought into focus.

Comparative Demographic Data

No sensible person would question the statement that higher education was never intended to serve everyone. No country in the world has designed its universities to fit the masses. Although some educators have postulated the notion of the accessibility and desirability of some kind of higher education for everyone, the realization of this vision will probably only be achieved at some distant point in the future. A hundred years ago, a relatively small proportion of Americans—barely 3 or 4 percent—proceeded beyond the secondary school to undertake formal, institutionalized academic training (Crossland 1971). But in the past century enrollment in the colleges and universities of the United States has doubled every ten or twelve years. Instead of admitting just a select and privileged few, the establishment of institutions of higher learning in the United States—there are close to 2600 of these institutions—presently caters to approximately half of the nation's total population, calculated in 1970 to be 205 million persons. Minorities account for 15 percent or more of the total population. Census data for 1970 for the specific groups were estimated by Crossland as follows: black Americans, 23,550,000 (11.5 percent); Mexican Americans, 5 million (2.4 percent); Puerto Ricans, 1,500,000 (0.7 percent); American Indians, 700,000 (0.4 percent).

The magnitude of the higher education enterprise in the United States is unmatched by that in any other country in the world. The freshman enrollment for 1970 in the complex of junior (two-year) and senior (four-year) private and public institutions was estimated at just over 8 million students. Their distribution is given in Table 1.

As Table 1 shows, the estimated population of minorities is calculated to be 15 percent of the total, whereas the estimated college enrollment for all minority students stands at 6.8 percent in comparison

TABLE 1. Comparative Demographic Data

Group	POPULATION ESTIMATED FOR 1970		COLLEGE ENROLLMENT ESTIMATED FOR 1970	
	Number	Pro-portion	Number	Pro-portion
Black Americans	23,550,000	11.5%	470,000	5.8%
Mexican Americans	5,000,000	2.4	50,000	0.6
Puerto Ricans	1,500,000	0.7	20,000	0.3
American Indians	700,000	0.4	4,000	0.1
All others	174,250,000	85.0	7,506,000	93.2
Total	205,000,000	100.0	8,050,000	100.0

SOURCE: Crossland 1971, tables on pp. 10 and 13.

with "all others," a category comprising 85 percent of the population and 93.2 percent of the college enrollment. And although it is true that (in the short span of six years) the number of blacks and other minorities at college has doubled from 234,000 in 1964 to 470,000 in 1970, the fact remains that minorities are still grossly underrepresented when compared with the college enrollment for all others (Jacobson 1971). The extent of the disparity may be best determined by comparing minority enrollment with the estimated census figure expressed as a ratio; and by doing the same for all others, the comparison of the two ratios will then demonstrate the degree of underrepresentation of minorities.

While the ratios (expressed as percentages) of population of all others enrolled in colleges in 1970 were estimated to be 4.3, that of black Americans, Mexican Americans, and American Indians was 2.0, 1.0, and 0.6, respectively (Crossland 1971, p. 15). The attainment of proportional representation or multiethnic parity would, therefore, require dramatic gains in the enrollment of minorities: 116 percent for blacks, 330 percent for Mexican Americans, 225 percent for Puerto Ricans, and 650 percent for American Indians. Thus despite the sharp increase of participation of minorities in higher education since the onset of the civil rights movement in the 1960s, there is still a great distance to go if equal access to college is to be assured. Moreover, the escalation of numbers of minorities attending college in the 1970s may create the impression of overnight equality in the opportunities for higher education. In some of the ivy league institutions, however, the proportion of minority students is still pitifully small, and, in the words of Harleston (1965), many institutions "operate under the paternalistic shibboleth that it is unfair to encourage Negroes to enroll unless we know they can make it, for a failure would be psychologically harmful and would do them a grave disservice" (in Wilcox 1971, p. 180).

Barriers to Minority Admission to College

Although the legal barrier to the access of minorities to college, in existence for over half a century since the *Plessy* case, was removed by the judgment in the 1954 *Brown* case, many other barriers still remain. These include (1) the test barrier; (2) the barrier of poor preparation; (3) the money barrier; (4) the distance barrier; (5) the motivation barrier; and (6) the racial barrier (Crossland 1971).

As stated earlier, tests were not created with the deliberate purpose of screening out minority or lower socioeconomic candidates from the competition for higher education. They were originally devised as essential tools to help colleges and universities decide—on some rational basis—who should be admitted and what selection criteria should be employed. It would seem logical to say, therefore, that the traditional admissions tests, reflecting the criteria of those who govern the higher institutions, were designed and intended to sift out an intellectual elite. In the process, however, minorities have been affected to the greatest extent. Tests became the means by which blacks and other minorities were excluded from the race for the credentials of higher education and for eventual upward social mobility.

College entrance examinations were introduced even before 1900 in response to a felt need. As the *Report of the Commission on Tests* shows, the examination procedures of the late 1800s were based on criteria set by each individual institution, and a student was admitted to the college of his choice on the basis of the results he obtained on that particular college's examinations (CEEB 1970a). Such a system permitted each institution to become "an absolute dictator among a small coterie of preparatory schools, when the examination papers of each college were chiefly bundles of the eccentricities of one or two superannuated professors, full of tricks and puzzles, appealing to memory and guesswork" (CEEB 1970a, p. 14). The board, formed in 1900, was designed to reduce the inequities that a chaotic, disorganized, and unfair system had created; it was to provide common standards of admission and better examination procedures.

The early examinations of the board were oriented to elements of the subject matter instruction in schools. They specified and controlled the acceptable level and kind of curriculum and curbed the capricious variety of individual institutional examinations. But the emphasis upon quality of education; the shift from memorization of facts to a demonstration of reasoning, comparing, and correlating data from a broad field; together with the onset of standardized objective testing and the application of psychometrics to the measurement of "intelligence"—all these precipitated the development of the kinds of scholastic batteries presently in use. Men like Carl Brigham, who helped pioneer the first application of mass psychological testing (using the army Alpha intelligence test for personnel classification during World War I), also influenced the development of aptitude tests for college admissions. The new technology of standardized testing gradually began to replace subject-matter examinations, and by 1926 the original version of the SAT was offered.

What Does the SAT Measure?

The present SAT is still extensively used to select students for college, to advise them in choice of institution and career goals, and to form the basis of the rationale for admission or rejection of students. While it is true that such test scores are increasingly being supplemented by records of extracurricular activities, grade-point averages, and estimates of motivation, the college board scores still remain a deciding factor for students in general. They are of particular importance in the controversy surrounding the imbalance of minorities at colleges and universities.

The SAT purports to measure "the developed verbal and mathematical aptitude of students who aspire to attend one of the approximately 900 colleges that require it of at least some students for admissions. It is also extensively used as a criterion for the award of competitive scholarships" (CEEB 1970a, pp. 11–12). The use of the word "aptitude" implies that practice or coaching on item types should not substantially and significantly increase the performance of a student on such tests. It implies, also, that what the tests measure are either some innate capacity to reason or developed abilities that normally mature slowly over a long period of time and are influenced by factors not yet understood (Carroll, in CEEB 1970b, p. 12). The present battery comprises five main sections—English Composition, Humanities, Mathematics, Natural Science, and Social Science. The SAT provides two separate scores: the SAT-Verbal and the SAT-Mathematical. The verbal section emphasizes verbal skills reflected in knowledge of English vocabulary, word usage, and reading comprehension. The mathematical sections are concerned with the ability "to deal with quantitative and geometric-spatial concepts. Both sections also measure reasoning and inferential ability, the SAT-Verbal in the verbal domain and the SAT-Mathematical in the quantitative domain" (Carroll, in CEEB 1970b, p. 2).

Essentially, tests of scholastic aptitude are designed to measure four aspects of mental ability: (1) knowledge of vocabulary and the understanding of language; (2) facility with quantitative and spatial concepts; (3) ability to reason with concepts in verbal or quantitative terms; and (4) speed in test taking. Moreover, as Crossland (1971) stated, scores are reported in relation to a group of individuals who have taken the same test, that is, in relation to a mean or average. And the distribution of the universe of the population taking the test is assumed to follow the familiar symmetrical bell curve. Thus the performance of a student taking the SAT for admission into a college is usually reported as a standard score—not in terms of a raw score—on a scale ranging from 200 to 800 with a mean of 500 and a standard deviation of 100. For purposes of clarification, Figure 1 shows the shape and characteristics of the normal curve of probability.

As Figure 1 demonstrates, scores are preponderantly clustered around the mean in accordance with the proportions indicated. A score of 600—one standard deviation or S.D., above the mean—for example, would correspond to a percentile rank of 84.13 for a group of 100 students; in other words, a standard score of 600 would indicate a

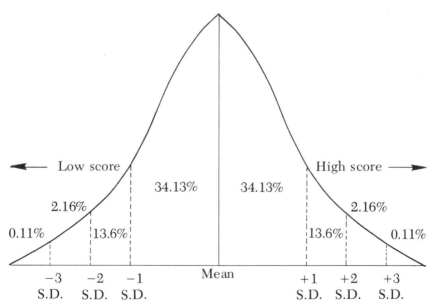

Figure 1. Distribution of Scores in the Normal Curve of Probability
SOURCE: Crossland 1971, p. 57.

TABLE 2. Comparative Performance of Minority Students

Score Range	All Others	Minority Students	Total
Absolute maximum			
	9		9
+3 S.D.		2	
	184		186
+2 S.D.			
	1156	32	1188
+1 S.D.			
	2901	204	3105
Mean			
	2901	512	3413
−1 S.D.		(minority mean)	
	1156	512	1668
−2 S.D.			
	184	204	388
−3 S.D.			
	9	34	43
Absolute minimum			

Source: Data from Crossland 1971, p. 59.

performance level superior to that of 84.13 percent of the students taking the test. Similarly, other scores can be computed by reference to Figure 1. The significant point to remember, when considering the performance of minority students is that the average minority score on tests of aptitude and achievement has been demonstrated to fall one standard deviation below the mean of the white students as a whole. Therefore, the average black student taking the SAT for admission to college would, in all probability, achieve a standard score of 400, where the average majority score is theoretically estimated to be 500. The logical consequences of the comparative performance of minority students are well illustrated in Table 2.

Table 2 shows the inevitable implications of the use of test scores, such as the SAT, when applied without discrimination and without reference to norms developed on a minority subgroup. It places the use of aptitude test scores in its true perspective—that is, as a major barrier to the access to college when such statistics are applied as a sorting and selecting device for admission. The strict application of test scores must, necessarily, result in the systematic exclusion of the vast majority of students of minority ethnic background from the educational opportunities of professional training. If the distribution shown in Table 2 were to be used strictly and impartially, it would follow that:

1. If a moderately selective university were to take all of its students from approximately the top one-sixth of the ability spectrum, its "talent

pool" would include only 2.5 per cent (34 out of 1,383) from the minority groups.

2. If American higher institutions collectively were to enroll everybody scoring above the arithmetic mean of "all others," only 5.3 per cent (238 out of 4,488) of that pool would come from the minority groups. Expressed another way, higher education would be serving 50 per cent of "all others" but only 15.9 per cent of all the minority youth.

3. Even if American higher institutions collectively were to enroll everybody scoring above the mean of the minority groups, only 9.5 per cent (750 out of 7,901) of that pool would come from the minority groups. Expressed another way, in order to serve 50 per cent of all minority youth, higher education would be obliged to enroll 84.1 per cent of all others. (Crossland 1971 pp. 59–60).

Tests of scholastic aptitude would undoubtedly have been discontinued had they failed to do a useful job. As culturally specific admission devices, they properly reflect the values and standards of officers of administration and instruction in colleges and universities. The basic assumption underlying the development of such tests resides in the belief that a certain minimum of formal knowledge and demonstrated ability to reason is indispensable for the prospective college student. However, as Thresher stated, "the present use of test scores introduces a competitive factor that was at most a minor part of the original plan" (CEEB 1970b, p. 134). And because minorities bear the brunt of this competition, test scores are seen as the single most invidious, pervasive, and potent exclusionary means of keeping them at the bottom of the social ladder. The paradox of aptitude testing lies in the fact that it was originally designed to remove the unfairness of privilege when access to higher education was restricted largely to the professional and managerial classes, who could afford to pay the fees for secondary schools that taught the curriculum required for college entrance. In practice, though, instead of removing class and racial biases from the selection processes of American higher education, aptitude tests have tended to reinforce them. Those who have been the hardest hit by such processes are the students of ethnic minority backgrounds.

It is no wonder that minority educators and social scientists have condemned the continued use of SAT-type tests as the criterion for deciding which students may or may not attend institutions of higher education. Therefore, demonstrating that such tests act as a barrier to minorities has been the cardinal challenge to the structured admissions procedures of the major universities throughout the country (Green 1969). Admissions formula based on board scores and high school records has resulted in the establishment of a collegiate student body from the middle and upper socioeconomic classes, to which few minorities belonged.

The chorus of public criticism of tests, outlined in the first chapter of this book, resulted in different reactions by the various universities, test producers, and psychometricians. Essentially, the argument against testing is that it involves (1) overemphasis on general academic ability to the exclusion of specialized abilities; (2) the operation of aptitude tests as self-fulfilling prophecies; (3) the questionable relationship between tests and college grades on the one hand, and professional or vocational effectiveness in postcollege life, on the other; (4) the ethnocentric bias of test content; (5) the endemic elitism of admission criteria that automatically exclude half of all the citizens and the vast majority of minorities from enjoying the privileges of higher education.

In his brilliant summation of the admissions testing quandary, B. Alden Thresher (1970) asserted that:

> Normative testing has led to a series of closed feedback loops through the following steps: 1) validation of tests (along with other predictors) against college performance (as expressed for example in grade-point averages); 2) prediction of performance based on a regression formula derived from this validation; and 3) selection of entering students according to the formula, thus maximizing correlation between predictor and criterion (CEEB 1970b, p. 131).

Consequently, the outcome of such built-in academic standards and procedures leads to a "collegiocentric" selection in which faculty preference and convenience often take precedence over the students' interest in their own long-range development and social effectiveness. Thresher seems to strike at the very heart of the issue in showing that officers of higher education are now faced with two broadly divergent philosophies of admission strategies governing the purposes of testing. Those university officials who accept the rationale of the criticisms of tests have tended to waive what they see as unfair admission criteria in the recruitment of minority students and have attempted to provide special support programs for the newcomers to college life. On the other hand, while they insist on applying the traditional test-score criteria and seek to recruit the "cream of the crop" of minority students, some officers of higher education argue that "spoon-feeding the minority student" and programming instruction to make up for past educational and cultural deprivation are not the proper roles of the university. Tests, they claim, are not unfair; they merely demonstrate the unfairness of the system. Next there are those extremists who insist on interpreting the relatively lower average score of minorities as indicative of the inherent incapacity of some ethnic groups to undertake serious academic pursuits and, therefore, condemn attempts to compensate for underachieving students.

Are Tests of Aptitude Fair to Minorities?

In responding to the charge of unfairness and bias in traditional aptitude tests, test makers and psychometricians contend that the major purposes of testing must necessarily be prediction and selection. Consequently, they have sought to examine whether the predictive validity of traditional aptitude tests is equivalent for different groups. Another approach to the problem of bias has been to study the actual content of aptitude tests to determine whether or not they are biased or whether the individual items favor one group over another.

Predictive Studies

A spate of studies on test bias has been conducted over the past ten years. Summaries of such studies are found in Anastasi (1972), Flaugher (1970), Stanley (1971), and Linn (1973). But perhaps the principal factor in determining bias has been the ambiguity of its definition or that of cultural fairness itself; different investigators examining the same data could come to very different conclusions depending on how fairness or bias is determined.

Many of the earlier pieces of research on test bias compared the test scores of white and black students to determine whether the same regression equation was appropriate for both groups (Linn and Werts 1971; Einhorn and Bass 1971; Temp 1971; Cleary 1968; Crooks 1972; and Pandey 1971). These studies used the Guilliksen and Wilks' method (1950), which tested the similarity of the regression lines for two or more samples. Such an approach, however, has been seriously criticized by recent authors (Thorndike 1971; Darlington 1971; Cole 1972).

A detailed examination of the literature on test bias and the predictive validity of aptitude tests with reference to minorities is beyond the scope of this section. Instead, this section highlights the main elements of the controversy—it examines the positions of those who, on the one hand, support the Cleary definition of bias and those who, on the other hand, base their findings on a definition similar to Thorndike's notion of culture fairness.

Cleary's study represented both the assertion of a definition of test bias and a report of empirical research based upon that definition. She was primarily interested in establishing whether or not a test, such as the SAT, could predict the performance of black freshmen college students as well as it did for their white peers. Cleary defined bias as follows:

A test is biased for members of a subgroup of the population, if in the prediction of a criterion for which the test was designed, consistent nonzero errors of prediction are made for members of the subgroup. In other words, the test is biased if the criterion score predicted from the common regression line is consistently too high or too low for members of the subgroup. With this definition of bias, there may be a connotation of "unfair," particularly if the use of the test produces a prediction that is too low. If the test is used for selection, members of a subgroup may be rejected when they were capable of adequate performance (Cleary 1968, p. 115).

This definition has been studied and supported by many educational researchers (Stanley and Porter 1967; Linn and Werts 1971; Pfeifer and Sedlacek 1971; Kallingal 1971; Einhorn and Bass 1971; Grant and Bray 1970; Cronbach 1970).

Cleary set out to challenge the kind of conclusions reached by Clark and Plotkin that "the SAT is not a valid predictor of academic success for Negroes in integrated colleges and that the academic performance of the students they studied was far beyond the level that would be indicated by such prediction indices as College Board Scores" (1968, p. 116). Essentially, Cleary's study compared the actual obtained freshman grades of black and white students attending three integrated colleges with that of the grades predicted by board scores. She found that the actual obtained grades of the black students were lower than had been predicted in all three integrated institutions, and in one of the colleges the difference was statistically significant. On the basis of this study Cleary concluded that the SAT, far from being biased against black students, did in fact tend to overpredict their potential for success by the use of the white or common regression lines, and, therefore, represented as fair a test for judging the performance of blacks as for estimating the performance of white students. Endorsed by several researchers in education and industry (Campbell, Pike, and Flaugher 1969; Gael and Grant 1972; Grant and Bray 1970; Guinn, Tupes, and Alley 1970; Tenopyr 1967), Cleary's findings led to the general rejection by many psychometricians of the notion that educational and employment tests, in their present form, are unfair or biased when used with minority groups.

Unlike the other writers just mentioned, Thorndike (1971) challenged Cleary's definition of test fairness and bias. Instead, he proposed an entirely different definition, which states that a test used for educational or employment selection is fair only if for any criterion of success the test admits or selects the same proportion of minority applicants that would be admitted or selected on the basis of the criterion itself or by using a perfectly valid test. Thorndike insisted that if one acknowledges that differences in average test performance may exist between two populations, then a judgment of test fairness must rest on the inferences that are made from the test rather than on a comparison of mean scores in the two populations. One must then focus attention on the fair *use* of the test scores rather than on the scores themselves. In a recent publication Schmidt and Hunter illustrated the implications of Thorndike's definition as follows:

> If it is known, based on past experience, that 37 percent of minority applicants equal or exceed the average majority group member in actual performance on the job or in an educational institution, and if the selection ratio is such as to admit 50 percent of the majority applicants, the test must admit 37 percent of the minority applicants to be considered fair (1974 p. 29).

Schmidt and Hunter criticized Thorndike's definition because it leads to a greater incidence of placement of individuals in educational and occupational roles for which they are unsuited. Moreover, "certain majority applicants will be rejected in favor of minority applicants with lower statistical probabilities of success on the criterion—a situation that could lead to reverse discrimination by many" (Schmidt and Hunter 1974, p. 6).

Thorndike's position seems to be basically geared to the optimization of equal opportunity in education and industry, given a situation in which psychometric strategies like the SAT play a significant role in selection of candidates and prediction of probable success on the job. This notion of test use, based essentially on the probability of matching, implies that the proportions of minority and majority groups selected by a given test should correspond with the probabilities of successful performance on a criterion when individuals are drawn at random from each of the groups. Thus the cutting score—the score that determines the minimum level of acceptability for admission—for minorities must always be determined by reference to on-the-job performance as the criterion.

Another definition of culture-fair use of tests, which approximates Thorndike's in that it also introduces the notion of differential cutting scores for different groups, is that of Darlington. But Darlington criticizes the view that cultural factors can be reduced to mechanical psychometric procedures. Wherever a conflict arises between the goals of maximizing a test's validity and minimizing the test's discrimination against certain cultural groups, then "a subjective, policy-level decision must be made concerning the relative importance of the two goals" (Darlington 1971, p. 71).

Stripped of their technical language, both of the latter definitions of culture-fairness stress the existence of bias in the *use* of test scores, not in the tests themselves. They also agree in the general approach to reaching the final goal—that of using cutting scores for minority-group selection, which would be different from that of the majority group. They both favor the introduction of a separate cutting score for minorities. In all probability this would allow for greater numbers of minority group admissions to colleges and the professions than would normally occur if selection and admission were based on scores from scholastic aptitude tests that use the common or white regression equation to establish the criteria for admission or rejection. Thorndike's definition would (at least, implicitly) determine the ratios of subjects from the different cultural groups by mechanical methods, whereas Darlington recommends that such ratios be "determined (indirectly) by a subjective policy-level decision" (1971, p. 71) that would take into account not only the differences between majority and minority students but also differences in cultural, educational, and socioeconomic backgrounds.

Studies of Content Analysis

Determination of test validity, as stated previously, comprises three basic dimensions—construct validity, predictive validity, and content validity. Content validity is determined by examining the content of the test as a whole as well as the individual test items. The controversy over test bias and whether a test measures the abilities of minority group individuals fairly has resulted in an intensive examination of the ways in which members of minority groups respond on test items in comparison with the responses of majority-group individuals.

In their study of test bias Cleary and Hilton (1968) explored the possibility of test bias in the comparative responses of black and white students on the PSAT. Bias was defined in the following manner:

> An item of a test is said to be biased for members of a particular group if, on that item, the members of the group obtain an average score which differs from the average score of other groups by more or less than expected from performance on other items of the same test (Cleary and Hilton 1968, p. 61).

The investigators sought to discover whether the performance of minorities on any given item was uncommonly divergent from that of the majority students taking the test. Three basic questions were asked: Are test items equally difficult for all groups? Do group mean scores across items differ by group? Do both group means and relative scores on individual items change as a function of race, SES within race, or both?

From studying the bivariate plots of sums of item scores Cleary and Hilton found that few items produced any uncommon discrepancy between the performance of black and white students. They concluded "that given the stated definition of bias the PSAT, for practical purposes, is not biased for the groups studied" (1968, p. 70). However, they made no statement concerning individual items that appeared deviant for minority students. Despite such findings, the debate concerning bias in the item content of scholastic aptitude tests has increased rather than abated. Irvine's studies in Africa brought some evidence to bear upon the problems of cross-cultural testing. He administered the Raven Progressive Matrices (a nonverbal test) to individuals from various parts of Africa and found that, even in the scores derived from figural test items, cultural bias persists. Irvine demonstrated that the measure gained will not necessarily be unbiased, simply because it is based on figural or low verbal content. It will be biased in different and undefined ways (Irvine 1966).

Similarly, Flaugher (1970) cited a number of studies revealing serious discrepancies between the test performances of whites and blacks and demonstrating that the greatest deviance appeared to be in nonverbal items. Medley and Quirk (1972) and Angoff and Ford (1973) showed that items dealing with blacks and modern culture were more appropriate for black students than those relating to the past and to more remote concepts. Belcher and Campbell (1968) found that word association patterns for certain words were different for blacks than for whites. Taylor (1971) emphasized the notion that many common words do not have the same meanings for black subjects as they have for whites. Kagan (1973) stressed the need to consider the differential experiences of children from different ethnic backgrounds and the ways in which cultural experiences and attitudes are reflected in the familiarity with the particular content of items on tests.

Moreover, motivational factors and such extraneous variables as anxiety, suppression of aggressive tendencies, and the perceptions of hostility in the test environment have been cited as possible sources of contamination of minority student test scores (Rock 1970; Lennon 1966). But the real determinants of the lowered performance of blacks and other minorities seem closely connected with the psychological factors engendered by the discrepant social and economic conditions. Test producers are correct when they say that minority scores on tests of aptitude and achievement reflect the unfairness of life. But they also reflect the real cultural differences between groups whose ethnicity veers from the middle-class white norm. It would be remarkable if there were no such differences in the scores of different groups on test results, for some aspects of the values and content of tests are—to a lesser or greater extent—necessarily alien to a large proportion of minorities. If tests are to be used for selection, if cutting scores continue to form the grounds for admission into educational institutions or to the avenues of access to employment opportunities, then it follows that without differential points of entry minorities will remain at a disadvantage, equity of educational employment opportunities will be denied them, and the gap between the dominant majority and the striving minorities will increase.

Introduction
Culture-Free and
  Culture-Fair Tests
The Culture-Specific Movement
Measures of the Environment
Criterion-Referenced Testing
Summary: Trends and Alternatives

ALTERNATIVES TO
TRADITIONAL STANDARDIZED TESTS

6

INTRODUCTION

Intelligence tests, in their existing forms, have been deemed inadequate to provide accurate measurements of the intellectual functioning of lower-class members in general and ethnic groups in particular. Haggard has summarized the four areas in which intelligence tests have been found wanting:

> Among other things, (a) they have measured only a very narrow range of mental abilities, namely, those related to verbal or academic success, and have ignored other abilities and problem-solving skills which are perhaps more important for adjustment and success—even in middle-class society; (b) they have failed to provide measures of the wide variety of qualitative differences in the modes or processes of solving mental problems; (c) they have ignored the influences of differences in cultural training and socialization on the repertoire of experience and the attitude, motivation, and personality patterns of subgroups in our society, and the effects of such factors on mental test performance; and (d) they have considered mental functioning in isolation, thus, ignoring the interdependence of the individual's motivational and personality structure on the characteristics of his mental functioning, as seen, for example, in the differences between rote learning and the ability to use previous experiences creatively in new contexts (1954, pp. 180–181).

Turning to the Stanford-Binet test and to the particular way in which it was standardized, Haggard indicated that, according to Warner's estimates, this test is appropriate for "testing fifty or perhaps even sixty-five percent of the children in our population" (1952, p. 101).

The resultant waste of human potential and threats of educational shortage were emphasized by Davis at the Mid-Century White House Conference on Children and Youth (1950), by Eells et al. (1951) and by Clark (1963b). The argument centers on the fact that the continued use of the present intelligence tests limits the discovery of talents to the higher socioeconomic groups and leaves untapped the ability of the mass of children from the lower strata of society. Eells and his associates wrote:

> The question of the fairness of our present intelligence tests is one of great importance both to the individual pupils and to society as a whole. If, as many competent educators, psychologists, and sociologists believe, the intelligence tests are really unfair to children from certain kinds of backgrounds, and do not reveal the full abilities of these children, then grave injustices are done to these children when school people base curricular, instructional and guidance practices on the IQ as determined by such tests. Moreover, a serious loss to society may result through failure to identify and develop the real talent of all its members. No democratic society in today's world is in such a secure position that it can afford to waste, through non-recognition, the leadership or other talents of any large group of its people (1951, p. 3).

Clark expressed the same sentiment:

> The dangers inherent in not developing an effective approach to the discovery, stimulation and training of superior intellectual potential in all groups of American children seem to be greater than the danger inherent in an inefficient and wasteful exploitation of our natural material resources. It is now axiomatic that trained human intelligence is the most valuable resource of a civilized nation. Like other natural resources, it must be discovered and transformed creatively into its most effective and usable form. At this period in world history, no nation can afford to waste any of its potential intelligence through indifference, inefficiency, ignorance, or the anachronistic luxury of racial and social prejudices (1963b, p. 144).

Several approaches have been proposed in an effort to halt the perpetration of injustices in respect to the mass of children who find themselves isolated from the mainstream culture. This chapter therefore summarizes the principal trends in the development of alternatives to traditional measurement. Such approaches may be categorized in terms of (1) changes in the interpretation of scores of minority subjects derived from their performance on traditional norm-referenced tests (such as the WISC); (2) attempts to develop tests whose content would be, theoretically, equally fair or unfair to different cultural groups; (3) attempts to relate scores derived from the performance of minority subjects with measures of the environmental circumstances of the individual students; (4) attempts to develop tests in areas of skill mastery and to relate the individual's score or level of performance with a minimum level of performance or criterion rather than comparing the individual's performance with the average score of the standardization sample.

CULTURE-FREE AND CULTURE-FAIR TESTS

The culture-free and, subsequently, the culture-fair movement emerged as a possible response to the growing dissatisfaction with traditional intelligence testing. Faulting the existing tests for their lack of "sound research and theory concerning the nature of intelligence" and for the fact that they "measure a good deal of obviously acquired knowledge and skill, and that they are heavily weighted with scoring on special abilities distinct from intelligence," Cattell proposed to "wipe the slate clean of these earlier results . . . and begin afresh with sounder tests" (1940, p. 162). What came to be known as the Chicago Group gravitating around workers like Davis and Eells also felt the pressing need to develop measures of intelligence that would be free of cultural influences, since, they contended, when cultural factors are controlled, no significant differences exist between the average intellectual ability of children from different socioeconomic backgrounds.

As the name indicates, the culture-free test represented an attempt at stripping the individual of his cultural veneer in order to reveal and expose his true and inherent abilities. Implicit in such an intent was the notion that "native intelligence lies buried in pure form deep in the individual and needs only to be uncovered by ingenious mining methods" (Wesman 1968a, p. 269). As it became evident that the type of relationship between nature and nurture was not dichotomous, the emphasis shifted toward the development of culture-fair tests. This time the attempt was not to eliminate cultural influences, for "heredity and environmental factors interact at all stages in the organism's development, from conception to death, and . . . their effects are inextricably intertwined in the resultant behavior" (Anastasi, in Gronlund 1968b, p. 280). Rather, researchers endeavored to keep cultural differences from permeating the tests by selecting only those experiences, knowledge, and skills common to different cultures. Eells and his associates defined a culture-fair test in this way: "To be equally fair to all persons, an intelligence test should present problems which are either equally familiar or equally unfamiliar to them" (1951, p. 16). They also listed the following as one of the criteria to be met in the construction of a culture-fair intelligence test:

> In order to compare the genetic mental equipment of different individuals, the test maker must select those problems in each mental system area which are common to the culture and practice of all socioeconomic groups in the population to be tested. In addition, the test maker must learn how to express these problems in symbols, words, pictures, etc. common to all the socioeconomic groups to be tested. He must likewise find problems which motivate equally all the groups to be tested (1951, p. 23).

In contrast to conventional intelligence tests, culture-fair tests deemphasize those factors believed to mitigate against the performance of lower-class children, namely, speed, item content, and heavy stress on verbal content. Thus these tests are presented primarily as nonverbal tasks requiring neither written nor spoken language on the part of the test taker. Directions are given orally, in a simple and clear way (or by means of gestures or pantomime whenever foreign-speaking subjects are tested), and materials consist of pictures, drawings, diagrams, and the like. Items are selected on the basis of their universal quality, that is, only those samples of knowledge, skills, and experiences which are equally common or uncommon to all groups are retained. It is not sufficient for a test to be nonverbal in order to be culturally fair. The Army Examination Beta, for example, used during World War I to test foreign-speaking and illiterate soldiers, contained a picture-completion test including culturally loaded items—violin, piano, telephone, gun, and so on—which automatically disfavored certain cultural groups who lacked the required experiential background. Since speed on tests has been recognized to be a culturally determined factor (Klineberg, 1935b), neither penalization nor reward is administered for fast or slow performance on a culture-fair test, which generally provides for ample time limits.

Cattell Culture-Free Intelligence Test

Cattell's test represents one of the first attempts to develop an intelligence measure free of cultural influences. Upon its publication in 1944 by the Institute for Personality and Ability Testing, it received highly critical reviews all pointing to the fact that a culture-free test was simply an impossibility. By the middle and late 1950s, Cattell's new test, although basically the same as the earlier one, omitted the term "culture-free" and was called the Culture-Fair Intelligence Test. Its design was based on Cattell's theory of fluid intelligence; that is, the test claimed to measure Spearman's single ability g.

The culture-fair test consists of three scales: Scale I (ages four to eight); Scale II (ages eight to twelve and average adults); and Scale III (high school pupils and superior adults). Scale I consists of eight subtests involving symbol copying, classification of pictures, mazes, identification of similar drawings, selection of familiar objects when named, following directions, and identifying what is wrong with pictures of familiar objects and riddles (Milholland 1965, p. 719). The standardization sample for this scale was reported to consist of "more than 400 cases combining American and British samples." Scales II and III are composed of the following four subtests:

> Series, which requires that the examinee complete a sequence of four drawings by choosing one from among five options; Classifications, which requires that he pick out one of a set of five drawings that is different from the rest; Matrices, requiring the selection of a drawing to complete a matrix; and Conditions, which requires that the examinee select from among five drawings of overlapping geometric figures the one in which one or two dots could be placed to fit the specifications of a model (Milholland 1965, p. 719).

Both scales were standardized on a sample of 4328 boys and girls from various regions of the United States and Britain (p. 720). Repeatedly since its original publication, the test has been criticized for its lack of satisfactory manuals.

The claim made for the test's relative freedom from cultural bias rested on demonstrations that no significant differences were found in the performances of American, Australian, French, and British samples (Macfarlane Smith 1959, p. 474), as well as on Cattell's observation that only infinitesimal changes in IQs were found when the test was administered to a group of immigrants first upon their entry into the United States and then a short time later. As noted earlier, such an assumption was widely criticized. Milholland noted that the group of immigrants in question "were tested after living approximately fourteen months in this country and then re-tested after 77 more days" (1965, p. 721). Kidd, after conducting a study investigating which items of the test were more culture fair, concluded that "some items of the test are not culture fair in that the differences between national and economic groups as well as the interaction between economic level and sex, are significant" (1962, p. 353). Marquart and Bailey demonstrated that while Scales II and III gave results that corresponded to expectation, items comprising Scale I were as much influenced by socioeconomic status as the Stanford-Binet test (1955, pp. 357–358). Marquart and Bailey repeatedly raised doubts as to the possibility of ever designing a test free from cultural influences, for "it is difficult to select items that will be equally familiar to individuals of all areas and all social groups. . . . It is difficult to know whether cultural contexts can be completely removed from any scale. Almost all human reactions are culturally influenced" (1955, p. 357). Similarly, Kidd concluded that "a truly culture-free test appears to be an impossibility because even methods of manipulation of material objects are culturally determined" (1962, p. 352). In reviewing the Cattell tests for Buros' *Sixth Mental Measurements Yearbook,* Tannenbaum expressed the same skepticism as the preceding workers:

> Since the IPAT is designed to be culture-fair, one basic question is whether it succeeds in eliminating the so-called contaminating effects of culture. At best, one can only answer that the success is partial. On the credit side, the manuals refer to studies showing that test norms for Taiwan and France did not differ from our own. On the other hand, mention is made of findings that detect norm differences between Indian and British American populations; between Belgian Congo and American groups; and between Puerto Rican immigrants to American and native-born Americans. Moreover, there is reference to data revealing correlation between IPAT scores and socioeconomic status in this country.
>
> In essence, then, it must be admitted that the long pursued goal of demonstrating equality among national and international subpopulations on some measure of general ability has not been reached by this test (1965, p. 722).

Test of General Intelligence or Problem-Solving Ability or the Davis-Eells Games

Published in 1953, the Davis-Eells Games Test attempted to reduce if not eliminate entirely the effect of cultural differences upon test performance. Starting with the premise that conventional intelligence tests do not reveal the hidden potential of the mass of children who belong to the lower socioeconomic classes, the Chicago Group undertook to build a test that would repair such injustices. The novel test was to measure the present problem-solving ability of children, which was regarded by its authors as the basic criterion of intelligence. "What is wanted," Eells wrote, "is knowledge of the ability which a child has now for meeting and solving life-problems, for making adaptations, for thinking abstractly, or for doing whatever else is regarded as intelligent behavior" (1951, p. 74). Because low-status groups evince less familiarity with the academic or bookish vocabulary upon which traditional intelligence tests rely heavily, the Davis-Eells Games became a non-verbal test in which all items are presented in pictorial form and deal with school, home, play, and work situations equally familiar to all American and urban cultural groups (Davis and Eells 1953, p. 8). The subjects do not use any written language, nor are they required to read any of the materials, for all instructions are given orally by means of simple, everyday vocabulary comprehensible by all. Moreover, all the tasks are short and unspeeded. The test was devised for grades one through six. The Primary Form for grades one and two, and the Elementary Form for grades three to six consist of 46 items and 62 items, respectively, dealing with "best ways," "analogies," and "probability" problems. The tests yield an index of problem-solving ability (IPSA). Like the Cattell Culture-Free Test, the Davis-Eells Games did not generate enthusiasm. On the contrary, critics were unanimous in expressing their skepticism and in furnishing evidence that did not support the claim that the Chicago test was more fair than any other test of intelligence. Coleman and Ward (1955) administered the Davis-Eells and Kuhlman-Finch tests to 194 children of high socioeconomic level and 200 children of low socioeconomic level in Memphis, Nashville, and Knoxville, Tennessee. Their conclusion was:

> The data obtained did not support the claims for the Davis-Eells that its items are culturally more fair than items used in other group intelligence tests. The writers have questioned the appropriateness of the assumptions made by Eells, Davis, Haggard, Havighurst, et al., that mean differences in innate ability between children of high and low socioeconomic status are insignificant (Coleman and Ward 1955, p. 469).

Ludlow (1956) reported the findings of the preceding study along with those of Fowler (1955) and Rosenblum, Keller, and Papania (1955). The investigation conducted by Fowler with 355 Michigan ten-year-old elementary schoolchildren from white American, black, and Polish ethnicity showed that "he had discovered no distinct tendency for lower socioeconomic pupils to obtain higher IQs when the presently used culture controlled tests are given rather than the current conventional mental ability tests" (1955, p. 147). Similarly, the authors of the last investigation (Rosenblum, Keller, and Papania) concluded that for the lower-class mentally retarded boys with whom the experiment was made "the Davis-Eells Games do not uncover a hidden intellectual potential—at least, none not measured by presumably culturally biased

tests such as the Binet, California, and Wechsler Children's Scale"
(1955, p. 147). Noll (1960) administered the Davis-Eells test to 313
children enrolled in grades two through six in a medium-sized Midwestern industrial city. Information about the father's occupational
status was secured as well as scores on the Otis Quick-Scoring Beta,
Form C, and the California Achievement Test. It was the purpose of the
study to verify the claim that the Davis-Eells Test correlated only
moderately with other standardized tests of intelligence and achievement and was equally fair to urban children from all socioeconomic
levels (Noll 1960, p. 121). Pointing to its weaknesses—low reliability at
some levels, time required to administer it, and expense—the author
questioned the usefulness of such a test for practical purposes (p. 128).
The fact that lower-class children do not perform as well on this test as
expected (in fact, they scored as low as they did on conventional tests),
along with its low validity as a predictor of academic achievement,
accounted for its being withdrawn from the market.

Raven's Progressive Matrices

The Progressive Matrices test was originally developed by Penrose
and Raven and then by Raven in 1938 in Great Britain. A second
version of the test was published in 1947. This test consists of 60
designs, called matrices, all lacking a piece that the subject selects from
among a given number of alternatives. The matrices, organized into
five sets, are arranged in an order of increasing difficulty. The test is
primarily nonverbal, instructions are reduced to a minimum, and no
time limit is set. Although it has been acclaimed by Spearman himself
as "perhaps the best of all non-verbal tests of 'g' " recent critics have
come to accept such a statement with mixed feelings. There is also
ample evidence (Burke 1958) to question the culture-free aspect of the
Progressive Matrices, which is used extensively in Great Britain and in
various parts of the world (Spain, France, Israel, Australia, and so on)
but only on a restricted scale in the United States. A very comprehensive summary of the test has been provided by Burke, and it seems
worthwhile to quote it in its entirety:

> The evidence indicates that at least Progressive Matrices (1938) has been
> very widely used, especially in England, clinically and in the British
> Services, but that it could and should be improved with respect to both
> reliability and validity especially for use in important diagnostic deci-
> sions about an individual. It is not a substitute in any sense for the Binet
> or Wechsler tests, nor for any verbal or non-verbal group test of mental
> ability, but is perhaps an almost equally useful supplement, and shows
> intercorrelations with such tests perhaps as high as they show with one

another. The evidence is not unequivocal that it is largely a pure test of Spearman's construct "g" even if such a device were possible, it has, nevertheless, been a useful research tool especially in the study of growth and deterioration of mental efficiency. It has special value for use with special groups, such as the deaf and the spastics. Its value for cross-cultural studies needs to be explored further (1958, pp. 221–222).

Leiter International Performance Scale

The Leiter Scale is a nonverbal test in which both examiner and examinee perform rather than verbalize questions and answers. It is made up of a series of short but diverse tasks requiring children to match identical colors, forms, or pictures, to copy a block design, to complete or memorize series, and so on. (Anastasi 1968a, p. 244). The Leiter Scale mainly tests children's ability to organize perceptions and discriminate among them. It is a scale designed to be administered individually to children from ages two to eighteen with no time limit of any kind. Like its predecessors or contemporaries, this test cannot be said to be culture free. From a rather sparse published literature, Bachelor, Donnofrio, and Griffin-Mallory (n.d.) summarized some of the main studies of the Leiter Scale. They cite the findings of Tate (1952), who concluded that the test was no more culture free than the Stanford-Binet; of Orgel and Dreger (1955), who recognized the special value of such a tool primarily for children with verbal handicaps; and of Cooper (1958), who demonstrated that the Leiter Scale was a poor predictor of school achievement for fifth-grade bilingual pupils in Guam. Bachelor, Donnofrio, and Griffin-Mallory came to this conclusion:

> The LIPS apparently is not very popular and the literature on it is sparse and inconclusive. The instrument's claim to culture fairness is not clear. It tends to correlate rather highly with "culture-bound" tests (S-B) but the LIPS appears not to be interchangeable with them. Apparently, the test measures series of abilities partially overlapping, or at least, positively correlated with the series of abilities assessed by the more popular, more documented, and incidentally, far less expensive measures of IQ (p. 8).

Goodenough Draw-a-Man Test

The Draw-a-Man Test was first published in 1926 and revised in 1963 to become the Goodenough-Harris Drawing Test. While the original version required children to draw the picture of a man, the later edition included that of a woman and also of the examinee himself. In evaluating the test, special attention is paid not to the child's artistic ability but to his keenness of observation, his sense of proportion, his vision of perspective, and to the inclusion of several features such as body parts, clothing, and so on. Although the Draw-a-Man Test has not been as widely used as the more common intelligence tests, it has, nonetheless, "been administered widely in clinics as a supplement to the Stanford-Binet and other verbal scales" (Anastasi 1968a, p. 250). With respect to the culture-free aspect of this test, the authors themselves, Goodenough and Harris, recognized that it was not free from cultural influences and further concluded that "the search for a culture-free test, whether of intelligence, artistic ability, personal-social characteristics, or any other measureable trait, is illusory" (in Anastasi 1968a, p. 250). Both Anastasi and Lambert (1961) cite studies which show that "test performance reflects degree of acculturation to Western civilization" (Anastasi 1968a, p. 250).

Rulon's Semantic Test of Intelligence

The Semantic Test of Intelligence was introduced by its author, Philip Rulon, at the 1952 Invitational Conference on Testing Problems. In the words of its creator, it represents an attempt to avoid the pitfalls of both verbal and nonverbal tests while combining their respective advantages so as not "to give any advantage whatever to the Northern child over the Southern child, the white over the colored, or the time-server in school over the bright youngster with less schooling" (Rulon 1952, p. 88). This test is completely nonverbal—no language is spoken by either examiner or examinee—and directions are given by way of pantomime. Materials include only those objects, animals, verbs, and actions familiar to all Western cultures. It is a semantic test of intelligence because it requires "the subject to associate an arbitrary symbol with a worldly referent, to indicate his mastery of this association and then to combine these symbols into groups in which the relationships between the symbols in each group are semantic or syntactical relationships" (Rulon 1952, p. 87).

In summary, the culture-fair movement has attempted to substitute pictorial material for verbal material so as to avoid unfair discrimination between high and low socioeconomic groups, between white and nonwhite subjects; and to use figural reasoning, along with figure analogies, to measure intellectual ability. In addition, efforts have been directed toward devising tests that are concerned with drawings of the human figure, completion of gestalt patterns, and the production of meaningful representations from abstract materials. Questions have been raised as to the usefulness of such endeavors, however, especially in the light of the findings that have demonstrated that those so-called culture-fair tests are actually affected by socioeconomic status and ethnicity.

Tannenbaum (1965), Dyer (1960), and Lorge (1952), to name but a few, all stressed the futility of the culture-fair movement. At the 1952 Invitational Conference on Testing Lorge faulted the Chicago Group and its followers for having fallen into what he called the "difference ergo bias" trap. That is to say, Eells and his associates have presumed that mental ability is equally distributed among the population and hence that differences in test performance stem not from an inadequate use of the test but from the test itself, which favors children of the higher strata of society. Thus by removing from the test those items that create the difference, the test is supposedly devoid of its bias. What does such a test measure? "It neither would be a test of intelligence nor would it give any evidence about the impact of status or culture on test performance," Lorge contends, and unbiased tests of intelligence are an impossibility because they ignore the proposition that "difference as difference is not bias."

Dyer also rejects the claim that tests can be devised that are free of culture on the ground that, since it is the nature of a test "to be made up of a series of pieces of the environment to which the pupil is expected to react in one way or another" (1960, p. 397), any attempt to eliminate all elements which are not common or uncommon to all groups will result in "a test whose score may not be very helpful in predicting school success" (p. 397). It is not the test that is unfair, Dyer continues, but the hard facts of social circumstance. Therefore, what the differential test performance reflects is the differential quality of educational opportunity.

Tannenbaum also questions the very goal of the culture-fair movement and its pursuits. He wrote:

> Even if it were possible to devise a test so antiseptic as to clean out inequality not only among sub-cultures but also among other groups showing differences in test intelligence, such as those classified by sex, age, education, geographic origin, body type, physical health, personality structure, and family unity—what kind of instrument would we then have? Since such a test must, perforce, be so thoroughly doctored as to omit tasks that reveal these group differences or substitute others that show "no difference" what could it possibly measure? What could it predict? Covering up group differences in this way does not erase test bias. Rather, it delimits drastically the kinds of information one can gather about problem-solving strength and weaknesses associated with groups as well as individuals (1965, pp. 722–723).

It is the consensual opinion of psychometricians and psychologists that culture-free or culture-fair tests have proved disappointing and have fallen short of their goals, for minority students have been shown to perform, if not more poorly, at least just as badly as they do on conventional intelligence measures. Notwithstanding their limitations and weaknesses, such ventures as the Davis-Eells Games, for instance, have been recognized to constitute a novel approach that brought in new theories and techniques and represented "a magnificent example of scientific penetration" (Ludlow 1956, p. 148; Haggard 1952).

THE CULTURE-SPECIFIC MOVEMENT

Aside from culture-fair tests, several other approaches have been suggested in an effort to resolve the issues raised by cross-cultural testing. Most common among these procedures has been the translation of existing intelligence tests into Spanish. There are Spanish versions of both the Stanford-Binet and the WISC, as well as of Cattell's Culture-Free Test. However, evidence suggests (Keston and Jiminez 1954; Moran 1962; Coyle 1965) that the quality of Spanish spoken at home or in the community and that used in the tests, as well as the fact that test content is still primarily culture bound hence cannot be simply transposed from one culture to another, all conspire to limit drastically the value of the translation approach. As Mercer remarked,

> Simply translating the content of a test designed for persons socialized in one culture into the language of another culture does not eradicate the cultural differences. Persons from backgrounds other than the culture in which the test was developed will always be penalized. It is difficult to interpret the meanings of IQs when this is the case (1971, p. 325)

Another approach, which dates back to the advent of World War I and the Army Examination Beta, has been to administer nonlanguage tests to those who cannot speak English. Yet the existing data are inconclusive in regard to their value as substitutes for verbal tests. Anastasi pointed out that what they assess is necessarily different from what conventional intelligence tests measure, for "it is a psychological impossibility to eliminate the verbal content of a test without altering the intellectual processes involved" (1958, p. 558). Still another approach has been the attempt to develop intelligence tests relevant to each major cultural group in the United States. Such a view holds that comparisons can only be made among individuals belonging to the same linguistic and cultural background. The major limitation of such an attempt, aside from the enormous expense in the standardization of a multiplicity of tests, concerns the extreme difficulty and complexities involved in delimiting the boundaries of each cultural group for which tests should be developed. Schwarz (1963) in his extensive work in Africa identified the obstacles that test adaptation presents. Moreover, when such tests are undertaken on a large scale, it is difficult to imagine the usefulness of culture-specific tests for the individual interacting with the larger society, since no performance on these tests can possibly be generalized beyond the culture for which they were developed.

There has emerged, particularly out of the work of Mercer (1971) in Riverside, California, the proposition of a new trend in the evaluation of children who do not belong to the dominant culture, namely, Mexican Americans and blacks. The rationale underlying what Mercer calls pluralistic evaluation is based on the observation that sociocultural factors account for 30.3 percent of the variance in IQ among Mexican Americans, blacks, and whites (28 percent is due to ethnicity and 10.9 to SES). Unlike culture-specific or conventional tests of intelligence—which both ignore the multicultural aspects of the American society and treat individuals as if they were culturally homogeneous—Mercer's approach would view and compare each individual within his own sociocultural background. Membership in a given group would be determined on the basis of certain family characteristics, which were found to differentiate most highly between Mexican American and black families and "the modal sociocultural configuration of the community" (Mercer 1971, p. 329). Mercer demonstrated in a dramatic fashion that whenever intelligence test scores are applied and interpreted literally, the black and Mexican-American children who come from families closely resembling the modal sociocultural community make IQ scores comparable to those of the middle-class children. Conversely, minority children whose families are least like the dominant culture receive scores that relegate them to the borderline of mental retardation. Table 3 indicates the various means and standard deviations as calculated by Mercer for the Mexican-American and black children whom she studied in relation to their correspondence with the white norm.

In the 1–0 group, for Mexican-American children (only one sociocultural characteristic in common with the dominant culture), the cutoff score for subnormality would be 61.9 or below (minus 2 Mexican-American standard deviations) as contrasted with the usual score of 75. A child belonging to this group would be considered normal if his score ranged from 73.2 (minus 1 Mexican-American standard deviation) to 95.8 (plus 1 Mexican-American standard deviation), and superior in the case of an IQ of 107.1 or above. Thus Mercer's pluralistic approach "would evaluate the intelligence of each person

TABLE 3. Sociocultural Groupings and IQ for Mexican-American and Black Children

RESEMBLANCE TO	RESEMBLANCE TO MODAL SOCIOCULTURAL CONFIGURATION OF THE COMMUNITY					
	Most 5	4	3	2	Least 1–0	All Groups
Full-scale WISC IQ	(n = 25)	(n = 174)	(n = 126)	(n = 146)	(n = 127)	(n = 598)
	(4.2%)	(29.1%)	21.1%)	(24.4%)	(21.2%)	
Mexican-American mean	104.4	95.5	89.0	88.1	84.5	90.4
Standard deviation	10.4	12.1	11.8	11.6	11.3	12.7
	(n = 17)	(n = 68)	(n = 106)	(n = 101)	(n = 47)	(n = 339)
	(5.0%)	(20.0%)	(31.3%)	(29.8%)	(13.9%)	
Negro mean	99.5	95.5	92.8	87.1	82.7	90.5
Standard deviation	12.1	11.3	11.0	10.5	11.4	—

SOURCE: This table is reprinted from "Institutionalized Anglocentrism: Labeling Mental Retardates in the Public Schools," by Jane R. Mercer in P. Orleans and Wm. R. Ellis, Jr. (eds.) *Urban Affairs Annual Reviews* (1971), Vol. 5, p. 333 by permission of the Publisher, Sage Publications, Inc.

only in relation to others who have come from similar sociocultural backgrounds and who have had approximately the same opportunity to acquire the knowledge and skills needed to answer questions on an intelligence test designed for an Anglo-American society" (1971, p. 335). Moreover, such a procedure "defines a person as intellectually subnormal only if he scores in the lowest 3 percent of his own sociocultural group" (1971, p. 336). The adoption of a pluralistic perspective would thus drastically reduce the number of children in EMR or MR classes and provide, instead, for the placement of those students who do not conform to the dominant culture into programs specifically designed to cater to individually identified educational needs and to prepare them for participation in the life of the mainstream culture. Mercer recapitulated her pluralistic approach as follows:

> Specifically, in a pluralistic IQ evaluation, the WISC is administered and scored in the usual fashion. The Full Scale, Verbal, and Performance IQs are calculated using procedures published in the manuals. Questions are asked in an interview with the parents to determine the extent to which the sociocultural background of the child conforms to the modal sociocultural configuration of the community. Each child is then assigned to the sociocultural group within ethnic group to which he belongs on the basis of family characteristics. The IQ of the child is interpreted according to the norms for his sociocultural group (1971, p. 336).

Minority psychologists have claimed that intelligence tests such as the Stanford-Binet and the WISC are culture-specific tests; that is, they relate primarily and almost exclusively to the white Anglo-Saxon experience. Recently, Robert Williams and Adrian Dove each designed instruments that are intentionally geared toward the experience of blacks. The Dove Counterbalance General Intelligence Test, published in 1966, for grades ten to twelve and for adults, is made up of questions which, the author feels, are easily answered by disadvantaged black children but rarely answered correctly by white middle-class children.

Williams' Black Intelligence Test of Cultural Homogeneity (BITCH) for adolescents and adults is a vocabulary test comprising 100 items of the multiple-choice variety that deal exclusively with the black experience. The original standardization sample included 100 blacks and 100 whites. According to the author, those black children who score high (above eighty) on the test demonstrate that they do possess the ability to learn, a fact that the Stanford-Binet or the WISC may not have revealed. When applied to white subjects, the test becomes a measure of their sensitivity and responsiveness to the black culture. Thus those white individuals who make high scores reveal that they have had intimate contact with and knowledge of blacks' life styles, values, folkways, and so on.

MEASURES OF THE ENVIRONMENT

Measuring the environmental determinants of intelligence is not new. But there has been widespread failure in finding an adequate instrument to measure these determinants. Bloom (1964), Wolf (1964), and Anastasi (1968a) observed that while there are many instruments for assessing individual characteristics, very few exist that can evaluate the environment. Of those that do exist, almost all are limited to yielding an index of social status and economic well-being with the consequent result that they "give little information about the specific ways in which environmental factors might affect the development of specific behavioral characteristics" (Wolf 1964, p. 95).

Wolf has undertaken to remedy such a deficit and to focus upon a procedure that would utilize measures of the environment in order to bolster and supplement the scores obtained from traditional intelligence tests. Departing from a position that posits the environment as a single global entity, Wolf adopted the following view:

> Our approach to the measurement of environments has been characterized by conceiving of specific environments for the development of particular characteristics, attempting to measure environmental variables which were hypothesized to be directly related to the development

of particular characteristics, summarizing and treating environmental data through the use of psychometric procedures, and relating environmental measurements to individual measurements (1964, p. 96).

Wolf's approach concentrates on the identification and description of the optimal characteristics of an environment that facilitate the development of general intelligence, academic achievements, physical growth, creativity, and so on. Thus an environment that is good for the development of physical growth may inhibit the development of general intelligence. The environment then becomes a series of subenvironments, each one geared to the enhancement of a specific characteristic.

The principal aim of the study, involving 60 homes and 1062 fifth graders enrolled in the schools of a medium-sized Midwestern community of urban, suburban, and rural characteristics, was to investigate the effects of the home on general intelligence and academic achievement. More specifically, the author was concerned not so much with the economic and occupational status of the parents or the physical amenities of the home, but rather with what parents *do* in their interactions with their children. From the information collected during the interview sessions with the families, an instrument measuring the environment for general intelligence was devised. It comprised 13 processed characteristics (21 for measuring the environment for academic achievement) listed as follows (Bloom 1964, p. 78):

A. Press for Achievement Motivation
1. Nature of intellectual expectations of child
2. Nature of intellectual aspirations for child
3. Amount of information about child's intellectual development
4. Nature of rewards for intellectual development
B. Press for Language Development
5. Emphasis on use of language in a variety of situations
6. Opportunities provided for enlarging vocabulary
7. Emphasis on correctness of usage
8. Quality of language models available
C. Provision for General Learning
9. Opportunities provided for learning in the home
10. Opportunities provided for learning outside the home (excluding school)
11. Availability of learning supplied
12. Availability of books (including reference works), periodicals, and library facilities
13. Nature and amount of assistance provided to facilitate learning in a variety of situations

Results of this investigation indicate that "the newer approach to the measurement of the environment accounts for about three times as much of the variance in general intelligence as a measure of social status" (Wolf 1964, p. 100). By obtaining a measure of what parents do in the home with their children, academic achievement can be predicted with a fairly high degree of accuracy. By combining measures of the individual's environment with measures of his performance on standardized tests of intelligence, it is possible, employing methods of multiple correlation, to raise the coefficient of correlation to +0.87, which represents practically the upper limit of such a relationship when the reliability of the instruments used is taken into account. Of importance for educational purposes is the finding that the measurement of environments implies better indices of prediction and provides useful information for "the development of new curricula designed to help overcome identified environmental deficiencies among students. Useful information about the ingredients for programs of compensatory education could be obtained from careful examination of the environmental measures" (Wolf 1964, p. 103).

CRITERION-REFERENCED TESTING

The controversy over testing and the teaching-learning process has led to a serious reevaluation of the traditional modes of assessment and prompted a number of innovations. Among the more fashionable notions of the 1960s and 1970s are those of individualized instruction, learning for mastery, the hierarchical sequencing of instruction, computer-assisted instruction, programmed instruction, and models of learning linked to the concept of formative and summative evaluation. But the core concept, one that is essentially associated with the latest trends in measurement and instruction, is that of criterion-referenced testing. What, at first glance, seems like a pioneer trend in the education and measurement of cognitive abilities turns out to be nothing more than the rebirth of a very old practice. The novelty lies not so much in the technicalities of item writing but in the approach to learning and teaching within an advancing decade of renewed focus on technology in the instructional process.

The idea of criterion-referenced testing is far older than the science of statistics, for it predates the systematic study of psychometrics by thousands of years. In essence, it is the same method as that employed by the Greeks and Romans, by the tutors of aristocrats (who, incidentally, also practiced along the lines of individualized instruction) in the Middle Ages, and, indeed, by pedagogues prior to the introduction of standardized norm-referenced testing in the twentieth century. The percentage-mastery grades, in determining and reporting the level of performance of students in schools and colleges in Europe and America, represent one type of criterion-referenced measurement (Ebel 1970). Work samples and performance measures employed in personnel selection and evaluation in industry represent another (Jackson 1971).

The impetus for the reawakening and implementation of an age-old concept seems to have begun in recent years when Robert Glaser introduced experiments in a program of "Individually Prescribed Instruction" at the Pittsburgh Learning Research and Development Center. A similar trend may also be identified in the work of Patrick Suppes and Richard Atkinson, whose experimental focus on computer-assisted instruction required the discrimination of learning tasks and the use of criterion-referenced measures to make judgments concerning the incremental progression of learning. Yet as far back as 1913, E. L. Thorndike had pointed out the inadequacy and limitations of standardized achievement-test scores and class grades as indicators of knowledge because they did not reveal the amount or type of knowledge possessed by the pupil. They merely reported how the pupil stood in relation to the performance of the rest of his class or some other referent group. It was Glaser (1963) who seemed to have coined the term and developed the distinction between criterion-referenced and norm-referenced types of tests.

More recently, Glaser and Nitko defined a *criterion-referenced test* as "one that is deliberately constructed to yield measurements that are directly interpretable in terms of specified performance standards" (1971, p. 653). In contrast to a norm-referenced test, a criterion-referenced measure is used to compare an individual with some established criterion or performance standard and not with other individuals. It tells what the individual can do, not how he stands in comparison to others (Popham and Husek 1969, p. 2). On this basis, a criterion-referenced test is distinctly different from a test of intelligence or aptitude, which implies "some average level of performance for a particular group of individuals" (Ebel 1970, p. 282) and also infers an individual's future performance on the basis of test results such as board scores. On the other hand, the meaning of an individual's test score on a criterion-referenced test "comes directly from the discrepancy between the examinee's test score and the criterion test score and is independent of scores obtained by other examinees on the same test" (Shoemaker 1971, p. 61). Sherman and Zieky have also emphasized the fact that "the essential difference in norm and criterion-referenced tests is their purposes which influence the form, the content, and the way the results are reported" (1974, pp. 3–4).

In debating the differences between the two forms of tests, Popham and Husek (1969) have claimed that it is not possible to tell one from the other by simply examining the test items and content, since a criterion-referenced test could also be used as a norm-referenced test. However, Simon (1969) has contested such a claim on the basis that a distinction applies not to the test itself but to the interpretation and the use of the test scores. It is important to recognize that criterion-referenced measures depend on absolute standards of quality, whereas norm-referenced measures depend on relative standards that are compared with the average performance of a group. As Glaser and Klaus (1962) defined it, the term "criterion," within the context of employment, does not necessarily refer to final on-the-job behavior, but rather to criterion levels established at any point in the training process; also it implies cumulative levels of achievement. Consequently, criterion standards are established in terms of the behavioral content itself rather than in terms of comparisons with groups or dispersion around a mean.

Even though criterion-referenced testing is a significant step toward the systematic sequencing of learning tasks leading to proficiency or mastery in any given body of knowledge or skills, the method does, however, have its special problems. The development of a good criterion-referenced test requires careful attention to certain essential questions. Boehm (1973, p. 120) listed the following: (1) Who determines the objectives? (2) Who sets the behavioral criterion levels? (3) Do test items accurately reflect the behavioral criteria? (4) What constitutes a sufficient sample of criterion levels? (5) Do the test scores obtained describe an individual's response pattern?

Evidently, problems exist in the determination of test reliability and test validity whether the measure is norm referenced or criterion referenced. But what is significant in the case of the latter is that such a measure helps in pinpointing the level of performance on a given task or set of subtasks within a skill or body of knowledge. Furthermore, it indicates how an individual responds in relation to a criterion, what he knows or does not know, and where his knowledge or skill mastery is deficient. Consequently, criterion-referenced measures permit the development of programs and instructional procedures matched to the particular individual's needs. This is especially important for minorities, who suffer most in the invidious comparison with normative groups from a different social and economic background.

In addition, criterion-referenced tests can help teachers determine whether or not a particular instructional program is suitable for a particular individual or set of individuals. In regard to the content of the tests, norm-referenced measures may or may not match the specific classroom objectives of a particular milieu, since sampling is conducted within the context of the larger task domain of the thing to be measured. Criterion-referenced assessment, on the other hand, must necessarily relate to the individual teacher's objectives determined before instruction begins, or to a standard of mastery against which the examinee's level of achievement can be assessed. Moreover, mastery levels can be fixed at any point along a continuum. The level of acceptable performance can be specified at a certain predetermined minimal level of competence. Furthermore, the statistic of primary importance is not related to any group but to the raw difference obtained by subtracting the examinee's test scores from the criterion test score defining the minimally acceptable level of achievement (Shoemaker 1971). Group variability on the test, therefore, becomes irrelevant. But what is important is the way in which each individual performs in relation to the criterion. Thus instead of masking what particular students can or cannot do, the scores reflect the pattern and extent of each individual's performance.

As Fremer has pointed out "we lack experimental support confirming the value of detailed hierarchical instructional sequences that would serve as a framework for using test results to route individuals to the next level of instruction" (1973, p. 9). And it is undeniable that individual students differ in the rate of sequencing of the learning of subtasks within a skill or body of knowledge. Moreover, suitable criterion measures are lacking and need to be developed. But it is significant that criterion-referenced testing is not an isolated phenomenon, for it goes hand-in-glove with educational innovations in scheduling, counseling, and administering programs. It is linked to the new technology of education that brings a new promise to the instruction of minorities. It represents a new philosophy that must, in time, drastically influence other parts of the educational system. Within the application of individualized instructional programs, criterion-referenced testing becomes an essential, integral part of teaching, rather than, as has so often been the case, an independent activity "performed at the teacher's whim or to meet some arbitrary school regulation" (Coulson and Cogswell 1965).

In what other ways do criterion-referenced tests, and the associated trends, add to our paraphernalia of educational technology? How can such devices and trends help to eliminate the problems associated with the measurement and instruction of minority students? As Benjamin Bloom (1968) shows, if we merely want to apply selective and sorting devices to exclude a large proportion of the population from higher education, if testing is used as a sorting mechanism, then the use of norm-referenced external examinations serve ideally. Even when applied impartially, the continued use of such devices can have, as previously outlined, devastating effects on minorities. The normal curve has come to be regarded as God-given, and tests have too often been used to ask and to determine answers to irrelevant questions: Are ethnic differences due to nature or nurture? Are levels of intelligence and aptitudes fixed? Such questions lead nowhere; at best they represent interesting academic exercises or rationalizations for guilty consciences. More appropriately, the questions asked should be: How can we optimize the potential of everyone? How can we engender a level of mastery in the key areas of knowledge and skills that will enable the black or Puerto Rican or Mexican-American youngster to enter into and benefit from the training program of his choice? How can we combine forces with the technology of cybernetics to make our instructional processes more efficient? How can we stem the waste of human potential and bring hope and motivation where frustration and despair exist?

Criterion-referenced testing represents the wave of the future. This direction in psychometrics was well summarized in the following quotation from Coulson and Cogswell:

> Extrapolating these trends in testing to a future school system, we envision frequent individualized diagnoses, based on several different measures of immediate and long-term performance. But a system having these capabilities will require an extremely powerful and flexible control mechanism. It is difficult for a teacher or experimenter to make the necessary sequencing decisions even for a program with a highly simplified branching structure. Furthermore, any branching procedures built into the materials themselves, as in a programmed text, must necessarily be quite elementary if they are to avoid an undesirable bookkeeping burden on the student. Modern computers offer the speed and memory necessary for complex branching, and for this reason a number of organizations have been experimenting with the use of computers to control individualized instruction. It seems a safe prediction that, within the next decade, operational schools will begin to use computers to control instruction and to record and analyze student responses, as well as for routine data processing (1965, p. 60).

These authors may have been a little ahead of their time, for computer-based systems of instruction have not proved as successful as it was hoped they might be. However, as technology becomes more adaptive and as the need arises to cater to masses of students on an individual level, the conceptual notions of learning for mastery, computer-based instruction, individualized instruction, and criterion-referenced assessment will become part of the armamentarium of pedagogy. Testing, instead of retarding the drive of minorities for parity in educational opportunity, could become the boon of a large portion of the population who suffer the consequences of a system that imposes unfair standards unrelated to the individual's needs and background. Criterion-referenced testing, though still in its infancy, could help to revolutionize the teaching-learning process and assist educators and social scientists in taking one giant step for mankind.

SUMMARY: TRENDS AND ALTERNATIVES

Expansion and elaboration—rather than abolition—of psychometric strategies may very likely result from the attacks on the testing industry. But changes are mandatory if the makers and users of tests are to discharge their functions responsibly. The direction of such changes can be seen in the various responses to the exposure of the limitations of the use of standardized tests with minority students, in particular, and with the general application of tests to the education of any student. These responses or trends can be dichotomized into two major categories—namely, one that seeks to retain the concepts of aptitude or fitness to perform in future situations from the results on a standardized repertoire of behavioral tasks; and one that emphasizes the purposes and goals of testing as essentially descriptive and prescriptive leading from an analysis of function levels and cognitive styles to the prescription of learning experiences matched to the individual needs of each student.

The first general trend is illustrated by the response of the majority of test producers to the charge that testing serves to keep minority groups in a relatively inequitable educational situation, to label as educationally mentally retarded many who are able to do normal work in an appropriate learning situation suited to their needs, and to serve a gatekeeping function to the institutions of higher education by unfairly depressing true potential of minority students through comparison with middle-class norms. Test producers claim that tests have been misused and misinterpreted by counselors, teachers, admission officers, and administrators. They also claim that those who use the tests should be aware of the meaning of the results and should not interpret the scores on IQ tests as implying permanent, innate, or irremediable deficiency. For test results merely indicate the degree of the individual's atypical level of function. They point up the unfairness of life—not the unfairness of the test. Thus it is the job of the school to gear instruction to the special needs of the student and to bring him up to par. Such a stance predicates a certain standard of behavioral responses; it emphasizes the fact that IQ tests are predictors of future achievement and that the school does exist as a middle-class institution that trains people to fit into a certain kind of society. As long as the norms of society remain what they are, IQ tests of the individual or group variety do fulfill a necessary and vital function. The need, therefore, is to train test users to ensure that test scores are properly obtained and interpreted.

The second trend is somewhat similar to the first in that it advocates the need for training and sensitizing test users to the possible misinterpretations of test scores as a result of technical and psychological contamination. Such a position has been enunciated by a division of APA, the Society for the Psychological Study of Social Issues, in the well-publicized "Guidelines for Testing Minority Group Children" (Fishman et al. 1964). The article deals specifically with three basic critical issues in the testing of minorities: lack of reliable differentiation in the range of minority group scores, which tend to cluster at the lower end of the total range; lack of predictive validity when scores are compared with standardization samples of a different sociocultural background; emphasis on adequate understanding of sociocultural background of the group being tested in order to make a true interpretation of scores. Fishman and his associates call for a thorough reexamination of the "use of tests" and for the retraining of those who administer and interpret them. In addition, they suggest certain modifications in the structure of existing tests, as well as in the procedures and test-taking situations; but the main thrust of their recommendations is directed toward the need to interpret test results with the understanding that certain variables, extraneous to test content, influence them. It is the opinion of these workers that tests should continue to be used as a means of comparing the performance of the minority child with that of advantaged white, middle-class children in order to determine "the magnitude of the deprivation to be overcome" (Fishman et al. 1964, p. 144). The essential philosophy of the "Guidelines" seems to follow the lines of the cultural deprivation theory or deficit model, whereby tests are viewed as gauging the success of the student in overcoming the deficiencies that an unfair social system has forced upon him.

The third trend focuses on measures of the environment in order to bolster and supplement the scores from traditional intelligence tests. Its essential thesis is that "the addition of a measure of the environment greatly enhances the estimation of academic achievement" (Wolf 1964, p. 102). Wolf empirically demonstrated that by measuring not only the economic and occupational status of the family or the physical amenities of the home but also what parents do in their interactions with their children, school achievement can be predicted with a high degree of accuracy. Thus by combining measures of the individual's environment with measures of his performance on standardized tests of intelligence and by employing methods of multiple correlation, it is possible to raise the coefficient of correlation to +0.87, which is practically the upper limit of such a correlation when the reliability of the instruments used is taken into account. Measurements of the environment, therefore, imply better indices of prediction and provide useful information for the development of "new curricula designed to help overcome identified environmental deficiencies among students. Useful information about the ingredients for programs of compensatory education could be obtained from careful examination of the environmental measures" (Wolf 1964, p. 103). Throughout almost all of the 1960s, there was a tacit and underlying acceptance of the deficit model and of the emphasis upon the environment as the principal factor in determining the deprived state of the minority person. Spawned in the period of the Kennedy and Johnson administrations, such positions typified the drive to right the balance and furnish the enrichment necessary to ameliorate the "cultural disadvantage" of an impoverished environment. Essentially, Wolf believes that because the development of the particular individual's characteristics is greatly influenced by environmental variables, one can discover how particular traits are learned, maintained, or altered by systematically relating data about the individual to data about the environment.

The fourth trend, espoused particularly by Jane Mercer and her associates at Riverside, California, calls for a "pluralistic sociocultural" perspective on the testing of minorities. Such a position is consistent with the modified use of standardized measures of IQ but requires that

> a culturally aware pluralistic interpretation would thus evaluate the intelligence of each person only in relation to others who have come from similar socio-cultural backgrounds and who have had approximately the same opportunity to acquire the knowledge and skills to answer questions on an intelligence test designed for an Anglo-American society (Mercer 1971, p. 335).

The implication of the pluralistic sociocultural perspective is that norms would be developed for each distinct sociocultural group within the ethnic group to which the individual belongs on the basis of family characteristics. The individual's IQ would be determined and interpreted, therefore, in relation to norms developed for his own sociocultural group, so that intellectual subnormality becomes associated with the lowest 3 percent of intelligence-test scores for his sociocultural group. The adoption of Mercer's pluralistic perspective would result in the placement of students in programs specifically designed to provide for individually identified educational needs, and comparison would be made only with peers from the same sociocultural group within those special programs designed to prepare the individual for participation in the mainstream of American life.

The fifth trend departs from traditional testing and involves the development of new measures consistent with the special language characteristics of minority individuals. This movement is fundamentally opposed to the notion that the black vernacular is nothing more than an underdeveloped form of standard English and that black children fail to learn appropriately at school because they have certain developmental or maturational deficits in the areas of language, learning set attitudes, and capacity for logical thought. Labov and the Baratzes take the position that standardized tests are, by their very nature, biased against black and other minority children and therefore greatly contribute to making normally intelligent children look stupid when their scores are compared with those of white, middle-class children. Although they stress a linguistic or anthropological frame of reference, this school of thought has vital implications for measurement. These authors hold that (1) tests that make use of standard English can only judge the abilities of those individuals who have been accustomed to using standard English; (2) the verbal-deprivation theory is bolstered by the fallacious use and interpretation of traditional tests of mental ability; (3) there is no reason to believe that any nonstandard vernacular is, in itself, an obstacle to learning; (4) the frequently monosyllabic verbal expression of black and lower-class children in the school represents a form of response to a formal and threatening situation rather than a lack of verbal capacity or verbal deficit; (5) evidence of the use of formal speech patterns does not necessarily coincide with logical thought; and (6) so long as we continue to use traditional standardized measures of mental ability with minorities and to explain their atypical results on the basis of a verbal-deprivation theory, we will continue to rationalize the failure of the school and the educational system in terms of the personal deficiencies of the individual. Such a trend implies the development of new measures matched to the language style and vernacular of the individual while ensuring that the circumstances of testing are such that the minority child feels free to respond without anxiety or emotional threat.

The sixth and final trend is a culmination of several schools of thought and theories related to the measurement and education of minorities. It calls for an emphasis on description and prescription rather than on selection and prediction in order to facilitate equal educational opportunities (Gordon 1972). Such a position radically departs from traditional testing, particularly in the purposes of psychometrics, since it focuses, essentially, on the descriptive, diagnostic, and qualitative analysis of behavioral function. It represents an integration and extension of several theoretical positions and the application of research findings to the education of minorities, as well as an extension of educational opportunity for the mass of people through individualized prescriptive educational planning. Instead of seeking to abolish tests, this trend regards psychometrics as a fundamental means by which we can begin to make education more accessible to the underprivileged elements of society without penalizing the individual for not belonging to the middle-class mainstream culture. The primary objective of testing becomes not just one of discovering where the individual is on a scale of attainment or of estimating his chances of success in a particular course of study, but it consists of diagnosing, in some detail, what he can and cannot do so as to plan those strategies that will optimize learning. It further recognizes that in order to gear instruction to individual needs, something must be known about the verbal and cognitive style of the child. By testing within the context of the individual's linguistic frame of reference, we can gauge the level and quality of his intellectual functioning and of his academic attainment. But judgments of mental capacity must take into account such factors as health and nutritional status, as well as the social and cultural environmental factors impinging upon academic and social development. Such a trend implies an extension of existing tests whereby patterns of achievement in any given subject area would provide qualitative descriptions or profiles in terms of the level of skill or knowledge as well as an account of those particular gaps or deficiencies toward which instruction should be focused. Thus test procedures would be directed toward broadening the varieties of competencies and skills—not merely through objective-type items but through open-ended probes designed to incorporate atypical patterns and varieties of learning. Also, by incorporating the work of McClelland within the body of psychometric technology, emphasis would be placed on measures of ego development and motivation and upon operant (or free-associative) thought patterns in assessing nonacademic learning such as social competence, coping skills, and political and avocational skills.

In the final analysis, we need to look at our purposes for testing. If testing is to serve a selective and sorting function and if, indeed, psychometric technology is intended to preserve an elite, then it follows that traditional procedures for measuring intelligence and scholastic aptitude, tied to a set of middle-class ethnocentric norms, will serve that function very well. However, if it is our purpose to serve the mass of citizens and if it is our goal to use measurement to facilitate the education of the poor, of the minority student, and of the atypical individual, then we will need to expand our research endeavors. Psychometric technology must become the handmaiden of educational innovation in optimizing the individual's competence through qualitative analysis of achievement and weaknesses so as to point the way toward the modification of instruction matched to the individual needs of individual students. Such a philosophy of testing can, hopefully, achieve true educational opportunity within the limits of the existing social system.

REFERENCES

ALPERT, R., AND HABER, R. N. Anxiety in academic achievement situations. *Journal of Abnormal and Social Psychology*, 61 (1960), 207–215.

ANASTASI, ANNE. *Differential psychology*. 2nd ed. New York: The Macmillan Company, 1958.

———. Psychology, psychologists and psychological testing. *American Psychologist*, 22 (1967), 297–306.

———. *Psychological testing*. 3rd ed. The Macmillan Company, 1968a.

———. Culture-fair testing. In *Readings in measurement and evaluation*, ed. N. E. Gronlund. New York: The Macmillan Company, 1968b, pp. 280–286.

———. Test bias. Paper Presented at Educational Testing Service, Princeton, N.J., January 1972.

———, AND CORDOVA, F. A. Some effects of bilingualism upon the intelligence test performance of Puerto Rican children in New York City, *Journal of Educational Psychology*, 44 (1953), 1–19.

ANGOFF, W., AND FORD, S. Item-race interaction on a test of scholastic aptitude. *Journal of Educational Measurement*, 10 (1973), 95–105.

ARMES, W. H. Medical Aspects of 1967 summer Head Start programs: Memphis and Shelby County. *Memphis and Mid-South Medical Journal*, 43 (1968), 203–206.

ARNEZ, NANCY L. Enhancing the black self-concept through literature. In *Black self-concept*, eds. J. A. Banks and J. D. Grambs. New York: McGraw-Hill, 1972, pp. 93–116.

ASHER, E. J. The inadequacy of current intelligence tests for testing Kentucky Mountain children. *Journal of Genetic Psychology*, 46 (1935), 480–486.

AUSUBEL, D. P. How reversible are the cognitive and motivational effects of cultural deprivation? Implications for teaching the culturally deprived child. *Urban Education*, 1 (1964), 16–38. In *Education of the disadvantaged*, eds. A. H. Passow, M. Goldberg, and A. J. Tannenbaum. New York: Holt, Rinehart and Winston, 1967, pp. 306–326.

———. Negativism as a phase of ego development. *American Journal of Orthopsychiatry*, 20 (1950), 796–805. In *The child*, ed. J. M. Seidman. New York: Holt, Rinehart and Winston, 1963, pp. 475–485.

———, AND AUSUBEL, P. Ego development among segregated Negro children. In *Education in depressed areas*, ed. A. H. Passow. New York: Teachers College Press, Columbia University, 1963, pp. 109–141.

159

BACHELOR, D., DONOFRIO, R., AND GRIFFIN-MALLORY, G. *Cognitive strengths and learning styles: Analysis and review of the Leiter International Performance Scale and the Peabody Picture Vocabulary Test*. Prepared by the Research and Evaluation Component of the Child Support Center, University of New Mexico (no date).

BANKS, J. A., AND GRAMBS, J. D. (Eds.) *Black self-concept*. New York: McGraw-Hill, 1972.

BARATZ, S. S., AND BARATZ, J. C. Early childhood intervention: The social science base of institutional racism. *Harvard Educational Review*, 40 (1970), 29–50.

BARKER LUNN, J. C. *Streaming in the primary school*. London: National Foundation for Educational Research in England and Wales, 1970.

BAUGHMAN, E. E. *Black Americans: A psychological analysis*. New York: Academic Press, 1971.

BELCHER, L. H., AND CAMPBELL, J. T. An exploratory study of word associations of Negro college students. *Psychological Report*, 23 (1968), 119–134.

BENNETT, G. K. Response to Robert Williams. *The Counseling Psychologist*, 2 (1970), 88–89.

BEREITER, C., ET AL. An academically oriented pre-school for culturally deprived children. In *Pre-school education today*, ed. F. M. Hechinger. New York: Doubleday, 1966, pp. 105–135.

BERNSTEIN, B. Language and social class. *British Journal of Sociology*, 11 (1960), 271–276.

———. Social structure, language, and learning. *Educational Research*, 3 (1961), 163–176. In *Education of the disadvantaged*, ed. A. H. Passow, M. Goldberg, and A. J. Tannenbaum. New York: Holt, Rinehart and Winston, 1967, pp. 225–244.

BERNSTEIN, L. The examiner as an inhibiting factor in clinical testing. *Journal of Consulting Psychology*, 20 (1956), 287–290. In *Readings in educational and psychological measurement*, ed. C. I. Chase and H. G. Ludlow. Boston: Houghton Mifflin, 1966, pp. 376–380.

BIAGGIO, A. Relative predictability of freshman grade point averages from SAT scores in Negro and white Southern colleges. *Technical Report No. 7*, Research and Development Center for Learning and Re-education, Univ. of Wisconsin, Madison, 1966.

BINET, A., AND SIMON, T. *The development of intelligence in children*. Tr. Elizabeth S. Kite. Baltimore: The Williams and Wilkins Company, 1916.

BIRCH, H. G., AND GUSSOW, J. D. *Disadvantaged children, health, nutrition and school failure*. New York: Harcourt, Brace and World; Grune and Stratton, 1970.

BLACK, H. *They shall not pass*. New York: Morrow, 1963.

BLOOM, B. *Stability and change in human characteristics*. New York: John Wiley and Sons, 1964.

———. Learning for mastery. *CSEIP Evaluation Comment*, 1 (1968).

BODMER, W. F. Race and IQ: The genetic background. In *Race and intelligence*, ed. K. Richardson and D. Spears. Baltimore: Penguin Books, 1972, pp. 83–113.

BOEHM, ANN E. Criteria-referenced assessment for the teacher. *Teachers College Record*, 75 (1973), 117–126.

BORG, W. R. *Ability grouping in the public schools*, 2nd ed. Madison, Wisconsin: Dembar Educational Research Services, Inc., 1966.

BOUVIER, L. F., AND LEE, E. S. Black America. *Population Profiles*, No. 10 (1974), 1–8.

BOYD, W. *Genetics and the races of man*. Boston: Little, Brown, 1950.

BRIGHAM, C. C. *A study of American intelligence*. Princeton, N.J.: Princeton Univ. Press, 1923.

BROOKOVER, W. B., AND ERIKSON, E. L. *Society, schools and learning*. Boston: Allyn and Bacon, 1969.

BROWN, B. The assessment of self-concept among four-year-old Negro and white children: A comparative study using the Brown-IDS Self-Concept Referents Test. New York: Institute for Developmental Studies (mimeo.), 1967.

BURKE, B., BEAL, V. A., KIRKWOOD, S. B., AND STUART, H. C. Nutrition studies during pregnancy. *American Journal of Obstetrics and Gynecology*, 46 (1943), 38–52.

BURKE, H. R. Raven's progressive matrices: A review and critical evaluation. *Journal of Genetic Psychology*, 93 (1958), 199–228.

BURKS, B. S. The relative influence of nature and nurture upon mental development: A comparative study of foster parent-foster child resemblance and true parent-true child resemblance. *Yearbook Natural Social Studies Education*, 27 (1928), 219–316.

BURT, C. Mental capacity and its critics. *Bulletin of the British Psychological Society*, 21 (1968), 11–18.

——. The genetic determination of differences in intelligence: A study of monozygotic twins reared together and apart. *British Journal of Psychology*, 57 (1966), 137–153.

——. The inheritance of mental ability. *American Psychologist*, 13 (1958), 1–15.

CALDWELL, M. B. An analysis of responses of a Southern urban Negro population to items on the Wechsler Intelligence Scale for children. Unpublished doctoral dissertation, Penn. State College, 1954.

CAMPBELL, J. T., PIKE, L. W., AND FLAUGHER, R. L. *A regression analysis of potential test bias: predicting job knowledge scores from an aptitude battery*. Project Report 69–6. Princeton, N.J.: Educational Testing Service, April 1969.

CANADY, H. G. The psychology of the Negro. In *The encyclopedia of psychology*, ed. P. L. Harriman. Philosophical Library, 65 (1946), 407–416.

——. The problem of equating the environment of Negro-white groups for intelligence testing in comparative studies. *The Journal of Social Psychology*, 17 (1943), 3–15. In *The psychological consequences of being a black American*, ed. R. C. Wilcox. New York: John Wiley & Sons, 1971, pp. 89–101.

——. Individual differences among freshmen at West Virginia State College and their educational bearings. *West Virginia State College Bulletin*, 23 (1936), 42.

CARROLL, J. B. Possible directions in which college board tests of abilities and learning capacities might be developed. In *Report of the Commission on Tests: II. Briefs*. New York: CEEB, 1970, pp. 1–12.

CASTANEDA, A., MCCANDLESS, B. R., AND PALMERO, D. S. The children's form of the Manifest Anxiety Scale. *Child Development*, 27 (1956), 317–326.

CATTELL, J. McK. Mental tests and measurements. *Mind*, 15 (1890), 373–381.

CATTELL, R. B. A culture-free intelligence test: I. *Journal of Educational Psychology*, 31 (1940), 161–179.

——, AND SCHEIER, I. H. *The meaning and measurement of neuroticism and anxiety*. New York: Ronald Press, 1961.

CLARK, K. B. Educational stimulation of racially disadvantaged children. In *Education in depressed areas*, ed. A. H. Passow. New York: Teachers College Press, Columbia University, 1963b, pp. 142–162.

——, AND PLOTKIN, L. *The Negro student at integrated colleges*. New York: National Scholarship Service and Fund for Negro Students, 1963.

——, AND CLARK, M. P. The development of consciousness of self and the emergence of racial identification in Negro pre-school children. *Journal of Social Psychology*, 10 (1939), 591–599.

——, AND PLOTKIN, L. A review of the issues and literature of cultural deprivation theory. In *The educationally deprived*, ed. K. B. Clark et al. New York: Metropolitan Applied Research Center, 1972, pp. 47–73.

——. Clash of cultures in the classroom. *Integrated Education*, 1 (1963a), 7–14.

——, AND CLARK, M. P. Emotional factors in racial identification and preference in Negro children. *Journal of Negro Education*, 19 (1950), 341–350.

——. Racial identification and preference in Negro children. In *Readings in social psychology*, eds. T. M. Newcomb and E. L. Hartley. New York: Holt, Rinehart and Winston, 1947, pp. 169–178.

CLEARY, ANNE T. Test bias: Prediction of grades of Negro and white students in integrated colleges. *Journal of Educational Measurement*, 5 (Summer 1968), 115–124.

——, AND HILTON, T. L. An investigation of item bias. *Educational and Psychological Measurement*, 28 (1968), 61–75.

CLEMANS, W. V. A note in response to a request by the editor to comment on R. L. Williams' article. *The Counseling Psychologist*, 2 (1970), 90–92.

CLINARD, M. B. The role of motivation and self-image in social change in slum areas. In *Psychological factors in poverty*, ed. L. A. Vernon. Chicago: The Institute for Research on Poverty Monograph Series, Markham Publishing Company, 1970, pp. 326–347.

CLOWARD, R. A., AND JONES, J. A. Social class: Educational attitudes and participation. In *Education in depressed areas*, ed. A. H. Passow. New York: Teachers College Press, Columbia Univ. 1963, pp. 190–216.

COFER, C. M., AND APPLEY, M. H. *Motivation: Theory and research*. New York: John Wiley and Sons, 1964.

COLE, M., GAY, J., GLICK, J. A., AND SHARP, D. W. *The cultural context of learning and thinking: An exploration in experimental anthropology*. New York: Basic Books, 1971.

COLE, N. S. Bias in selection. *Research Report No. 51*, Iowa City, Iowa: American College Testing Program, 1972.

COLEMAN, J. S., ET AL. *Equality of Educational Opportunity*. Washington, D.C.: U.S. Department of Health, Education and Welfare, 1966.

COLEMAN, W., AND WARD, A. W. A comparison of the Daviş-Eells and Kuhlmann-Finch scores of children from high and low socioeconomic status. *Journal of Educational Psychology*, 46 (1955), 465–69.

COLLEGE ENTRANCE EXAMINATION BOARD. *Report of the Commission on Tests: I. Righting the balance*. New York: CEEB, 1970a.

COLLEGE ENTRANCE EXAMINATION BOARD. *Report of the Commission on Tests: II. Briefs*. New York: CEEB, 1970b.

COLLINS, J. E. Relation of parental occupation to intelligence of children. *Journal of Educational Research*, 17 (1928), 157–169.

COMMITTEE ON MATERNAL NUTRITION/FOOD AND NUTRITION. *Maternal nutrition and the course of pregnancy: Summary report*. Washington, D.C.: National Research Council, U.S. Department of Health, Education and Welfare, Rockville, Md., 1970, pp. 1–23.

COON, C. S., GARN, S. M., AND BIRDSELL, J. B. *Races*. Springfield, Ill.: C. C Thomas, 1950.

COOPER, J. G. Predicting school achievement in bilingual pupils. *Journal of Educational Psychology*, 49, (1958), 31–36.

COOPER, R., AND ZUBEK, J. Effects of enriched and restricted early environments on the learning ability of bright and dull rats. *Canadian Journal of Psychology*, 12 (1958), 159–164.

CORNISH, R. D., AND DILLEY, J. S. Comparison of three methods of reducing test anxiety: Systematic desensitization, implosive therapy, and study counseling. *Journal of Counseling Psychology*, 20 (1973) 499–503.

COULSON, J. E., AND COGSWELL, J. F. Effects of individualized instruction on testing. *Journal of Educational Measurement*, 2 (1965), 59–64.

COURSIN, D. B. Undernutrition and brain function. *Borden's Review of Nutrition Research*, 26 (1965), 1–16.

COYLE, F. A. Another alternate wording on the WISC. *Psychological Reports*, 16 (1965), 1276.

CRONBACH, L. J. *Essentials of psychological testing*. New York: Harper & Row, 1970.

CROOKS, L. A. (Ed.). *An investigation of sources of bias in the prediction of job performance . . . a six-year study*. New York: Educational Testing Service, 1972.

CROSSLAND, F. E. *Minority access to college*. New York: Shocken Books, 1971.

DARLINGTON, R. B. Another look at cultural fairness. *Journal of Educational Measurement*, 8 (1971), 71–82.

DAVIDSON, H. H., AND GREENBERG, J. V. *Traits of school achievers from a deprived background*. New York: City College of the City University of New York, May 1967.

———, AND LANG, G. Children's perceptions of their teachers' feelings toward them related to self-perception, school achievement, and behavior. *Journal of Experimental Education*, 29 (1960), 107–118.

DAVIS, A., GARDNER, B. B., AND GARDNER, M. R. *Deep South.* Chicago: Univ. of Chicago Press, 1941.

———, AND EELLS, K. *Davis-Eells Test of General Intelligence or Problem-Solving Ability manual.* New York: World Book Company, 1953.

———, AND HAVIGHURST, R. J. Social class and color differences in child-rearing. *American Sociological Review*, 11 (1946), 698–710.

DAVIS, J. A., AND TEMP, G. Is the SAT biased against black students? *College Board Review*, 81 (1971), 4–9.

DEUTSCH, C. P. Environment and perception. In *Social class, race and psychological development*, eds. M. Deutsch, I. Katz, and A. Jensen. New York: Holt, Rinehart and Winston, 1968, pp. 58–85.

DEUTSCH, M. Minority groups and class status as related to social and personality factors in scholastic achievement. In *The disadvantaged child*, ed. M. Deutsch et al. New York: Basic Books, 1967, pp. 89–131.

———, ET AL. *The disadvantaged child.* New York: Basic Books, 1967.

———, AND BROWN, B. R. Social influences in Negro-white intelligence differences. In *The disadvantaged child*, eds. M. Deutsch et al. New York: Basic Books, 1967, pp. 295–307.

———, AND DEUTSCH, C. P. Brief reflections on the theory of early childhood enrichment programs. In *The disadvantaged child*, eds. M. Deutsch et al. New York: Basic Books, 1967, pp. 379–387.

DOBBING, J. The developing brain: A plea for more critical inter-species extrapolation. In: Effect of maternal nutrition on the development of offspring. *Nutrition Reports International*, 7 (1973), 401–406.

DOBZHANSKY, T. *Mankind evolving.* New Haven, Conn.: Yale Univ. Press 1962.

———. *Heredity and the nature of man.* New York: New American Library, 1964.

DOCKRELL, W. B. (Ed.). *On intelligence.* Toronto: The Ontario Institute for Studies in Education, 1970.

DRAKE, ST. C. The social and economic status of the Negro in the United States. In *The Negro American*, eds. T. Parsons and K. B. Clark. Boston: Beacon Press, 1966, pp. 3–46.

DREGER, R. M., AND MILLER, K. S. Comparative psychological studies of Negroes and whites in the United States. *Psychological Bulletin*, 57 (1960), 361–402.

DREWS, E. M., AND TEAHAN, J. E. Parental attitudes and academic achievement. *Journal of Clinical Psychology*, 13 (1957), 328–332.

DUBOIS, P. H. Increase in educational opportunity through measurement. In *Educational change: Implications for measurement.* Proceedings of the 1971 Invitational Conference on Testing Problems. Princeton, N.J.: Educational Testing Service, 1972.

DUNN, L. C., AND DOBZHANSKY, T. *Heredity, race and society.* Rev. ed. New York: New American Library, 1952.

DUNN, L. M. Special education for the mildly retarded. Is much of it justifiable? *Exceptional Children*, 35 (1968), 5–22.

DUROST, W. N., AND PRESCOTT, G. A. *Essentials of measurement for teachers.* New York: Harcourt, Brace and World, 1962.

DYER, H. S. A psychometrician views human ability. *Teachers College Record.* New York: Teachers College Press, Columbia Univer. 61 (1960), 394–403.

———. Is testing a menace to education? *New York State Education*, XLIX (October, 1961), pp. 16–19. In *Readings in educational and psychological measurement*, ed. C. I. Chase and H. G. Ludlow. Boston: Houghton-Mifflin, 1966, pp. 40–45.

EBEL, R. L. Must all tests be valid? *American Psychologist*, 16 (1961), 640–647.

———. The measurement responsibilities of teachers. In *Readings in educational psychology.* 2nd ed. Eds. V. H. Noll and R. P. Noll. New York: The Macmillan Company, 1968, pp. 383–391.

———. The social consequences of educational testing. *Proceedings of the 1963 Invita-*

tional Conference on Testing Problems. Princeton, N.J.: Educational Testing Service, 1963, pp. 130–143.

————. Some limitations of criterion-referenced measurement. Paper Prepared for AERA Symposium: Criterion-referenced measurement: Emerging issues, Minneapolis, March 1970.

EDWARDS, F. G. Community and class realities: The ordeal of change. In *The Negro American*, eds. T. Parsons and K. B. Clark. Boston: Beacon Press, 1966, pp. 280–302.

EELLS, K. ET AL. *Intelligence and cultural differences*. Chicago: Univ. of Chicago Press, 1951.

EINHORN, H. J., AND BASS, A. R. Methodological consideration relevant to discrimination in employment testing. *Psychological Bulletin*, 75 (1971), 261–269.

ERIKSON, E. The course of healthy personality development (Mid-Century White House Conference on Children and Youth). In *The adolescent*, ed. J. M. Seidman. New York: Holt, Rinehart and Winston, 1960.

ERLENMEYER-KIMLING, L., AND JARVIK, L. F. Genetics and intelligence: A review. *Science*, 142 (1963), 1477–1479.

FEIN, R. An economic and social profile of the Negro American. In *The Negro American*, eds. T. Parsons and K. B. Clark. Boston: Beacon Press, 1966, pp. 101–133.

FELDHUSEN, J. F., AND KLAUSMEIER, H. J. Anxiety, intelligence and achievement in children of low, average and high intelligence. *Child Development*, 33 (1962), 403–409.

FINDLEY, W. G., AND BRYAN, MIRIAM. *Ability grouping: 1970 status, impact, and alternatives*. Athens, Ga.: Center for Educational Improvement, Univ. of Georgia, 1971.

FISHMAN, J. A., ET AL. Guidelines for testing minority group children. *Journal of Social Issues Supplement*, 20 (1964), 129–145.

FLAUGHER, R. L. *Testing practices, minority groups and higher education: A review and discussion of the research. Research bulletin 70–41*. Princeton, N.J.: Educational Testing Service, 1970.

FLEMING, E. F., AND ANTTONEN, R. D. Teacher expectancies or My Fair Lady. In John Pilder, *Abstracts/1:1970*. Annual Meeting, Paper Session, Washington, D. C.: AERA, 1970, 66.

FOWLER, W. L. A comparative analysis of pupil performance on conventional and culture-controlled mental tests. Unpublished Ph.D. Thesis, Univ. of Michigan, 1955.

FREEMAN, F. N., HOLZINGER, K. J., AND MITCHELL, B. C. The influence of environment on the intelligence, school achievement and conduct of foster children. *27th Yearbook, National Society of Social Science Education*, Part I, 1928, pp. 103–217.

FREMER, J. Services in the area of criterion-referenced and objectives-referenced measurement: What, why, and where next. Paper Adapted from a Presentation at the Michigan School Testing Conference, Ann Arbor, Mich., March 14, 1973.

FRENCH, J. W., AND MICHAEL, W. B. The nature and meaning of validity and reliability. In *Readings in measurement and evaluation*, ed. N. E. Gronlund. New York: Macmillan Company, 1968, pp. 165–172.

FULLER, J. L., AND THOMPSON, W. R. *Behavior genetics*. New York: John Wiley and Sons, 1960.

GAEL, S., AND GRANT, D. L. Employment test validation for minority and non-minority telephone company service representatives. *Journal of Applied Psychology*, 56 (1972), 135–139.

GALTON, F. *Hereditary genius: An inquiry into its laws and consequences*. London: Macmillan, 1869. Cleveland, Ohio: The World Publishing Company, 1962.

————. Inquiries into human faculty and its development. London: Macmillan, 1883.

GARN, R. M. *Human races*. Springfield, Ill.: C. C Thomas, 1961.

GEISEL, P. N. IQ performance, educational and occupational aspirations of youth in a Southern city: A racial comparison. Unpublished doctoral dissertation. Vanderbilt Univ., 1962.

GEORGEOFF, P. J. *The elementary curriculum as a factor in racial understanding.* Lafayette, Ind.: Purdue Univ. Press, December 1967.

GIBBY, R. G., MILLER, D. B., AND WALKER, E. I. The examiner's influence on the Rorschach Protocol. *Journal of Consulting Psychology,* 17 (1953), 425–428.

GINZBERG, E. *The middle-class Negro in the white man's world.* New York: Columbia Univ. Press, 1967.

GLASER, R. Instructional technology and measurement of learning outcomes. *American Psychologist,* 18 (1963), 519–521.

————, AND KLAUS, D. J. Proficiency measurement: Assessing human performance. In *Psychological principles in system development,* ed. R. Gagne. New York: Holt, Rinehart and Winston, 1962, pp. 419–474.

————, AND NITKO, A. J. Measurement in learning and instruction. In *Educational measurement,* ed. R. L. Thorndike. Washington, D.C.: American Council on Education, 1971, pp. 625–670.

GLASS, B., AND LI, C. C. The dynamics of racial intermixture—an analysis based on the American Negro. *American Journal of Human Genetics,* 5 (1953), 1–20.

GOLDBERG, M. L., PASSOW, A. H., AND JUSTMAN, J. *The effects of ability grouping.* New York: Teachers College Press, 1966.

GOLDMAN, L. *Using tests in counseling.* New York: Appleton-Century-Crofts, 1961.

GOLDSCHMID, M. (Ed.). *Black Americans and white racism: Theory and research.* New York: Holt, Rinehart and Winston, 1970.

GOOD, W. R. Misconceptions about intelligence testing. *The Education Digest,* 20 (October, 1954), pp. 14–16. In *Readings in educational and psychological measurement,* ed. C. I. Chase and H. G. Ludlow. Boston: Houghton-Mifflin, 1966, pp. 177–179.

GOODMAN, M. E. *Race awareness in young children.* The Anti-Defamation League of B'nai B'rith. New York: Collier Books, 1964.

GORDON, E. W., AND WILKERSON, D. A. *Compensatory education for the disadvantaged.* New York: CEEB, 1966.

GORDON, E. W. Qualitative assessment and the design of learner behavior. Address to the Institute for Assessment of Minority Adolescents, May, 1972, Educational Testing Service, Princeton, N.J.

GORDON, H. *Mental and scholastic tests among retarded children.* London: Board of Education (Educational Pamphlet No. 44), 1923.

GOSLIN, D. A. Standardized ability tests and testing. *Science,* 159 (1968), 851–855.

————. The social consequences of predictive testing in education. Paper presented at the Conference on Moral Dilemmas of Public Schooling, School of Education, Univ. of Wisconsin, May 12–14, 1965.

GOTTESMAN, I. I. Biogenetics of Race and Class. In *Social class, race and psychological development,* eds. M. Deutsch, I. Katz, and A. Jensen. New York: Holt, Rinehart and Winston, 1968, pp. 11–51.

GOTTLIEB, D. Teaching and students: The views of Negro and white teachers. *Sociology of Education,* 37 (Summer 1964), 345–353.

GOZALI, J., AND MEYER, E. L. The influence of teacher expectancy phenomena on the academic performances of educably mentally retarded pupils in special classes. *Journal of Special Education,* 4 (1970), 417–424.

GRAMBS, J. D. Negro self-concept reappraised. In *Black self-concept,* ed. J. A. Banks and J. D. Grambs. New York: McGraw-Hill, 1972, pp. 171–220.

GRANT D. J., AND BRAY, D. W. Validation of employment tests for telephone company installation and repair occupations. *Journal of Applied Psychology,* 54 (1970), 7–14.

GRAY, S. W., AND KLAUS, R. A. An experimental preschool program for culturally deprived children. *Child Development,* 36 (1965), 887–898.

GREEN, R. L. After school integration—what? Problems in social learning. In *Guidance for urban disadvantaged youth,* ed. E. C. Hallberg. American Personnel and Guidance Association Reprint Series, No. 3, 1971a, pp. 28–38.

————. Black quest for higher education: An admission dilemma. *The Personnel and*

Guidance Journal, 47 (1969). In *The psychological consequences of being a black American*, ed. R. C. Wilcox. New York: John Wiley & Sons, 1971, pp. 261–271.

GRONLUND, N. E. *Measurement & evaluation in teaching*. 2nd ed. New York: The Macmillan Company, 1971.

GROSS, M. J. *The brain watchers*. New York: Random House, 1962.

GUILDFORD, J. P. *The nature of human intelligence*. New York: McGraw-Hill, 1967.

———. The structure of intellect. *Psychological Bulletin*, 53 (1956), 267–293.

GUINN, N., TUPES, E. C., AND ALLEY, W. E. *Cultural sub-group differences in the relationships between Air Force aptitude composites and training criteria*. (Technical Report 70–35), Brooks, Texas: Brooks Air Force Base, Air Force Human Resources Laboratory, September 1970.

GULLIKSEN, H., AND WILKS, S. S. Regression tests for several samples.*Psychometrika*, 15 (1950), 91–114.

GUSSOW, JOAN D. Nutrition and mental development. *ERIC/IRCD Urban Disadvantaged Series*, 36 (1974), 1–41.

HABERMAN, M. The relationship of bogus expectations to success in student teaching (or, Pygmalion's illegitimate son). In John Pilder, *Abstracts/1:1970*. Annual Meeting, Paper Session, Washington, D.C.: AERA, 1970, 66.

HAGGARD, E. A. Social status and intelligence: An experimental study of certain cultural determinants of measured intelligence. *Genetic Psychology Monographs*, 49 (1954), 141–186.

———. Techniques for the development of unbiased tests. *The 1952 Invitational Conference on Testing Problems*. Princeton, N.J.: Educational Testing Service, 1952, pp. 93–120.

HAGGERTY, M. E., AND NASH, H. B. Mental capacity of children and parental occupation. *Journal of Educational Psychology*, 5 (1924), 559–572.

HARLESTON, B. W. Higher education for the Negro. *The Atlantic Monthly*, 1965, 139–144. In *The psychological consequences of being a black American*, ed. R. C. Wilcox. New York: John Wiley & Sons, 1971, pp. 175–185.

HARRELL, R. F., WOODYARD, E., AND GATES, A. I. *The effects of mothers' diet on the intelligence of offspring*. New York: Bureau of Publications, Teachers College, Columbia Univ., 1955.

HAUBRICH, V. F. Teachers for big-city schools. In *Education in depressed areas*, ed. A. H. Passow. New York: Teachers College Press, Columbia Univ., 1963, pp. 243–261.

HAUSER, P. M. Demographic factors in the integration of the Negro. In *The Negro American*, ed. T. Parsons and K. B. Clark. Boston: Beacon Press, 1966, pp. 71–101.

HAVIGHURST, J., AND BREESE, F. H. Relations between ability and social status in a midwestern community III. Primary mental abilities. *Journal of Educational Psychology*, 38 (1947), 241–247.

HAWKES, T. H., AND FURST, N. F. Race, socioeconomic situation, achievement, IQ and teacher ratings of student behavior as factors relating to anxiety in upper elementary school children. *Sociology of Education*, 1971.

HEATHERS, G. Grouping. In *Encyclopedia of educational research*. 4th ed. Ed. R. L. Ebel. New York: The Macmillan Company, 1969, pp. 559–570.

HERRNSTEIN, R. IQ. *The Atlantic Monthly*, 1971, 43–64.

HESS, R. D., AND SHIPMAN, V. C. Early experience and the socialization of cognitive modes in children. *Child Development*, 36 (1965), 369–386.

HESS, R. D., SHIPMAN, B. C., BROPHY, J. E. AND BEAL, R. M. *The cognitive environments of urban pre-school children*. The Graduate School of Education, Univ. of Chicago, 1968.

HILGARD, E. R., AND ATKINSON, R. C. *Introduction to psychology*. 4th ed. New York: Harcourt, Brace and World, 1967.

HILL, R. *The strengths of black families*. National Urban League. New York: Emerson Hall Publishers, 1972.

HILLS, J. R., KLOCK, J. C., AND LEWIS, S. *Freshman norms for the University System of Georgia, 1961–1962*. Atlanta, Ga.: Office of Testing and Guidance, Regents of the University System of Georgia, 1963.

HIRSCH, J. Behavior-genetic analysis and its biosocial consequences. In *Intelligence: Genetic and environmental influences*, ed. R. Cancro. New York: Grune and Stratton, 1971, pp. 88–106.

HODGKINS, B., AND STAKENAS, R. C. A study of self-concepts of Negro and white youth in segregated environments. *Journal of Negro Education*, 38 (1969), 370–377.

HODGSON, G. Do schools make a difference? *The Atlantic Monthly*, 1973, 35–46.

HOFFMAN, B. *The tyranny of testing*. New York: The Crowell-Collier Press, 1962.

HOLLINGSHEAD, A. B. *Elmtown's youth*. New York: John Wiley and Sons, 1949.

HUNT, J. McV., AND KIRK, G. E. Social aspects of intelligence: Evidence and issues. In *Intelligence*, ed R. Cancro. New York: Grune and Stratton, 1971, pp. 262–306.

HUNT, J. McV. *Intelligence and experience*. New York: The Ronald Press, 1961.

————. The psychological basis for using pre-school enrichment as an antidote for cultural deprivation. In *Education of the disadvantaged*, eds. A. H. Passow, M. Goldberg, and A. J. Tannenbaum. New York: Holt, Rinehart and Winston, 1967, pp. 174–213.

————. Towards the prevention of incompetence. In *Research contributions from psychology to community health*, ed. J. W. Carter. New York: Behavioral Publications, 1968.

HURLOCK, ELIZABETH. A study of self-ratings by children. *Journal of Applied Psychology*, 11 (1927), 490–502.

HUTCHESON, R. H. Iron deficiency anemia in Tennessee among rural poor children. *Public Health Report*, 83 (1968), 939–943.

IRVINE, S. H. Towards a rationale for testing attainments and abilities in Africa. *British Journal of Educational Psychology*, 36 (1966), 24–32.

JACKSON, R. Developing criterion-referenced tests. TM Report No. 1 ERIC Clearinghouse on Tests, Measurement and Evaluation, Educational Testing Service, Princeton, N.J., June 1971.

JACOBSON, R. L. Black enrollment rising sharply, U.S. data show. *The Chronicle of Higher Education*, October 4, 1971.

JENCKS, C. *Inequality*. New York: Basic Books, 1972.

JENKINS, M. D. Problems incident to racial integration and some suggested approaches to these problems—a critical summary. In *The psychological consequences of being a black American*, ed. R. C. Wilcox. New York: John Wiley and Sons, 1971, pp. 45–56.

————. The upper limit of ability among American Negroes (1948). In *The psychological consequences of being a black American*, ed. R. C. Wilcox. New York: John Wiley and Sons, 1971, pp. 102–106.

JENSEN, A. R. How much can we boost IQ and scholastic achievement? *Harvard Educational Review*, 39 (1969), 1–123.

JOHN, V. P., AND GOLDSTEIN, L. S. The social context of language acquisition. In *The disadvantaged child*, ed. M. Deutsch et al. New York: Basic Books, 1967, pp. 163–175.

JOSÉ, J., AND CODY, J. J. Teacher-pupil interaction as it relates to attempted changes in teacher expectancy or academic ability and achievement. *American Educational Research Journal*, 8 (1971), 39–50.

KAGAN, J. The IQ puzzle: What are we measuring? *Inequality in Education*, 14 (1973), 5–13.

KALLINGAL, A. The prediction of grades for black and white students at Michigan State University. *Journal of Educational Measurement*, 8 (1971), 263–265.

KARMEL, L. J. *Measurement and evaluation in the schools*. New York: The Macmillan Company, 1970.

KATZ, I., GOLDSTON, J., AND BENJAMIN, L. Behavior and productivity in bi-racial work groups. *Human Relations*, 11 (1958), 123–141.

————, AND COHEN, M. The effects of training Negroes upon cooperative problem solving in bi-racial teams. *Journal of Abnormal and Social Psychology*, 64 (1962), 319–325.

————. Academic motivation and equal educational opportunity. *Harvard Educational Review*, 38 (Winter 1968a), 56–65.

————. Factors influencing Negro performance in the desegregated school. In *Social class, race and psychological development*, eds. M. Deutsch, I. Katz, and A. Jensen. New York: Holt, Rinehart and Winston, 1968b, pp. 254–289.

———, AND BENJAMIN, L. Effects of white authoritarianism in bi-racial work groups. *Journal of Abnormal and Social Psychology*, 61 (1960), 448–456.

———, ROBERTS, S. D., AND ROBINSON, J. M. Effects of difficulty, race of administrator and instructions on Negro digit-symbol performance. *Journal of Personality and Social Psychology*, 70 (1965), 53–59.

———, ROBINSON, J. M., EPPS, E. G., AND WALY, P. The influence of race of the experimenter and instructions upon the expression of hostility by Negro boys. *Journal of Social Issues*, 20 (1964), 54–59.

KELLER, S. The social world of the urban slum child: Some early findings. *American Journal of Orthopsychiatry*, 33 (1963), 813–822.

KENNEDY, VAN DE RIET, W. A., AND WHITE, J. C. A normative sample of intelligence and achievement of Negro elementary school children in the Southeastern United States. *Monograph of the Society in Research Child Development*, 28, No. 6 (1963).

KESTON, J. J., AND JIMINEZ, C. K. A study of the performance on English and Spanish editions of the Stanford-Binet Intelligence Test by Spanish-American children. *Journal of Genetic Psychology*, 85 (1954), 263–269.

KIDD, A. H. The culture-fair aspects of Cattell's Test of g: Culture-free. *Journal of Genetic Psychology*, 101 (1962), 343–362.

KIMBLE, G. A., AND GARMEZY, N. *Principles of General Psychology*. 3rd ed. New York: The Ronald Press, 1968.

KLINEBERG, O. (Ed.). *Characteristics of the American Negro*. New York: Harper & Row, 1944.

———. *Negro intelligence and selective migration*. New York: Columbia Univ. Press, 1935a.

———. *Race differences*. New York: Harper, 1935b.

———. A study of psychological differences between racial and national groups in Europe. *Archives of Psychology*, No. 13 (1931).

KNOBLOCH, H., AND PASAMANICK, B. Further observations on the behavioral development of Negro children. *Journal of Genetic Psychology*, 83 (1953), 137–157.

———, RIDER, R., HARPER, P., AND PASAMANICK, B. Neuropsychiatric sequelae of prematurity. *Journal of the American Medical Association*, 161 (1956), 581–585.

LABOV, W. Academic ignorance and black intelligence. *The Atlantic Monthly* (1971), 59–67.

LAMBERT, N. M. The present status of the culture-fair testing movement. *Psychology in the Schools* (1961), 318–330.

LANDRETH, C., AND JOHNSON, B. C. Young children's responses to a picture and inset test designed to reveal reactions to persons of different skin color. *Child Development*, 24 (1953), 63–79.

LARSON, R. G., ET AL. Kindergarten racism: A projective assessment. Unpublished report, Univ. of Wisconsin, Milwaukee, 1966.

LEAHY, A. M. Nature-nurture and intelligence. *General Psychological Monographs*, 17 (1935), 235–308.

LEE, E. S. Negro intelligence and selective migration: A Philadelphia test of the Klineberg hypothesis. *American Sociological Review*, 16 (1951), 227–233.

LENNON, R. T. Testing and the culturally disadvantaged child. Lecture delivered at the Mackey School, Boston, February 26, 1964. New York: Harcourt, Brace and World, 1964.

———. Testing: The question of bias. In *Evaluation in the inner city*, ed. T. J. Fitzgibbon. New York: Harcourt, Brace and World, 1970.

———. *Testimony of Doctor Roger T. Lennon as expert witness on psychological testing in the case of Hobson et al. versus Hansen et al. (Washington, D.C. School)*. New York: Harcourt, Brace and World, 1966.

LESAGE, W., AND RICCIO, A. C. Testing the disadvantaged—an issue of our time. *Focus on Guidance*, 3 (1970), 1–7.

LEVIN, H. A. A psycholinguistic investigation: Do words carve up the world differently for Negro and whites, boys and girls from city and suburban junior high schools? Unpublished doctoral dissertation. Rutgers, The State Univ., 1964.

LINDEN, K. W., AND LINDEN, J. D. *Modern mental measurement: A historical perspective. Guidance monograph series, III: Testing.* Boston: Houghton-Mifflin, 1968a.

LINDEN, J. D., AND LINDEN, K. W. *Tests on trial. Guidance monograph series, III: Testing.* Boston: Houghton-Mifflin, 1968b.

LINN, R. L., AND WERTS, C. E. Considerations for studies of test bias. *Journal of Educational Measurement,* 8 (1971), 1–4.

LINN, R. L. Fair test use in selection. *Review of Educational Research,* 43 (1973), 139–161.

LORETAN, J. O. Alternatives to intelligence testing. *Proceedings of the 1965 Invitational Conference on Testing Problems.* Princeton, N.J.: Educational Testing Service, 1966, 19–30.

LORGE, I. Differences or bias in tests of intelligence. *Proceedings of the 1952 Invitational Conference on Testing Problems.* Princeton, N.J.: Educational Testing Service, 1952, pp. 76–83.

LOUGHLIN, L. J., O'CONNOR, H. A., POWELL, M., AND PARSLEY, K. An investigation of sex differences by intelligence, subject-matter area, grade and achievement on three anxiety scales. *Journal of Genetic Psychology,* 106 (1965), 207–215.

LOWELL, E. L. The effect of need for achievement on learning and performance. *Journal of Psychology,* 33 (1952), 31–40.

LUDLOW, H. G. Some recent research on the Davis-Eells games. *School and Society,* 84 (1956), 146–148.

LYND, R. S., AND LYND, H. M. *Middletown: A study in American culture.* New York: Harcourt, Brace and World, 1929.

———. *Middletown in transit.* New York: Harcourt, Brace and World, 1937.

MACFARLANE SMITH, I. IPAT culture-free intelligence test. In *Fifth Mental Measurement Yearbook,* ed. O. Buros. (Tests and Reviews: Intelligence Group), 1959, pp. 473–474.

MACKLER, B., AND GIDDINGS, M. G. Cultural deprivation: A study in mythology. *Teachers College Record,* 66 (1965), 608–613.

MALINA, R. M. Growth and physical performance of American Negro and white children. *Clinical Pediatrics,* 8 (1969), 476–481.

MANDLER, G., AND SARASON, S. B. A study of anxiety and learning. *Journal of Abnormal and Social Psychology,* 47 (1952), 166–173.

MARQUART, D. I., AND BAILEY, L. L. An evaluation of the culture-free test of intelligence. *Journal of Genetic Psychology,* 86 (1955), 353–358.

MASLOW, A. H. What intelligence tests mean. *Journal of General Psychology,* 31 (1944), 85–93.

MAURER, S. The effect of early partial depletion of vitamin B upon learning in rats. *Journal of Comparative Psychology,* 20 (1935), 309–318.

———. Vitamin B deficiency and learning ability. *Journal of Comparative Psychology,* 11 (1930), 51–62.

———, AND TSAI, L. S. Vitamin B deficiency in nursing young rats and learning ability. *Science,* 70 (1929), 456–458.

MAYER, K. B. *Class and society.* Rev. ed. Studies in Sociology. New York: Random House, 1959.

MAYESKE, G., ET AL. *A study of our nation's schools.* Washington, D.C.: Government Printing Office, 1970.

MAYR, E. *Animal species and evolution.* Cambridge, Mass.: Harvard Univ. Press, 1963.

MCCLELLAND, D. C. Testing for competence rather than for intelligence. *American Psychologist,* 28 (1973), 1–14.

———, ET AL. *The achievement motive.* New York: Appleton-Century-Crofts, 1953.

MCCLELLAND, D. C. Toward a theory of motive acquisition. *American Psychologist,* 20 (1965), 321–333.

McGRAW, M. B. A comparative study of a group of Southern white and Negro infants. *Genetic Psychology Monograph*, 10 (1931), 1–10.

——. Need for denial. *American Psychologist*, 19 (1964), 56.

McKEACHIE, W. J., POLLIE, D., AND SPEISMAN, J. Relieving anxiety in classroom examinations. In *Readings in the social psychology of education*, ed. W. M. Charters and N. L. Gage. Boston: Allyn and Bacon, 1963, pp. 212–218.

McKELPIN, J. P. Some implications of the intellectual characteristics of freshmen entering a liberal arts college. *Journal of Educational Measurement*, 2 (1965), 161–166.

McREYNOLDS, P. The assessment of anxiety: A survey of available techniques. In *Advances in psychological assessment*, Vol. 1, ed. P. McReynolds. Palo Alto, Calif.: Science and Behavior Books, 1968, pp. 244–264.

MEDLEY, D. M., AND QUIRK, T. J. Race and subject-matter influences on performance on general education items of the National Teacher Examination. *Research Bulletin 72-43*, Princeton, N.J.: Educational Testing Service, 1972.

MEHRENS, W. A., AND LEHMANN, I. J. *Standardized tests in education*. New York: Holt, Rinehart and Winston, 1969.

MERCER, J. R. "Institutionalized anglocentrism: Labeling mental retardates in the public schools." In *Race, change, and urban society*, ed. Peter Orleans and William Russell, Jr. Urban Affairs Annual Review, Vol. V. Los Angeles: Sage Publications, 1971.

MEREDITH, H. V. Body weight at birth of viable human infants: A worldwide comparative treatise. *Human Biology*, 42 (1970), 217–264.

MESSICK, S., AND ANDERSON, S. Educational testing, individual development and social responsibility. *The Counseling Psychologist*, 2 (1970), 80–88.

MILHOLLAND, J. E. Culture-fair Intelligence Test. In *Sixth Mental Measurement Yearbook, Tests and Reviews: Intelligence Group*, ed. O. Buros, 1965, pp. 719–721.

MILNER, E. A study of the relationship between reading readiness in grade one school children and patterns of parent-child interaction. *Child Development*, 22 (1951), 95–112.

MONTAGU, A. M. F. (ed.), *Frontiers of Anthropology*. New York: G. P. Putnam's Sons, 1974.

——. *Man's most dangerous myth, the fallacy of race*. New York: Harper and Bros., 1952.

MORAN, R. E. Observations and recommendations on the Puerto Rican version of the Wechsler Intelligence Scale for children. *Pedagogia*, Rio Piedras, 10 (1962), 89–98.

MORLAND, J. K. Racial self-identification: A study of nursery school children. *The American Catholic Sociological Review*, 24 (1963), 231–242.

MOSTELLER, F., AND MOYNIHAN, D. P. (Eds.). *On equality of educational opportunities*. New York: Vintage Books, 1972.

MOYNIHAN, D. P. Employment, income and the ordeal of the Negro family. *Daedalus*, 1965, 745–770.

MUELLER, K. H., AND MUELLER, J. H. Class structure and academic and social success. *Educational and Psychological Measurement*, 13 (1953), 486–496.

MURRAY, H. A. *Explorations in personality*. New York: Oxford University Press, 1938.

MUSSEN, P. H. Differences between the TAT responses of Negro and white boys. *Journal of Consulting Psychology*, 17 (1953), 373–376.

——. *The psychological development of the child*. Foundations of Modern Psychology Series, Englewood Cliffs, N.J.: Prentice-Hall, 1963.

NATIONAL EDUCATION ASSOCIATION, RESEARCH DIVISION. *Ability grouping*, Research Summary 1968-S3. Washington, D.C.: National Education Association, 1968.

NEWMAN, H. H., FREEMAN, F. N., AND HOLZINGER, K. J. *Twins: A study of heredity and environment*. Chicago: Univ. of Chicago Press, 1937.

NOLL, V. H. Relation of scores on Davis-Eells games to socio-economic status, intelligence test results, and school achievement. *Educational and Psychological Measurement*, 20 (1960), 119–129.

NORTH, R. D. *The intelligence of American Negroes*. New York: Anti-Defamation League of B'nai B'rith, 1957.

NUNN, SIR P. *Education: Its data and first principles*. 3rd ed. London: Edward Arnold and Company, 1945.

OGLETREE, E. Homogeneous ability grouping—British style. *Peabody Journal of Education*, 47 (1969), 20–25.

ORGEL, A. R., AND DREGER, R. M. A comparative study of the Arthur-Leiter and Stanford-Binet Intelligence Scales. *Journal of Genetic Psychology*, 86 (1955), 359–365.

OSTERHOUSE, R. A. Desensitization and study-skills training as treatment for two types of test-anxious students. *Journal of Counseling Psychology*, 19 (1972), 301–307.

OTIS, S., AND LENNON, R. T. *Otis-Lennon Mental Ability Test: Manual for administration*. New York: Harcourt, Brace and World, 1967.

OWEN, G. M., AND KRAM, K. M. Nutritional status of preschool children in Mississippi. *Journal of the American Diet Association*, 54 (1969), 490–494.

PACKARD, V. *The hidden persuaders*. New York: David McKay, 1957.

PANDEY, R. E. The SAT and race. *Psychological Report*, 28 (1971), 459–462.

PASAMANICK, B. A comparative study of the behavioral development of Negro infants. *Journal of Genetic Psychology*, 69 (1946), 3–44.

———, AND KNOBLOCH, H. The contribution of some organic factors to school retardation in Negro children. *Journal of Negro Education*, 27 (1958), 4–9.

———. Early language behavior in Negro children and the testing of intelligence. *Journal of Abnormal Psychology*, 50 (1955), 401–402.

PASANELLA, A., MANNING, W. H., AND FINDIKYAN, N. Bibliography of test criticism. *Commission on tests: Background papers*. New York: CEEB, 1967, pp. 73–127.

PETERSON, J. *Early conceptions and tests of intelligence, measurement and adjustment series*, ed. Lewis M. Terman. New York: World Book Company, 1925.

———. The comparative abilities of white and Negro children. *Comparative Psychology Monograph*, 5 (1923), 1–141.

PETTIGREW, T. F. *A profile of the Negro American*. Princeton, N.J.: D. Van Nostrand, 1964.

PFEIFER, C. M., JR., AND SEDLACEK, W. E. The validity of academic predictors for black and white students at a predominantly white university. *Journal of Educational Measurement*, 8 (1971), 153–161.

PINTNER, R. *Intelligence testing: Methods and results*. Holt, 1931.

POLLITZER, W. S. The Negroes of Charleston, S.C.: A study of hemoglobin types, serology and morphology. *American Journal of Physical Anthropology*, 16 (1958), 241–263.

POPHAM, W. J., AND HUSEK, T. R. Implications of criterion-referenced measurement. *Journal of Educational Measurement*, 6 (1969), 1–9.

PRESSEY, S. L., AND RALTON, R. The relation of the general intelligence of school children to the occupation of their fathers. *Journal of Applied Psychology*, 3 (1919), 336–373.

PROSHANSKY, H., AND NEWTON, P. The nature and meaning of Negro self-identity. In *Social class, race and psychological development*, ed. M. Deutsch, I. Katz, and A. Jensen. New York: Holt, Rinehart and Winston, 1968, pp. 178–218.

RADKE, M., SUTHERLAND, J., AND ROSENBERG, P. Racial attitudes of children. *Sociometry*, 13 (1950), 154–171.

RAINWATER, L. *Behind ghetto walls*. Chicago: Aldine, 1970.

REX, J. Nature versus nurture: The significance of the revived debate. In *Race and intelligence*, eds. K. Richardson and D. Spears. Baltimore, Md.: Penguin Books, 1972, pp. 167–178.

RICCIUTI, H. N. *Malnutrition and psychological development*. Proceedings of the Association for Research in Nervous and Mental Disease, 1973.

RIDER, R., TABACK, M., AND KNOBLOCH, H. Associations between premature birth and socioeconomic status. *American Journal of Public Health*, 45 (1955), 1022–1028.

RIESSMAN, F. *The culturally deprived child*. New York: Harper & Row, 1962.

RIST, R. C. Student social class and teacher expectations: The self-fulfilling prophecy in ghetto education. *Harvard Educational Review*, 40 (1970), 411–451.

ROBERTS, D. F. The dynamics of racial intermixture in the American Negro—some anthropological considerations. *American Journal of Human Genetics*, 7 (1955), 361–367.

ROBERTS, S. O. Studies in identification of college potential. Nashville, Tenn.: Department of Psychology, Fisk Univ., 1962 (mimeo.).

ROCK, D. A. Motivation, moderators and test bias. *Toledo Law Review* (1970), 527–537.

ROEDER, L. M., AND CHOW, B. F. Maternal undernutrition and its long-term effects on the offspring. *The American Journal of Clinical Nutrition*, 25 (1972), 812–821.

ROSEN, B. C. Race, ethnicity, and the achievement syndrome. *American Sociological Review*, 24 (1959), 47–60.

ROSENBLUM, S., KELLER, J. E., AND PAPANIA, N. Davis-Eells (Culture-fair) Test Performance of Lower-Class Retarded Children. *Journal of Consulting Psychology*, 19 (1955).

ROSENTHAL, R., AND JACOBSON, LENORE. *Pygmalion in the classroom. Teachers' expectation and pupils' intellectual development.* New York: Holt, Rinehart, and Winston, 1968.

ROTH, R. W. The effects of black studies on Negro fifth-grade students. *The Journal of Negro Education*, 38 (1969), 435–439.

RULON, P. J. A semantic test of intelligence. *The 1952 Invitational Conference on Testing Problems.* Princeton, N.J.: Educational Testing Service, 1952, pp. 84–92.

SACKS, E. L. Intelligence scores as a function of experimentally established social relationships between child and examiner. *Journal of Abnormal and Social Psychology*, 47 (1952), 354–358.

SARASON, S. B., DAVIDSON, K., LIGHTHALL, F., AND WAITE, R. A test anxiety scale for children. *Child Development*, 29 (1958), 105–113.

SARASON, S. B., AND MANDLER, G. Some correlates of test anxiety. *Journal of Abnormal and Social Psychology*, 47 (1952), 810–817.

———, AND CRAIGHILL, P. G. The effects of differential instructions on anxiety and learning. *Journal of Abnormal and Social Psychology*, 47 (1952), 561–565.

SCHAEFER, A. E. The national nutrition survey. *Journal of the American Diet Association*, 54 (1969), 371–375.

SCHMIDT, F. L., AND HUNTER, J. E. Racial and ethnic bias in psychological tests: Divergent implications of two definitions of test bias. *American Psychologist*, 29 (1974), 1–8.

SCHRAG, P. America's dual system of education (1967). In *Crucial issues in education.* 4th ed. Ed. H. Ehlers. New York: Holt, Rinehart and Winston, 1969, pp. 74–77.

SCHWARZ, P. A. Adapting tests to the cultural setting. *Educational and Psychological Measurement*, 23 (1963), 673–686.

SEASHORE, H., WESMAN, A., AND DOPPELT, J. The standardization of the Wechsler Intelligence Scale for Children. *Journal of Consulting Psychology*, 14 (1950), 99–110.

SEWARD, G. *Psychotherapy and culture conflict.* New York: Ronald Press, 1956.

SHERMAN, M., AND KEY, C. B. The intelligence of isolated mountain children. *Child Development*, 3 (1932), 279–290.

SHERMAN, M., AND ZIEKY, M. (Eds.). *Handbook for conducting task analyses and developing criterion-referenced tests of language skills.* Project Report 74–12. Educational Testing Service, Princeton, N.J., March 1974.

SHIELDS, J. *Monozygotic twins brought up apart and brought up together.* London: Oxford Univ. Press, 1962.

SHIMBERG, M. E. An investigation into the validity of norms with special reference to urban and rural groups. *Archives of Psychology*, No. 104 (1929).

SHOEMAKER, D. M. Criterion-referenced measurement revisited. *Educational Technology* (March 1971), 61–62.

SHUEY, A. M. *The testing of Negro intelligence.* Lynchburg, Va.: J. P. Bell, 1958. Second Edition, New York: Social Science Press, 1966.

SIMON, G. B. Comments on implications of criterion-referenced measurement. *Journal of Educational Measurement*, 6 (1969), 259–260.

SINNOTT, E. W., DUNN, L. C., AND DOBZHANSKY, T. *Principles of genetics.* 5th ed. New York: McGraw-Hill, 1958.

SKODAK, M., AND SKEELS, H. M. A final follow-up study of one hundred adopted children. *Journal of Genetic Psychology*, 75 (1949), 85–125.

SNOW, R. E. Unfinished Pygmalion, Review of Rosenthal and Jacobson, *Pygmalion in the classroom* in *Contemporary Psychology*, 1969, 14, 197–199.

SOKAL, M. M. The unpublished autobiography of James McKeen Cattell. *American Psychologist*, 26 (1971), 626–635.

SOMMER, J. Response to Robert Williams. *The Counseling Psychologist*, 2 (1970), 92.

SPEARMAN, C. *The abilities of man.* New York: Macmillan Company, 1927.

SPIELBERGER, C. D. The effects of anxiety on complex learning and academic achievement. In *Anxiety and behavior*, ed. C. D. Spielberger. New York: Academic Press, 1966.

———, AND KATZENMEYER, W. G. Manifest anxiety, intelligence, and college grades. *Journal of Consulting Psychology*, 23 (1959), 278.

STANDARDS FOR DEVELOPMENT AND USE OF EDUCATIONAL AND PSYCHOLOGICAL TESTS (3rd Draft). *APA Monitor*, 4, No. 2 (February 1973), I–XV.

STANDIFORD, P. Parental occupation and intelligence. *School and Society*, 23 (1926), 117–119.

STANLEY, J. C., AND PORTER, A. C. Correlation of Scholastic Aptitude Test scores with college grades for Negroes versus whites. *Journal of Educational Measurement*, 4 (1967), 199–218.

STANLEY, J. C. Predicting college success of the educationally disadvantaged. *Science*, 171 (1971), 640–647.

TANNENBAUM, A. J. Culture-fair Intelligence Test. In *Sixth mental measurement yearbook, tests and reviews: Intelligence—group*, ed. O. Buros, 1965, pp. 721–723.

TATE, M. E. The influence of cultural factors on the Leiter International Performance Scale. *Journal of Abnormal and Social Psychology*, 47 (1952), 497–501.

TAYLOR, J. A. A personality scale of manifest anxiety. *Journal of Abnormal and Social Psychology*, 48 (1953), 285–290.

TAYLOR, O. L. Some sociolinguistic concepts of black language. *Today's Speech* (1971), 19–26.

TEMP, G. *Test bias: Validity of the SAT for blacks and whites in thirteen integrated institutions: Research bulletin 71-2.* Princeton, N.J.: Educational Testing Service, 1971.

TENOPYR, M. L. Race and socioeconomic status as moderators in predicting machine-shop training success. A Paper Presented in a Symposium on "Selection of Minority and Disadvantaged Personnel" at the APA Meeting, Washington, D.C., 1967.

TERMAN, L. M., AND MERRILL, M. A. *Measuring intelligence.* Boston: Houghton-Mifflin, 1937.

THRESHER, B. A. Diversification in educational assessment. *Report of the Commission on Tests, II. Briefs.* New York: CEEB, 1970, pp. 125–138.

THORNDIKE, R. L. Concepts of culture-fairness. *Journal of Educational Measurement*, 8 (1971), 63–70.

———. Review of Rosenthal and Jacobson's *Pygmalion in the classroom, American Educational Research Journal*, 1968, 5(4), 708–711.

TIBER, N., AND KENNEDY, W. A. Effects of incentives on the intelligence test performance of different social groups. *Journal of Consulting Psychology*, 28 (1964), 187.

TURNBULL, W. W. *Foreword of educational change: Implications for measurement.* Princeton, N.J.: Educational Testing Service, 1972.

TYLER, LEONA E. *Tests and measurements. Foundations of modern psychology series*, ed. R. S. Lazarus. Englewood Cliffs, N.J.: Prentice-Hall, 1963.

———. *The psychology of human differences.* New York: Appleton-Century-Crofts, 1956.

———. (Ed.). *Intelligence: Some recurring issues.* New York: Van Nostrand Reinhold Company, 1969.

U.S. COMMISSION ON CIVIL RIGHTS. *Racial isolation in the public schools*, I. Washington, D.C.: Government Printing Office, 1967.

U.S. DEPARTMENT OF COMMERCE, Bureau of the Census, *The social and economic status of the black population in the United States*, 1972, Current Population Reports, Series P—23, No. 46 (July 1973).

U.S. DEPARTMENT OF HEALTH, EDUCATION AND WELFARE. *How children grow. Clinical research advances in human growth and development*, Washington, D.C.: U.S. Government Printing Office, 1973, pp. 22–26.

VEGA, M. The performance of Negro children on an oddity discrimination task as a function of the race of the examiner and the type of verbal incentive used by the examiner. Unpublished Doctor's dissertation, Florida State University, 1964.

VEROFF, J., ATKINSON, J. W., FELD, S., AND GURIN, G. The use of thematic apperception to assess motivation in a nationwide interview study. *Psychological Monographs*, 74, No. 12 (1960).

WAITE, R. R., SARASON, S. B., LIGHTHALL, F. AND DAVIDSON, K. A study of anxiety and learning in children. *Journal of Abnormal and Social Psychology*, 57 (1958), 267–270.

WARNER, R. L., HAVIGHURST, R. J., AND LOEB, M. B. *Who shall be educated?* New York: Harper & Row, 1944.

WARNER, W. L., ET AL. *Democracy in Jonesville*. New York: Harper and Brothers, 1949.

——, AND LUNT, P. S. *The social life of a modern community*. New Haven, Conn.: Yale Univ. Press, 1941.

WATSON, J. B. *Behaviorism*. Rev. ed. Chicago: The Univ. of Chicago Press, 1963.

WECHSLER, D. The IQ is an intelligent test. *New York Times Magazine*, June 26, 1966. In *Contributions to general psychology: Selected readings for introductory psychology*, ed. C. D. Spielberger, R. Fox and B. Masterton. New York: The Ronald Press, 1968, pp. 304–309.

WEINER, B. *Theories of motivation*. Chicago: Markham Publishing Company, 1972.

WESMAN, A. G. Intelligent testing. *American Psychologist*, 27 (1968a), 267–274.

——. Reliability and confidence. *Test Service Bulletin, No. 44*. New York, The Psychological Corporation, 1952. In *Readings in measurement and evaluation*, ed. N. E. Gronlund. New York: The Macmillan Company, 1968, pp. 193–202.

WEST, J. *Plainville, U.S.A.* New York: Columbia Univ. Press, 1945.

WHEELER, L. R. The intelligence of East Tennessee mountain children. *Journal of Educational Psychology*, 23 (1932), 351–370.

WHITEMAN, M., AND DEUTSCH, M. Social disadvantage as related to intellective and language development. In *The disadvantaged child*, M. Deutsch and Associates. New York: Basic Books, 1967, pp. 337–356.

WICKES, T. A. Examiner influence in a testing situation. *Journal of Consulting Psychology*, 20 (1956), 23–26.

WILLIAMS, R. L. Abuses and misuses in testing black children. *The Counseling Psychologist*, 2 (1971), 62–73.

WINICK, M. (Ed.). *Current concepts in nutrition, Volume I: Nutrition and development*. New York: John Wiley and Sons, 1972.

WOLF, R. The measurement of environments. *Proceedings of the 1964 invitational conference on testing problems*. Princeton, N.J.: Educational Testing Service, 1964, pp. 93–106.

WOODWORTH, R. S. *Heredity and environment: A critical survey of recently published materials on twins and foster children*. New York: Social Science Research Council Bulletin, No. 47 (1941).

WRIGHTSTONE, J. W. Relation of testing programs to teaching and learning. The impact and improvement of school testing programs. In *The sixty-second yearbook of the national society for the study of education, Part II*, ed. W. G. Findley. Chicago: Univ. of Chicago Press, 1963, pp. 45–61.

WYLIE, RUTH. *The self-concept*. Lincoln: Univ. of Nebraska Press, 1961.

YATES, A. *Grouping in Education*. New York: John Wiley and Sons, 1966.

YOUNG, FLORENCE M., AND BRIGHT, H. A. Results of testing 81 Negro rural juveniles with the Wechsler Intelligence Scale for Children. *Journal of Social Psychology*, 39 (1954), 219–226.

ZEE, P., WALTERS, T., AND MITCHELL, C. Nutrition and poverty in school children. A nutritional survey of preschool children from impoverished black families, Memphis. *Journal of the American Medical Association*, 213 (1970), 739–742.

COURT CASES

Brown v. Board of Education of Topeka, Kansas, United States Supreme Court, 347 U.S. 483 (1954).

Hobson v. Hansen, 269 F. Supp. 401 (1967).

Larry P. et al. v. Wilson Riles et al., No. C-71 2270 RFP, U.S. District Court, Northern District of California (June 1972).

Plessy v. Ferguson, 163 U.S. 537, 16 Sup. Ct. 1138, 41 L. Ed. 256 (1896).

APPENDIX

COMPENDIUM OF TESTS
FOR MINORITY ADOLESCENTS AND ADULTS

Introduction

The *Compendium of Tests for Minority Adolescents and Adults* is an attempt to list and describe instruments that are designed for or advertised as being appropriate for minorities or the educationally disadvantaged. Only measures appropriate for grades 7 through 12 and/or adolescents and adults are included. For the purposes of this bibliography, minority groups are: blacks, Puerto Ricans, Mexican Americans or Spanish Americans, Native Americans, the Appalachian poor, and those in the lower socioeconomic strata. Tests specifically developed for, or separately normed on, Title I and Title III schools are also included. Some of the measures listed are designed for the educationally disadvantaged—those who are illiterate or whose educational skill level is lower than grade 12, or below the level associated with the highest grade completed. (For example, a high school graduate who reads on an 8th-grade level is considered educationally disadvantaged.) The assumption is made that the individual has the ability to acquire the skills but has failed to do so because of intrinsic or extrinsic factors. Tests available in Spanish editions and measures for which norms are reported separately for minorities are within the scope of this compendium.

The measures in this bibliography were found through a search of publishers' catalogs, advertisements, and the instruments included in the Educational Testing Service Test Collection. Since the Test Collection—a specialized library of tests and assessment devices—does not evaluate or endorse any of its holdings, I have included in this listing any test that the publisher asserts is appropriate for any of the populations under discussion. Each of the tests is currently available from a publisher or organization within the United States for use within the United States. With one exception, instruments intended exclusively for research use have been excluded.

The compendium is divided into four sections: Achievement; Aptitude; Personality, Interests, Attitudes, and Opinions; and Miscellaneous and Sensory-Motor. Within each section, tests are listed alphabetically by title. The title is followed by the name of the author(s)—if any; the copyright date (indicated by c) or the date of publication; the age, grade, or skill level for which the test is appropriate; the length of time required to administer the test; the availability of equivalent forms; the publisher; the type of personnel required to administer the test; and references to test reviews or descriptions—if any.

The American Psychological Association (APA) has developed a system of categorizing tests according to the qualifications required to properly administer and interpret the measure. The APA administrator levels are:

Level A: Tests that can be administered, scored, and interpreted adequately with the aid of the test manual and a general orientation to the type of organization in which one is working.

Level B: Measures that require some technical knowledge of test construction and use, and of supporting psychological and educational fields such as statistics, personnel psychology, guidance, and so on.

Level C: Tests that require a thorough understanding of testing and supporting psychological fields, plus supervised experience in the use of assessment aids in this category.

See the *Standards for Educational and Psychological Tests and Manuals*, prepared by a joint committee of the APA, the American Educational Research Association, and the National Council on Measurement in Education for a more detailed discussion of qualifications for test administrators. The *Standards* was published in 1966 by the APA, Inc. Most of the tests in this bibliography are Level A. Therefore, the administrator level is listed only for measures that are Level B or C.

Many of the tests have been critically reviewed in one or more volumes in the *Mental Measurements Yearbook* (MMY) series edited by Oscar K. Buros. The yearbooks are a source of information on commercially available psychological, educational, and vocational tests published in English. Each yearbook covers tests published or revised during a specified period. The last item in the test citation is a reference to descriptions or reviews appearing in the MMY. The abbreviations used for the volumes in the *Mental Measurements Yearbook* series are:

7MMY   *Seventh Mental Measurements Yearbook* (1972)
6MMY   *Sixth Mental Measurements Yearbook* (1965)
5MMY   *Fifth Mental Measurements Yearbook* (1959)
4MMY   *Fourth Mental Measurements Yearbook* (1953)
3MMY   *Third Mental Measurements Yearbook* (1949)*

The annotation or body of the entry is a general description of the test including the factor(s) assessed, subscores or subtests available. A description of the sample on which the test was normed and distinguishing features are mentioned. The reader can assume that evidence to support the reliability and validity of the test is available unless there is a statement to the contrary.

No attempt has been made to evaluate the tests, the evidence to support reliability or validity, or the adequacy of norms. If the reader finds a test of interest, he is advised to obtain a specimen set and examine the test, test accessories, manuals, and technical reports in detail before making a final decision on the appropriateness of the measure for his needs. Write directly to the publisher for specimen sets or specific information. Addresses are provided at the end of the bibliography.

Achievement

Adult Basic Education Student Survey by Elvin Rasof and Monroe C. Neff; c1966–1967; Educational Level Grades 1–4; Untimed; Two Equivalent Forms; Follett Educational Corporation. 7MMY: Entry 2.

A battery of tests designed for use in the class placement of adult basic education students and in the assessment of academic progress. Subtests are Reading Comprehension, Word Recognition, Arithmetic Computation, and Arithmetic Problems. The tests have been standardized on a multiethnic, disadvantaged adult sample representative of urban and nonurban populations.

Adult Basic Learning Examination: Level I (ABLE I) by Bjorn Karlsen, Richard Madden, and Eric F. Gardner; c1967; Educational Level Grades 1–4; Testing Time 145 Minutes; Two Equivalent Forms; Harcourt Brace Jovanovich, Inc. 7MMY: Entry 3.

> A measure of achievement in basic skills for adults who have not completed a formal 12-year education. Subtests are Reading, Vocabulary, Spelling, Arithmetic Computation, and Arithmetic Problem Solving. The Vocabulary, Spelling, and Arithmetic Problem Solving tests are administered as listening tests to eliminate the contamination of scores by reading ability. Preliminary norms are reported for a group of 3rd and 4th graders, Job Corps trainees, and adults enrolled in basic education courses.

Adult Basic Learning Examination: Level II (ABLE II) by Bjorn Karlsen, Richard Madden, and Eric F. Gardner; c1967; Educational Level Grades 5–8; Testing Time 145 Minutes; Two Equivalent Forms; Harcourt Brace Jovanovich, Inc. 7MMY: Entry 3.

> Reading, Vocabulary, Spelling, Arithmetic Problem Solving, and Arithmetic Computation are the subtests in this battery designed for adults who have not completed a formal 12-year education. Normative data is reported for a group of 6th- and 7th-grade students, Job Corps trainees, and adults enrolled in basic education courses.

Adult Basic Learning Examination: Level III (ABLE III) by Bjorn Karlsen, Richard Madden, and Eric F. Gardner; c1970–1971; Educational Level Grades 9–12; Testing Time 130 Minutes; Two Equivalent Forms; Harcourt Brace Jovanovich, Inc. 7MMY: Entry 3.

> A battery of tests in basic skills for adults who have not completed a formal 12-year education. Subtests are Reading, Vocabulary, Spelling, Arithmetic Computation, and Arithmetic Problem Solving. Normative data is presented for persons enrolled in vocational training and high school equivalency programs. ABLE III has been equated to subtests of the *Stanford Achievement Tests: High School Battery* to provide a measure of high school equivalency.

Adult Basic Reading Inventory by Richard W. Burnett; c1966; Reading Level Grades 2–5; Testing Time 50–60 Minutes; One Form; Scholastic Testing Service, Inc. 7MMY: Entry 769.

> Designed for use in the identification of absolute illiterates, functional illiterates (a person who reads at the 4th-grade level or below), and the identification of individuals who are not illiterate but have reading difficulties originating from other problems. Subscores are Sight Words (Vocabulary), Sound and Letter Discrimination, Word Meaning (Reading), Word Meaning (Listening), and Context Reading. No normative data are presented.

American Literacy Test by John J. McCarthy; c1962; Adults; Testing Time Approximately 4 Minutes; One Form; Psychometric Affiliates. 6MMY: Entry 328.

> The respondent is required to select one of four options that has the same meaning as the stimulus word. Construction of the test is based on the premise that a literacy test must bear a "reasonable" relation to knowledge of grammar and the mechanics of the English language. Norms are reported for illiterates, technical trade candidates, and university seniors.

Basic Reading Inventory.

> See *Adult Basic Reading Inventory.*

Basic Reading Rate Scale by Miles A. Tinker and Ronald P. Carver; c1970; Grades 3–16 and Adults; Testing Time Approximately 5 Minutes; Two Equivalent Forms; Revrac Publications.

> Measures the rate at which an individual can read very easy material. The test is appropriate for use in assessing reading rate at all levels of reading ability. Median scores are reported for students classified as beginning, good, better, and best readers in grades 3 through 12.

Basic Skills in Arithmetic Test by William L. Wrinkle, Juanita Sanders, and Elizabeth H. Kendel; c1945; Adolescents and Adults; Untimed; Two Equivalent Forms; Science Research Associates, Inc. 3MMY: Entry 335.

> Assesses an individual's ability to perform 43 fundamental skills in arithmetical operations involving whole numbers, fractions, decimals, and percentages. Test results can be used in determining group and individual instructional needs. In industrial settings test results can be used as an aid in the selection and placement of personnel in positions that require basic computational skills. Percentile norms are reported for grades 6 through 12. Data are presented concerning the reliability of the test.

Black Intelligence Test of Cultural Homogeneity by Robert L. Williams; c1972; Adolescents and Adults; Untimed; One Form; Williams and Associates.

A culture-specific, multiple-choice vocabulary test using items drawn from the black experience. The test may be used as a measure of a person's capacity to learn or as a measure of sensitivity and responsibility of whites to the black experiences.

Brief Tests of Literacy: Basic Skills Survey—Reading and Writing by Thomas Donlon and W. M. McPeek; c1966; Educational Level Grade 4 or Below; Testing Time Approximately 10 Minutes; One Form; Test Development Division, Educational Testing Service.

This test is designed to facilitate the classification of individuals as literate or illiterate rather than differentiate levels of literacy. There are two subtests, Reading and Writing. Validity data is provided in *Development of Brief Tests of Literacy*, a publication available from the U.S. Department of Health, Education, and Welfare.

Brown-Holtzman Survey of Study Habits and Attitudes: Spanish Edition.

See *Encuesta de Hábitos y Aptitudes Hacia el Estudio.*

CIA Pruebas de Lectura.

See *Cooperative Inter-American Series: Tests of Reading.*

CIA Uso del Lenguaje.

See *Cooperative Inter-American Series: Tests of Language Usage.*

CIA Vocabulario e Interpretación de Material de Lectura

See *Cooperative Inter-American Series: Tests of Natural Sciences: Vocabulary and Interpretation of Reading Materials* and the *Cooperative Inter-American Series: Tests of Social Studies: Vocabulary and Interpretation of Reading Materials.*

Comprehensive English Language Test for Speakers of English as a Second Language: Listening by Dale P. Harris and Leslie A. Palmer; c1970; Grades 9–16 and Adults; Testing Time Approximately 45 Minutes; One Form; McGraw-Hill Book Company. 7MMY: Entry 260.

A measure of the English proficiency of persons high school age and above who are learning English as a second language. The Listening Test is concerned with the comprehension of short statements, questions, and dialogues as spoken by native speakers of English. It is designed for use in programs of English as a second language at the intermediate and advanced levels. The test is administered orally or with the aid of a tape recording. The development of local norms is recommended. Tentative norms are reported for adult foreign students accepted for undergraduate and graduate programs at a small private Eastern university, adult foreign students taking full-time intensive language training in a university-related English language institute in the Western United States, foreign adults participating in an advanced-level program in English as a second language in a Midwestern community college, a group of French-speaking Canadians beginning the first year of college, and a group of teenage foreign students enrolled in grades 10 through 12 of a large Eastern suburban high school. Included in the norming study were individuals from Europe, the Middle East, the Far East, and Latin America.

Comprehensive English Language Test for Speakers of English as a Second Language: Structure by Dale P. Harris and Leslie A. Palmer; c1970; Grades 9–16 and Adults; Testing Time Approximately 55 Minutes; One Form; McGraw-Hill Book Company. 7MMY: Entry 260.

Assesses the ability to manipulate the grammatical structures occurring in spoken English. The examinee is required to read and select the construction that is acceptable and idiomatic in word order or choice of words. The test is appropriate for students of high school age or older who are participating in programs of English as a second language at the intermediate and advanced levels. Included in the standardization population were individuals from Europe, the Middle East, the Far East, and Latin America. Tentative norms are reported for adult foreign students accepted for undergraduate and graduate programs at a small private Eastern university, adult foreign students taking full-time intensive language training in a university-related English language institute in the Western United States, foreign adults participating in an advanced-level program in English as a second language in a Midwestern community college, French-speaking Canadians beginning the first year of college, and a group of teenage foreign students enrolled in grades 10 through 12 of a large Eastern suburban high school. The publisher recommends the construction of local norms.

Comprehensive English Language Test for Speakers of English as a Second Language: Vocabulary by Dale P. Harris and Leslie A. Palmer; c1970; Grades 9–16 and Adults; Testing Time Approximately 45 Minutes; One Form; McGraw-Hill Book Company. 7MMY: Entry 260.

A test of the understanding of the kinds of lexical items that occur in advanced reading materials such as those assigned in general college courses. The test is designed for use in intermediate and advanced level programs of English as a second language for persons of high school age or older. The publisher recommends the development of local norms. Tentative norms are provided for adult foreign students accepted for undergraduate and graduate programs at a small private Eastern university, adult foreign students taking full-time intensive language training in a university-related English language institute in the Western United States, foreign adults participating in an advanced-level program in English as a second language in a Midwestern community college, a group of French-speaking Canadians beginning the first year of college, and teenage foreign students enrolled in grades 10 through 12 of a large Eastern suburban high school. Included in the norming study were individuals from Europe, the Middle East, the Far East, and Latin America.

Cooperative Inter-American Series: Tests of Language Usage by Herschel T. Manuel; c1950; Grades 8–13; Testing Time 35 Minutes; Two Equivalent Forms in English and Spanish; Guidance Testing Associates. 4MMY: Entry 176.

This test, available in parallel English and Spanish editions, measures the ability to use English and Spanish, as distinguished from the ability to understand the languages. The examinee is required to recall a word that is appropriate in a given context (Active Vocabulary) and to recognize idiomatic expressions (Expression). The development of local or regional norms is advocated by the publisher. Preliminary norms are presented for Mexican and Puerto Rican students. No reliability and validity data are provided.

Cooperative Inter-American Series: Tests of Natural Sciences: Vocabulary and Interpretation of Reading Materials by Herschel T. Manuel; c1950; Grades 8–13; Testing Time Approximately 40 Minutes; Two Equivalent Forms in Each Language; Guidance Testing Associates. 4MMY: Entry 577.

Provides an estimate of the ability to read and understand scientific materials. The publisher cautions that the test does not sample the most recent scientific materials. Parallel English and Spanish forms are available. Preliminary norms are reported for Mexican and Puerto Rican students. However, the publisher recommends the development of local or regional norms. Information concerning the reliability and validity of the test is not provided.

Cooperative Inter-American Series: Tests of Reading: Advanced Tests by Herschel T. Manuel; c1950; Grades 8–13; Testing Time Approximately 50 Minutes; Two Equivalent Forms in Each Language; Guidance Testing Associates. 6MMY: Entry 818.

A measure of reading comprehension available in parallel English and Spanish editions. Subscores are Vocabulary and Comprehension. Preliminary norms are reported for Mexican and Puerto Rican students. The development of local and regional norms is encouraged. No data on the reliability and validity of the test are provided.

Cornell Learning and Study Skills Inventory: College Form by Walter Pauk and Russell N. Cassel; c1970; Grades 13–16+; Testing Time Approximately 45 Minutes; One Form; Psychologists and Educators, Inc.

Although designed for students at the college and graduate level, the inventory can be administered to students with a reading level of grade 9 or above. Subscales are: Goal Orientation (Goal Setting, Goal Compatibility, Goal Striving, Goal Involvement, and Goal Achievement Progress); Activity Structure (Physical Setting, Sense of Order, Use of Time, Mental Setting and Assignments); Scholarly Skills (Academic Involvement, Principles of Learning, Verbal Facility, and Concentration); Lecture Mastery (Objective in Note Taking, Taking Notes and Listening, Use of Abbreviations, Use of Shorthand, Rewriting of Longhand Notes, Notes in One's Own Words, Reflecting on Ideas During Lecture); Textbook Mastery (Overview and Skimming, Reading for Ideas, Underlining the Textbook, Marginal Notes and Note Taking, Reflecting and Integrating, and Preparing for Examinations); Examination Mastery (Examination Preparation, Writing the Essay Exam, Taking the Objective Exam, and the Mechanics of Examinations); Self Mastery (Self Reliance, Attitude Toward Work, Attitude Toward College, Social Relations, and Emotional Strength). Included in the inventory is a Reading Validity Index, which serves as an indication of whether students read and carefully considered the items or responded randomly. Normative data are presented for college freshmen and upperclassmen.

Cornell Learning and Study Skills Inventory: Secondary School Form by Walter Pauk and Russell N. Cassel; c1970–1971; Grades 7–13; Testing Time Approximately 45 Minutes; One Form; Psychologists and Educators, Inc.

> An aid in the assessment of factors that are related to learning problems and school performance. The inventory can be used with a 6th-grade or higher reading level. Subscales are: Goal Orientation (Goal Setting, Goal Compatibility, Goal Striving, Goal Involvement, and Goal Achievement Progress); Activity Structure (Physical Setting, Sense of Order, Use of Time, Mental Setting and Assignments); Scholarly Skills (Academic Involvement, Principles of Learning, Verbal Facility, and Concentration); Lecture Mastery (Objective in Note Taking, Taking Notes and Listening, Use of Shorthand, Rewriting of Longhand Notes, Notes in One's Own Words, and Reflecting on Ideas During Lecture); Textbook Mastery (Overview and Skimming, Reading for Ideas, Underlining the Textbook, Marginal Notes and Note Taking, Reflecting and Integrating, and Preparing for Examinations); Examination Mastery (Examination Preparation, Writing the Essay Exam, Taking the Objective Exam, and the Mechanics of Examinations); Self Mastery (Self Reliance, Attitude Toward Work, Attitude Toward College, Social Relations, and Emotional Strength). Included in the inventory is a Reading Validity Index, which provides an indication of whether students responded randomly or read and carefully considered the items. Norms are reported separately for junior high, senior high, and junior college populations.

Dove Counterbalance General Intelligence by Adrian Dove; c1966; Grades 10–12 and Adults; Untimed; One Form; Adrian Dove.

> Designed to demonstrate that intelligence tests—especially the general information type questions—are heavily weighted against minority groups whose experiences are different from those in the mainstream of society. The author felt that questions on this test could be answered easily by disadvantaged blacks and rarely answered correctly by middle class whites. Therefore, test results would show that disadvantaged blacks are more "intelligent" than middle class whites.

Effective Study Test: College Level by William F. Brown; c1964; Grades 11–13; Testing Time Approximately 40 Minutes; One Form; Effective Study Materials.

> Measures knowledge of effective study techniques. The subscores are: Reality Orientation, Study Organization, Reading Behavior, Writing Behavior, and Examination Behavior. The test has been translated and adapted for use with Spanish-speaking students. Norms are presented for high school juniors, seniors, and college freshmen enrolled in schools and colleges in Texas. Norms are not reported separately for Spanish speakers. Provisional validity data are reported.

Effective Study Test: High School Level by William F. Brown; c1964; Grades 9–12; Testing Time Approximately 40 Minutes; One Form; Effective Study Materials.

> Tests knowledge of effective study techniques. The subscores are: Reality Orientation, Study Organization, Reading Behavior, Writing Behavior, and Examination Behavior. A Spanish translation of the test is available. Norms are reported for students enrolled in the 9th through 12th grades of schools in Texas.

Encuesta de Hábitos y Aptitudes Hacia el Estudio, Translated and Adapted by Fernando Garcia, Eduardo Garcia, and Luis Laosa. (Original edition authored by William F. Brown and Wayne H. Holtzman); c1964–1971; Grades 9–16; Untimed—Approximately 25 Minutes Required; One Form; The Psychological Corporation (APA Level B). 7MMY: Entry 782.*

> An authorized Spanish-American edition of the *Survey of Study Habits and Attitudes* developed in Mexico but appropriate for use in other Hispano-American countries. The survey is designed to assist the counselor in identifying and helping students whose study habits and attitudes may prevent them from obtaining maximal benefit from their educational experiences. The diagnostic profile and Counseling Key serve as an aid in planning remedial activities. The survey yields four basic scale scores and three combined scores: Delay Avoidance, Work Methods, Study Habits (subtotal), Teacher Approval, Education Acceptance, Study Attitudes (subtotal), and total Study Orientation score. Norms are reported separately for freshmen enrolled in a Mexican university and a group of students in grades 9 through 12 (combined sample) of a technical institute.

Individual Reading Placement Inventory: Field Research Edition by Edwin H. Smith and Weldon G. Bradtmueller; c1969; Reading Level Grade 7 or Below; Testing Time

---

* Reviews of the English edition, *Survey of Study Habits and Attitudes,* are included in the 7MMY.

Approximately 10–35 Minutes; Two Equivalent Forms; Follett Educational Corporation. 7MMY: Entry 730.

> An individually administered aid in determining the level at which a student can read easily without assistance, the level at which instruction should begin; the level that is beyond the student's ability, and the level at which the student could read with comprehension if he possessed the necessary reading skills (Present Language Potential). The inventory is designed specifically for illiterate and semiliterate adolescents and adults. Subscores are Word Recognition and Analysis, Oral Paragraph Reading, Present Language Potential, Auditory Discrimination, and Letters of the Alphabet. After administering the inventory, the examiner completes the *Checklist of Reading Difficulties*, a form for recording observations concerning possible posture problems, emotional symptoms, reading-rate difficulties, and sight-sound perceptual problems.

Inter-American Series: Tests of Reading, Level 4 by Herschel T. Manuel; c1962–1967; Grades 7–9; Testing Time Approximately 50 Minutes; Two Equivalent Forms in Each Language; Guidance Testing Associates.

> A measure of Vocabulary, Level of Comprehension, and Speed of Comprehension available in parallel English and Spanish editions. Data to support the equivalence of the English and Spanish editions are presented. Normative data are reported—some based on estimations derived by calibrating the *Inter-American Tests* with measures for which norms have been published. Norms are reported separately for 7th graders enrolled in urban public, rural public, and private schools in Puerto Rico. Some performance data are available for students in the schools of Venezuela, Chile, and Central America. The development of local and regional norms is recommended by the publisher.

Inter-American Series: Tests of Reading, Level 5 by Herschel T. Manuel; c1962–1967; Grades 10–13; Testing Time Approximately 50 Minutes; Two Equivalent Forms; Guidance Testing Associates. 6MMY: Entry 818.

> A reading test designed for use in bilingual communities or in cross-cultural educational research. Subscores are: Speed of Comprehension, Level of Comprehension, and Vocabulary. Parallel English and Spanish editions are available. Evidence to support the equivalence of the English and Spanish editions is reported. The development of local and regional norms is recommended by the publisher. Limited normative data are presented—some based on estimations derived by calibrating the *Inter-American Tests* with other tests for which norms have been published. Percentile scores are reported separately for 10th-grade students enrolled in urban public and private schools in Puerto Rico. Also norms are reported for students in Venezuela, Chile, and Central America.

McGraw-Hill Basic Skills System: Mathematics Test by Alton L. Raygor; c1970; Grades 11–14; Testing Time Approximately 50 Minutes; Two Equivalent Forms; California Test Bureau/McGraw-Hill. 7MMY: Entry 477.

> The *McGraw-Hill Basic Skills System* (MHBSS) is an integrated series of tests and instructional materials designed to provide training in the basic academic skills that are prerequisites for success in college. The program is geared to the college-bound student with educational deficiencies and the college student in need of remedial activities. The four components of the MHBSS are: diagnosis, prescription (test performance is related to prescriptive units of instruction), instruction (learning materials consist of printed self-instructional programs, workbooks, audiotapes, etc.), and evaluation. The test components can be used independently of the instructional materials.
>
> The *Mathematics Test* consists of three sections: Basic Mathematics, Elementary Algebra, and Intermediate Algebra. The Basic Mathematics section covers operations with whole numbers, negative numbers, rational numbers, and decimals; solution of first-degree equations in one variable; concepts of percentage, ratio, and proportion; use of exponents and powers of ten; and the significance of numbers generated by operations using rounded figures or measurements. In the Elementary Algebra section there are items concerned with the more complex uses of negative and rational numbers; the language of algebra; solutions of first-degree equations in one variable; graphical representation of first-degree equations in two variables; solution of first-degree equations in two variables; and solution of pairs of first-degree equations in two variables. The characteristics of polynomials in one variable; operations of rational expressions in one variable; simplification of expressions in many variables; interpretation of radical expressions and solution of equations containing radicals; use of exponents, rational and negative; and the use of logarithms are topics included in the Intermediate Algebra section. In the *MHBSS Mathematics Test* the emphasis is placed on traditional mathematics. Norms are reported for freshmen in four-year

colleges, first-year students in two-year colleges, and college-bound high school juniors and seniors.

McGraw-Hill Basic Skills System: Reading Test by Alton L. Raygor; c1970; Grades 11–14; Testing Time Approximately 76 Minutes; Two Equivalent Forms; CTB/McGraw-Hill. 7MMY: Entry 704.

See preceding entry for a description of the MHBSS.

The *Reading Test* consists of passages taken from college textbooks. Scores are provided for Reading Rate and Comprehension (retention of factual information); Skimming and Scanning (the ability to search for specific facts, definitions, words, and numbers); and Paragraph Comprehension (the ability to recognize and understand the main idea, recognize specific facts and understand their importance and function, recognize and understand general scientific principles in the physical and social sciences, recognize paragraph organization and structure, and the ability to critically evaluate a written passage). Norms are reported for freshmen in four-year colleges, first-year students in two-year colleges, and college-bound high school juniors and seniors.

McGraw-Hill Basic Skills System: Spelling Test by Alton L. Raygor; c1970; Grades 11–14; Testing Time Approximately 30 Minutes; Two Equivalent Forms; CTB/McGraw-Hill. 7MMY: Entry 230.

See previous entry for a description of the MHBSS.

The *Spelling Test* measures the ability to recognize a misspelled word within the context of a sentence. Normative data are reported for freshmen in four-year colleges, first-year students in two-year colleges, and college-bound high school juniors and seniors.

McGraw-Hill Basic Skills System: Study Skills Test by Alton L. Raygor; c1970; Grades 11–14; Testing Time Approximately 56 Minutes; Two Equivalent Forms; CTB/McGraw-Hill. 7MMY: Entry 781.

See previous entry for a description of the MHBSS.

Subscores in the *Study Skills Test* are: Problem Solving; Underlining (mastery of effective underlining technique is a skill considered necessary for quickly and effectively reviewing study material without rereading complete passages); Library Information; and Study Skills Information (knowledge of study aids and techniques). Included in the test component of the *MHBSS: Study Skills* is a self-report *Inventory of Study Habits and Attitudes* designed to elicit information concerning the student's study habits and attitudes toward studying. Subscores for the inventory are: Listening and Note-taking, General Study Habits, Relationships with Teachers and Courses, Motivation, Organization of Effort, Concentration, and Emotional Problems. Normative data are reported for freshmen in four-year colleges, first-year students in two-year colleges, and college-bound high school juniors and seniors.

McGraw-Hill Basic Skills System: Vocabulary Test by Alton L. Raygor; c1970; Grades 11–14; Testing Time Approximately 22 Minutes; Two Equivalent Forms; CTB/McGraw-Hill. 7MMY: Entry 236.

See previous entry for a description of the MHBSS.

The *Vocabulary Test* measures knowledge of word meanings and knowledge of the meanings of word stems or elements. For the first part of the test, the words are drawn from the social and natural sciences. In the second part, artificial words are used to determine the student's mastery of the meanings of word parts. The first and second parts of the test do not yield subscores. Normative data are reported for freshmen in four-year colleges, first-year students in two-year colleges, and college-bound high school juniors and seniors.

McGraw-Hill Basic Skills System: Writing Test by Alton L. Raygor; c1970; Grades 11–14; Testing Time Approximately 55 Minutes; Two Equivalent Forms; CTB/McGraw-Hill. 7MMY: Entry 214.

See previous entry for a description of the MHBSS.

The *Writing Test* has subscores in Language Mechanics (capitalization, punctuation, and grammar); Sentence Patterns (the classification of sentence types, choice of pronouns, detection of nonparallel constructions, and the use of appropriate transitional words and phrases to introduce or connect sentences); and Paragraph Patterns (the identification of appropriate topic sentences, development sentences, concluding sentences, awareness of proper sequence of sentences, and appropriate division of sentences into paragraphs). Norms are reported for college-bound high school juniors and seniors, first-year students in two-year colleges, and freshmen in four-year colleges.

Peabody Individual Achievement Test (PIAT) by Lloyd M. Dunn and Frederick C. Markwardt, Jr.; c1970; Kindergarten–Grade 12; Testing Time Approximately 30 Minutes (Paced Administration); One Form; American Guidance Service, Inc. 7MMY: Entry 417.

An individually administered, wide-range achievement battery with subtests in Mathematics, Reading Recognition, Reading Comprehension, Spelling, and General Information. No written responses are required by the subject—he responds orally or by pointing. The Mathematics subtest measures basic skills such as matching, discrimination, and number recognition—as well as advanced concepts in geometry and trigonometry. In the Reading Recognition subtest the examinee is required to match letters of the alphabet, name individual letters, and read aloud individual words. The items in this subtest range in difficulty from the preschool through high school level. For the Reading Comprehension subtest the examinee silently reads a sentence and then must select the one of four illustrated options that best represents the meaning of the sentence. The item difficulty range for the Spelling subtest is kindergarten through high school. For this subtest, the examinee is asked to select the letter of the alphabet as being different from the other items pictured, identify the letter that represents a speech sound or named letter, and point out the correct spelling for individual words that have been pronounced and used in sentences by the examiner. Topics such as science, social studies, fine arts, and sports are included on the General Information subtest, designed to tap general knowledge that can be acquired in situations other than school. The publisher states that the test is appropriate for culturally disadvantaged adults, those with reading disabilities, subjects with motor handicaps, and the mentally retarded. The PIAT has been standardized on a sample representative of the national population. All members of the norming group were enrolled in public education programs, kindergarten through grade 12. Norms are reported in terms of four derived scores: grade equivalents, age equivalents, percentile ranks, and standard scores.

In addition to the review in the 7MMY, the PIAT has been reviewed in the Fall-Winter 1970 issue of the *Journal of Special Education* (Vol. 4, No. 4, pp. 461–467).

Pruebas de Lectura

See the *Inter-American Series: Tests of Reading: Levels 4 and 5.*

RBH Basic Reading and Word Test; c1968–1969; Adults; Untimed (can be completed in 25 to 30 minutes); One Form; Richardson, Bellows, Henry & Company, Inc. 7MMY: Entry 700.

An aid in establishing minimum reading skills or literacy by measuring reading vocabulary and comprehension. The test, which covers a broad reading and vocabulary range, is recommended for use in situations in which a quick measure of reading level is necessary. The publisher states that the test is most commonly used in the selection of blue-collar workers, unskilled laborers, routine factory workers, basic white-collar and sales and service positions. Percentile and standard scores are reported.

SRA Arithmetic Index; c1968; Ages 14–Adults; Untimed (approximately 50–60 minutes); One Form Available; Science Research Associates, Inc. 7MMY: Entry 20a.

Designed for use with adolescents and adults whose basic skills are too low to be reliably evaluated by traditional standardized tests. The *Index* covers a broad range of ability, from the minimal levels of proficiency to the competence level expected of lower-level high school students. Scores reflect proficiency at various levels. Levels are: Addition and Subtraction of Whole Numbers, Multiplication and Division of Whole Numbers, Basic Operations Involving Fractions, and Basic Operations Involving Decimals and Percentages. An individual's score is the highest developmental level passed. Percentile norms are reported for adult education trainees. Data to support the reliability of the test are provided. The publisher has prepared a comparison of *Arithmetic Index* levels and job tasks to assist personnel officers in the determination of the appropriate minimum proficiency level necessary to qualify for employment requiring varying degrees of competence in arithmetic.

SRA Reading Index; c1968; Ages 14–Adults; Untimed (approximately 50–60 minutes); One Form; Science Research Associates, Inc. 7MMY: Entry 20b.

Designed for use with adolescents and adults whose basic skills are too low to be reliably evaluated by traditional standardized tests. The *Index* covers a broad range of ability, from the minimal levels of proficiency to the competence level expected of lower-level high school students. The test is scored to reflect proficiency at five levels: Picture-Word Association, Word Decoding, Phrase Comprehension, Sentence Comprehension, and Paragraph Comprehension. An individual's score is the highest developmental level passed. The publisher has prepared a comparison of *SRA Reading Index* levels and job tasks to assist personnel officers in the determination of the appropriate minimum proficiency level necessary to qualify for employment requiring varying degrees of competence in reading. Adult education trainees participated in the standardization of the *Index*. Reliability data are reported.

Study Skills Survey by William F. Brown; c1965–1970; Grades 9–16; Working Time Approximately 15 Minutes; One Form in Each Language; Effective Study Materials.

> A series of three questionnaires designed to identify deficiencies in study skills and habits that will hinder academic achievement. Questionnaires are: Study Organization, Study Techniques, and Study Motivation. The *Survey* has been translated and adapted for use with Spanish-speaking students. Norms are reported for high school and college freshmen. Data concerning test validity are provided.

Test of Individual Needs in Reading: 1970 Seventh Revision by Hap Gilliland; c1966–1970; Reading Levels Primer-College; Testing Time Approximately 50 Minutes; One Form; The Reading Clinic, Eastern Montana State College.

> An individually administered screening device for use by the classroom teacher or reading specialist as an aid in assigning appropriate instructional materials. Subscores are: Oral Reading, Comprehension, Basic Reading Level, Silent Reading Speed, Use of Context, Words Beginning Alike and Word Analysis Skills (Beginning Consonants, Ending Consonants, Consonant Substitution, Speech Consonants, Consonant Blends, Reversals, Long and Short Vowels, Vowel Blends, Blending Letter Sounds, Prefixes, Suffixes, Compound Words, Recognizing Syllables, Syllabication). The author states that the test is an aid in diagnosing weaknesses in reading rather than a vehicle for comparing the achievement of one student with another. Normative data are not provided. The reliability and validity of the instrument are discussed but not documented.

> The sixth edition of the *Test of Individual Needs in Reading* is reviewed in the 7MMY: Entry 726.

Test of Retail Sales Insight by Russell N. Cassel; c1971; Grades 9–12 and Adults; Testing Time Approximately 30 Minutes; One Form; Psychologists and Educators, Inc.

> A measure of knowledge of selling and sales transactions that can be administered to persons whose reading level is grade 6 or higher. The author suggests that the test be administered orally to individuals whose reading level is questionable or below grade 6. Subscores are: General Sales Knowledge, Customer Motivation and Need, Merchandise Procurement and Adaptation, Sales Promotion Procedures, and Sales Closure. Norms are reported for high school students in beginner sales courses, novice, and experienced salesmen.

Tests of Adult Basic Education, Level D (Difficult) (TABE–D) by Ernest W. Tiegs and Willis W. Clark; c1957–1967; Reading Level Grades 7–9; Testing Time Approximately 200 Minutes (Administered in 3 Sessions); Two Equivalent Forms; CTB/McGraw-Hill. 7MMY: Entry 32.

> Level D of TABE is an adaptation of the junior high school level of the *California Achievement Tests: 1957 Edition*. TABE–D is designed for use in the identification of the individual's instructional needs in the basic skills. Subtests are: Reading Vocabulary, Reading Comprehension, Arithmetic Reasoning, Arithmetic Fundamentals, Mechanics of English and Spelling. The grade placement norms reported are identical to the 1963 school-based norms for the *California Achievement Tests*. The validity of the battery is discussed; no reliability data are reported.

Test of Adult Basic Education, Level E (Easy) (TABE–E) by Ernest W. Tiegs and Willis W. Clark; c1957–1967; Reading Level Grades 2–4; Testing Time Approximately 120 Minutes (Administered in 2 sittings); Two Equivalent Forms; CTB/McGraw-Hill. 7MMY: Entry 32.

> Level E of TABE is a battery of tests designed for use in the identification of the instructional needs of individuals with severe educational limitations. TABE–E is an adaptation of the upper primary level *California Achievement Tests: 1957 Edition*. Subtests are: Reading Vocabulary, Reading Comprehension, Arithmetic Reasoning, and Arithmetic Fundamentals. The grade placement norms reported are identical to the 1963 school-based norms for the *California Achievement Tests*. Information to support the reliability and validity of the battery is not provided.

Tests of Adult Basic Education, Level M (Medium) (TABE–M) by Ernest W. Tiegs and Willis W. Clark; c1957–1967; Reading Level Grades 4–6; Testing Time Approximately 180 Minutes (Administered in 3 Sessions); Two Equivalent Forms; CTB/McGraw-Hill. 7MMY: Entry 32.

> An adaptation of the elementary level of the *California Achievement Tests: 1957 Edition* designed as an aid in the identification of the instructional needs of individuals with educational

deficiencies. Subtests are: Reading Vocabulary, Reading Comprehension, Arithmetic Reasoning, Arithmetic Fundamentals, Mechanics of English, and Spelling. The grade placement norms reported are identical to the 1963 school-based norms for the *California Achievement Tests*. Reliability and validity data are not presented.

Tests of Adult Basic Education: Practice Exercises and Locator Test by Ernest W. Tiegs and Willis W. Clark; c1957–1970; Reading Level Grades 2–9; Testing Time Approximately 30 Minutes; One Form; CTB/McGraw-Hill. 7MMY: Entry 32.

The *Locator Test* is a means of determining which of the levels of the TABE are appropriate for an individual. The *Practice Exercises* are designed to help overcome resistance to testing and to provide some experience in test-taking procedures.

Tests of General Educational Development (GED); c1944–Present; Educational Level Grades 9–12 and Candidates for High School Equivalency Certificates; Testing Time Approximately 600 Minutes (120 Minutes for Each Test); New Form Issued Annually in September; General Educational Development Testing Service of the American Council on Education. 7MMY: Entry 34.

Scores on the GED are used as the criteria for granting high school equivalency certificates. GED scores can be used to gain admission to licensing examinations for professions that require the completion of the 9th, 10th, 11th grades. Critical scores for these grades must be obtained upon request to the Director, Commission on Accreditation of Service Experiences, General Educational Development Testing Service of the American Council on Education. The tests included in the GED battery are Correctness and Effectiveness of Expression, Interpretation of Reading Materials in the Social Studies, Interpretation of Reading Materials in the Natural Sciences, Interpretation of Literary Materials, and General Mathematical Ability. The GED is not available on an open-sale basis. Test administrations are scheduled throughout the year at official GED test centers. Civilian Restricted Forms are administered to civilians and veterans; military personnel on active duty are given the Military Restricted Forms through the U.S. Armed Forces Institute. Special forms are available for the blind and partially sighted. Normative data are provided.

Tests of General Educational Development (GED): *Spanish Edition*; c1971–Present; Educational Levels Grades 9–12 and Candidates for High School Equivalency Certificates; Testing Time Approximately 600 Minutes (120 Minutes for Each Test); New Form Issued Annually in September; General Educational Development Testing Service of the American Council on Education.

The *Spanish Edition* of the GED was developed for Spanish-speaking Puerto Ricans residing in the United States. Norms are reported for this group. The publisher states that the test may be suitable for individuals from Cuba, Mexico, and other Latin American countries. Although the test is administered to candidates seeking high school equivalency certificates, GED scores can be used to gain admission to licensing examinations for professions that require completion of the 9th, 10th, 11th grades. Critical scores for these grades must be obtained upon request to the Director, Commission on Accreditation of Service Experiences, General Educational Development Testing Service of the American Council on Education. The tests are administered at official GED test centers on dates scheduled throughout the year. The Civilian Restricted Forms of the test are administered to veterans and civilians, while military personnel on active duty are given the Military Restricted Forms provided through the U.S. Armed Forces Institute.

Tests of Reading.

See the *Inter-American Series: Tests of Reading, Level 4 and Level 5*.

Aptitude

Arthur Point Scale of Performance Tests, Form I by Grace Arthur; c1925–1947; Ages 5.5–Superior Adults; Testing Time Approximately 90 Minutes; One Form; Stoelting Company (APA Level C). 4MMY: Entry 335.

An individually administered test of intelligence appropriate for deaf children, the blind, those suffering from reading disabilities, those with delayed speech or speech difficulties, non-English speakers, and native Americans enrolled in Indian schools. The scale consists of the following tests: the Knox Cube, Seguin Form Board, Two-Figure Form Board (Pintner), the Casuist Form Board (Knox), the Manikin (Pintner), Feature-Profile (Knox and Kempl), Mare and Foal (Healy Modified Form), Healy Picture Completion I, the Porteus Maze (1924 Series) and the Kohs Block Design. Props needed for the tests are available from the publisher. The test was standardized on middle-class children 5 to 15 years of age. Raw scores on each test are translated into a point score that weights each test in proportion to its ability to discriminate among successive age levels. The point scores are totaled and converted into a mental age, from which a ratio intelligence quotient is computed.

Arthur Point Scale of Performance Tests, Revised Form II by Grace Arthur; c1947; Ages 4.5–Superior Adults; Testing Time Approximately 90 Minutes; One Form; The Psychological Corporation (APA Level C). 4MMY: Entry 335.

An individually administered test of intelligence that can be used with youngsters, the reading disabled, those with defective speech, the non-English speaking, native Americans enrolled in Indian schools. During the development of Form II, efforts were made to prepare directions that would be suitable for deaf children. There is minimal use of language in the administration of the scale. Five tests are included on Form II. They are: the Knox Cube Test (Arthur Revision), the Seguin Form Board (Arthur Revision), the Arthur Stencil Design Test I, the Healy Picture Completion Test II, and the Porteus Maze Test (Arthur Modification). The props needed for the test are available from the publisher. Form II was standardized on middle-class children 5 to 15 years of age. Raw scores on each test are translated into a point score that weights each test in proportion to its ability to discriminate among successive age groupings. The point scores are totaled and then converted into a mental age, from which a ratio intelligence quotient is computed.

Barranquilla Rapid Survey Intelligence Test (BARSIT) By Francisco del Olmo; c1956–1958; Grades 3–6 and Adults with Elementary School Education; Testing Time Approximately 10 Minutes; One Form; The Psychological Corporation.

Provides an index of learning potential by evaluating verbal intelligence and numerical reasoning through items covering general knowledge, vocabulary, verbal reasoning, logical reasoning, and numerical reasoning. The test is appropriate for Latin American children in the 3rd through 6th grades and adults with an elementary school education. A thorough knowledge of Spanish is necessary for administering the BARSIT, since both the test and manual are in Spanish. Norms are reported for Venezuelan industrial workers classified according to the number of years of education and for children in grades 3 through 6.

Benge Employment Tests.

See *Employment Test, Form B.*

CIA Tests of General Ability.

See the *Cooperative Inter-American Series: Tests of General Ability: Intermediate Level* and *Advanced Level.*

Cattell Culture Fair Intelligence Tests.

See *IPAT Culture Fair Intelligence Test: Scales I, II, and III.*

Chicago Non-Verbal Examination by Andrew W. Brown; c1936–1963; Ages 6–Adults; Testing Time Approximately 50 Minutes; One Form; The Psychological Corporation (APA Level B). 1940 MMY: Entry 1387.

An intelligence test designed specifically for children who are handicapped in the use of the English language, such as the deaf, those with reading difficulties, and those who have been brought up in a foreign-language environment. Information is provided concerning the use of the measure with the mentally retarded. The test can be administered with either verbal or pantomime directions. The verbal directions can be used with children as young as age 6. However, the pantomime directions are not usable below the age of 8. Norms, stated in terms of mental-age equivalents, standard scores and percentile ranks, are reported separately for the verbal and pantomime test administrations. The *Chicago Non-Verbal Examination* was standardized on normal hearing children residing in middle-class areas of Chicago. The standardization sample was 70 percent white and 30 percent foreign-born. High school students from various parts of Chicago and adults employed in a government agency located in Chicago also participated in the standardization.

Cooperative Inter-American Tests: Tests of General Ability: Advanced Level by Herschel T. Manuel; c1950–1967; Grades 8–13; Testing Time Approximately 50 Minutes; Two Equivalent Forms in Each Language; Guidance Testing Associates. 4MMY: Entry 325.

A series of tests of general mental ability. The test yields a Nonverbal Score, which is a composite of the scores obtained on the Classification, Figure Analogies, and Number Series sections, and a Verbal Score obtained from the Word Relations section. Parallel English and Spanish editions were developed by equating and balancing linguistic and cultural materials from the two languages. The tests were developed for use in Puerto Rico, but they have also been used in Mexico and the continental United States. The publisher recommends that the user develop local norms. General norms are not available for the series. The *1967 Supplement to the Examiner's Manual for the Cooperative Inter-American Tests, 1950 Edition* does include some normative data obtained by the publisher from various sources. Information is provided to support the reliability of the test. Data on the validity of the test are not reported.

Cooperative Inter-American Tests: Tests of General Ability: Intermediate Level by Herschel T. Manuel; c1950–1967; Grades 4–7; Testing Time Approximately 50 Minutes; Two Equivalent Forms in Each Language; Guidance Testing Associates. 6MMY: Entry 507d.

A measure of general mental ability that yields a Nonverbal Score, which is a composite of the scores obtained on the Classification, Figure Analogies, and Number Series sections, and a Verbal Score obtained from the Word Relations section. The test is available in parallel English and Spanish editions, which were developed by equating and balancing linguistic and cultural materials from the two languages. The tests originally were developed for use in Puerto Rico, but have also been used in Mexico and the continental United States. The publisher recommends the development of local norms by the user. General norms are not available for the series. However, the *1967 Supplement to the Examiner's Manual for the Cooperative Inter-American Tests, 1950 Edition*, does include some normative data obtained by the publisher from various sources. Some data on the reliability of the test are reported, but no information on validity is provided.

Culture Fair Intelligence Tests.

See *IPAT Culture Fair Intelligence Test: Scales I, II and III.*

Employment Test Form B by Eugene J. Benge; c1942; Educational Level Grade 8 or Below; Testing Time Approximately 20 Minutes; One Form; Management Service Company. 3MMY: Entry 221.

A measure of mental ability also referred to as the *Benge Employment Tests.* Subscores are Memory, Mathematical Ability, Vocabulary, Space Perception, and Reasoning. No data are provided concerning the reliability or validity of the test. Norms are reported.

Escala de Inteligencia Wechsler para Adultos by David Wechsler; Translated and adapted by R. F. Green and J. N. Martinez; c1955–1968; Ages 16–Adults; Testing Time Approximately 60 Minutes; One Form; The Psychological Corporation (APA Level C).

An authorized Spanish-American edition of the *Wechsler Adult Intelligence Scale* (WAIS) translated and adapted to Spanish culture and standardized in Puerto Rico. The test is individually administered and requires the use of props, which are available from the publisher. Subtests are: Information, Comprehension, Arithmetic, Similarities, Digit Span, Vocabulary, Digit Symbol, Picture Completion, Block Design, Picture Arrangement and Object Assembly.

The English edition of the test is reviewed in Entry 429 of the 7MMY.

Escala de Inteligencia Wechsler para Niños by David Wechsler; Translated by Pablo Roca; c1949–1951; Ages 5–15; Testing Time Approximately 60 Minutes; One Form; The Psychological Corporation (APA Level C).

An authorized Spanish-American translation and adaptation of the *Wechsler Intelligence Scale for Children* (WISC) developed in Puerto Rico. The props required for the performance sections of the individually administered test are identical to those used with the English edition and are available from the publisher. The questions used in the verbal subtests and the directions for administering the verbal and performance scales are included in the Spanish manual. Also in the Spanish manual are test results for several Puerto Rican groups expressed in terms of norms developed in the continental United States. The test yields an intelligence quotient based on scaled scores for each age rather than a mental age. An intelligence quotient can be derived from either the verbal or the performance scale. Included on the Verbal Scale are subtests in Comprehension, Information, Arithmetic, Similarities, Vocabulary, Digit Span (optional). The performance subtests are: Picture Completion, Picture Arrangement, Block Design, Coding, Object Assembly, and an optional Mazes Test. Also reported are a total Verbal and Performance Score, as well as a total test score.

The English edition of the WISC is reviewed in the 7MMY: Entry 431.

Examen de Percepción Mecánica: Edición Experimental by D. R. Miller; c1955–1968; Grades 9–12 and Adults; Testing Time Approximately 40 Minutes; One Form; CTB/McGraw-Hill.

> A Spanish edition of the *Survey of Mechanical Insight*, a test that measures aptitude for solving the type of mechanical problems found in the operation, maintenance, repair, and design of various types of machinery. Also measured is the ability to foresee resultant motion of various parts of a mechanism when a given part is operated. Items consist of a drawing of a mechanical device followed by a statement concerning an aspect of the machine's operation.
>
> The English edition, *Survey of Mechanical Insight*, is reviewed in Entry 886 of the 5MMY.

Fundamental Achievment Series (FAS) by George K. Bennett and Jerome E. Doppelt; c1965–1969; Educational Level Basic Literacy–Eighth Grade; Testing Time Approximately 30 Minutes Each Test; Two Forms; The Psychological Corporation. 7MMY: Entry 978.

> Designed to assess the knowledge and competencies that a job applicant may be expected to have acquired in the course of ordinary daily living and that will be relevant to actual job performance. Items are based on experiences assumed to be generally familiar to both the advantaged and the disadvantaged. The FAS Verbal Test consists of items that measure the ability to read signs, restaurant menus, apartment-house directories, to recognize correct spelling and meaning of commonly used words, to understand orally presented information, and the ability to write legibly. In the Numerical test are items concerned with the ability to tell time, recognize numbers, use calendars, and to solve problems ranging from simple arithmetic to the computation of interest. The FAS can be administered via tape recordings. The tape-recorded administration, which permits standardized oral presentation and accurate control of timing, is provided in order to reduce the contamination of test results by inadequate reading skills.
>
> There are two forms of the FAS. Form A is accessible to personnel departments for the testing of applicants and employees, while Form B is available to governmental and social agencies, business and industrial firms, and educators for use in employment and training. Norms are reported for several specific populations: blacks, whites, trainees in antiproverty programs, and Puerto Rican trainees in antipoverty programs, students in a Southern city school system by grade and race, students in a Northern city school system by grade and race, applicants and employees in a Southern food-processing plant, applicants to schools of practical nursing, steel-plant production employees in a Western city, entry-level bank trainees in an Eastern city, and antipoverty trainees in a small city in New England. There are some data on the validity of the FAS. The publisher encourages local prediction studies. Reliability data are provided for Form A only.

Gilliland Learning Potential Examination: 1970 Revision by Hap Gilliland; c1966–1970; Ages 6–Adults; Testing Time Approximately 50 Minutes; One Form; The Reading Clinic, Eastern Montana College.

> A measure of intelligence designed specifically for individuals who are either nonreaders or poor readers, native and rural Americans. Area scores reported are: Visual Memory, Symbolic Representation, Symbol Identification, Relationships, Listening Comprehension, Picture Completion, and General Information. Five of the seven sections of the test are unrelated to reading ability and are included in the Non-Reading and Non-Cultural IQ scores. Two of the subtests, Symbol Interpretation and General Information, are related to reading skill in order to provide information on the student's abilities in specific areas related to reading. The General Information test can also be used to determine student interest areas so that reading materials can be geared to individual interests. Some preliminary validity data are presented, but the author states that additional information on the validity of the test and data on reliability can be obtained by writing to the publisher. The test has been standardized on native Americans who reside on reservations, or in rural areas, adults, and a general population of students in six Western states.
>
> An earlier edition of the *Gilliland Learning Potential Examination* is reviewed in the 7MMY: Entry 351.

IPAT Culture Fair Intelligence Test: Scale II by Raymond B. Cattell and A. K. S. Cattell; c1949–1963; Ages 8–13 and Average Adults; Testing Time Approximately 30 Minutes; Two Equivalent Forms; Institute for Personality and Ability Testing (APA Level B). 6MMY: Entry 453a.

> An intelligence test designed to be relatively free of cultural and educational influences. The test can be used with the culturally, educationally, and socially disadvantaged. The four subtests —Series, Classification, Matrices, and Conditions (Topology)—are perceptual and nonverbal.

Norms are reported for women enrolled in a Job Corps program, children and adults administered the test under timed conditions, and children and adults administered the test under unspeeded conditions. A Spanish edition of the test has been prepared; norms are not available at this time.

IPAT Culture Fair Intelligence Test: Scale III by Raymond B. Cattell and A. K. S. Cattell; c1949–1963; Grades 9–12 and Superior Adults; Testing Time Approximately 30 Minutes; Two Equivalent Forms; Institute for Personality and Ability Testing (APA Level B). 6MMY: Entry 453a3.

An intelligence test designed for use with individuals having different national languages and cultures, or influenced by very different social status and education. Subtests are: Series, Classification, Matrices, and Conditions (Topology). Items are perceptual in nature. The test has been standardized with American high school students and adults. A Spanish edition of the test has been prepared; norms are not available at this time.

Inter-American Series: Tests of General Ability, Level 4 by Herschel T. Manuel; c1962–1967; Grades 7–9; Testing Time Approximately 65 Minutes; Two Equivalent Forms in Each Language; Guidance Testing Associates.

A series of tests of scholastic aptitude available in parallel English and Spanish editions. A Verbal score is obtained from the Sentence Completion and Word Relations subtests, a Nonverbal score from the Analogies and Figure Classification subtests, and a Number score from the Number Series and Computation subtests. The use of local norms is encouraged by the publisher. Some normative data based on results obtained by users and researchers are provided; there are no general norms. Some of the norms have been estimated by calibrating the *Inter-American Series* with other tests for which norms have been published. Information to support the reliability of the test is provided; information on validity is not.

Inter-American Series: Test of General Ability: Level 5 by Herschel T. Manuel; c1962–1967; Grades 10–13; Testing Time Approximately 65 Minutes; Two Equivalent Forms in Each Language; Guidance Testing Associates. 6MMY: Entry 507e.

A series of tests of scholastic aptitude available in parallel English and Spanish editions. A Verbal score is obtained from the Sentence Completion and Word Relations subtests, a Nonverbal score from the Analogies and Figure Classification subtests, and a Number score from the Number Series and Computation subtests. The use of local norms is recommended by the publisher; general norms are not available. However, the publisher is able to provide some limited normative data based on results obtained by users and researchers. Some of the norms have been estimated by calibrating the *Inter-American Series* with other tests for which norms have been published. Scores on the test have been equated with the College Entrance Examination Board's *Prueba de Aptitud Academica*, the Puerto Rican edition of the *Scholastic Aptitude Test*. There is information to support the reliability of the measure, but none for validity.

Job-Tests Program—Factored Aptitude Series: Blocks Test by Joseph E. King; c1948–1960; Adults; Testing Time Approximately 10 Minutes; One Form; Industrial Psychology, Inc. 6MMY: Entry 774a12.

A measure of quantitative space relations available in parallel English, Spanish, and French editions. The test is designed for use in the selection of semiskilled workers, factory machine operators, inspectors, skilled workers (linemen, machinists, maintenance, toolmakers, etc.), and designers (artists, draftsmen, etc.). The publisher provides a discussion of testing procedures and the applicability of the tests for minorities. Suggested qualification levels are provided for the various job categories for which the test is recommended. Research bulletins on validation studies involving the test are available from the publisher.

Job-Tests Program—Factored Aptitude Series: Dexterity Test by Joseph E. King; c1949–1960; Adults; Testing Time Approximately 10 Minutes; One Form; Industrial Psychology, Inc. 6MMY: Entry 774a14.

A paper-pencil measure of aptitude for fine and gross muscle control, dexterity, coordination of eye and hand. A score is obtained for each section of the test: Maze, Checks, and Dots. It is appropriate for clerical, mechanical, and technical job fields in which dexterity is required in job performance. One form of the test is available in parallel English, Spanish and French editions. The publisher provides a discussion of testing procedures and the applicability of the tests for minorities. Suggested qualification levels are provided for the various job categories for which the test is recommended. Research bulletins on validation studies involving the test are available from the publisher.

Job-Tests Program—Factored Aptitude Series: Dimensions Test by Joseph E. King; c1917–1960; Adults; Testing Time Approximately 10 Minutes; One Form; Industrial Psychology, Inc. 6MMY: Entry 774a13.

A measure of space relations aptitude available in parallel English, Spanish, and French editions. The test can be used in the selection of candidates for positions that require a high degree of spatial perception (designers, draftsmen, engineers, scientists, inspectors, etc.). The publisher provides a discussion of testing procedures and the applicability of the tests for minorities. Suggested qualification levels are provided for the various job categories for which the test is recommended. Research bulletins on validation studies involving the test are available from the publisher.

Job-Tests Program—Factored Aptitude Series: Factory Terms Test by H. B. Osborn, Jr.; c1957–1960; Adults; Testing Time Approximately 15 Minutes; One Form; Industrial Psychology, Inc. 6MMY: Entry 774a3.

Measures comprehension of high-level mechanical, engineering, and factory information needed by factory supervisors, skilled workers, engineers, and scientists. Parallel English, Spanish, and French editions are available. The publisher provides a discussion of testing procedures and the applicability of the tests for minorities. Suggested qualification levels are provided for the various job categories for which the test is recommended. Research Bulletins on validation studies involving the test are available from the publisher.

Job-Tests Program—Factored Aptitude Series: Fluency Test by Joseph E. King; c1947–1960; Adults; Testing Time Approximately 10 Minutes; One Form; Industrial Psychology, Inc. 6MMY: Entry 774a9.

Measures the ability to use words with ease. There are four sections: Words Ending in "tion," Words Beginning with "pre," Names of Jobs, and Types of Office Equipment. It is designed for use in the selection of sales and supervisory positions, some clerical and technical jobs. French, Spanish, and English editions are available. The publisher provides a discussion of testing procedures and the applicability of the tests for minorities. Suggested qualification levels are provided for the various job categories for which the test is recommended. Research bulletins on validation studies involving the test are available from the publisher.

Job-Tests Program—Factored Aptitude Series: Judgment Test by Joseph E. King; c1947–1960; Adults; Testing Time Approximately 10 Minutes; One Form; Industrial Psychology, Inc. 6MMY: Entry 774a7.

A measure of the ability to approach and solve difficult problems, think logically, foresee and plan, and deal with abstract relationships. It is a measure of intelligence. Recommended usage is the selection of personnel for higher level jobs such as sales engineers, supervisors, and scientists. The publisher provides a discussion of testing procedures and the applicability of the tests for minorities. Suggested qualification levels are provided for the various job categories for which the test is recommended. Research bulletins on validation studies involving the test can be obtained from the publisher. French, Spanish, and English editions are available.

Job-Tests Program—Factored Aptitude Series: Memory Test by Joseph E. King; c1948–1960; Adults; Testing Time Approximately 10 Minutes; One Form; Industrial Psychology, Inc. 6MMY: Entry 774a10.

A measure of the ability to recognize and recall associations such as names, faces, numbers, and prices. Designed for use in the selection of applicants for sales, supervisory, and some clerical and technical jobs. Parallel Spanish, French and English forms are available. The publisher provides a discussion of testing procedures and the applicability of the tests for minorities. Suggested qualification levels are provided for various job categories for which the test is recommended. Research bulletins concerning validation studies can be obtained from the publisher.

Job-Tests Program—Factored Aptitude Series: Motor Apparatus Test by Joseph E. King; c1948–1960; Adults; Testing Time Approximately 10 Minutes; One Form; Industrial Psychology, Inc. 6MMY: Entry 774a15.

Test apparatus consists of a board containing nuts, bolts, and washer. It is used to measure coordination ability. Recommended usage is in the selection of applicants for mechanical jobs. Instructions and record forms for the test are available in French, Spanish, and English. The publisher provides a discussion of testing procedures and the applicability of the tests for minorities. Suggested qualification levels are provided for various job categories for which the test is recommended. Research bulletins concerning validation studies of the tests are available from the publisher.

Job-Tests Program—Factored Aptitude Series: Numbers Test by Joseph E. King; c1947–1956; Adults; Testing Time Approximately 10 Minutes; One Form; Industrial Psychology, Inc. 6MMY: Entry 774a5.

Tests aptitude to work rapidly and accurately with numbers, files, codes, symbols, standard procedures, or any system in which symbols are manipulated by certain rules. The test is used in the selection of applicants for clerical, sales, technical, and supervisory positions involving systems. The publisher provides a discussion of testing procedures and the applicability of the tests for minorities. Suggested qualification levels are provided for various job categories for which the test is recommended. Research bulletins concerning validation studies can be obtained from the publisher. Parallel Spanish, French, and English forms of the test are available.

Job-Tests Program—Factored Aptitude Series: Office Terms Test by Joseph E. King; c1947–1960; Adults; Testing Time Approximately 10 Minutes; One Form; Industrial Psychology, Inc. 6MMY: Entry 774a1.

Measures the ability to understand information of an office or business nature. It is a measure of intelligence and also indicates overqualification (applicants who score very high will soon become bored and inefficient in positions requiring detailed, routine, and repetitive work). Recommended usage in the selection of clerical, technical, and supervisory personnel. Parallel editions are available in French, English, and Spanish. The publisher provides a discussion of testing procedures and the applicability of the tests for minorities. Suggested qualification levels are provided for various job categories for which the test is recommended. Validation studies are available from the publisher.

Job-Tests Program—Factored Aptitude Series: Parts Test by Joseph E. King; c1949–1956; Adults; Testing Time Approximately 10 Minutes; One Form; Industrial Psychology, Inc. 6MMY: Entry 774a11.

Designed for use in the selection of personnel for supervisory and technical jobs in which layout, planning, and organization are required. The test measures the ability to visualize sizes, shapes, and spatial relationships of objects in two and three dimensions. Subscores are Parts, Blocks, and Dimension. The publisher provides a discussion of testing procedures and the applicability of the tests for minorities. Suggested qualification levels are provided for various job categories for which the test is recommended. Validation studies are available from the publisher. Parallel French, Spanish, and English forms are available.

Job-Tests Program—Factored Aptitude Series: Perception Test by Joseph E. King; c1948–1960; Adults; Testing Time Approximately 10 Minutes; One Form; Industrial Psychology, Inc. 6MMY: Entry 774a6.

A measure of the ability to scan and locate details in words and numbers rapidly, to recognize likenesses and differences quickly. It can be used in the selection of applicants for any clerical position and certain technical and supervisory jobs. Parallel French, English, and Spanish editions are available. The publisher provides a discussion of testing procedures and the applicability of the tests for minorities. Suggested qualification levels are provided for various job categories for which the test is recommended. Validation studies are available from the publisher.

Job-Tests Program—Factored Aptitude Series: Precision Test by Joseph E. King; c1947–1960; Adults; Testing Time Approximately 10 Minutes; One Form; Industrial Psychology, Inc. 6MMY: Entry 774a8.

Provides a measure of the ability to recognize likenesses and differences of objects. It can be used in the selection of applicants for inspection-type positions and some technical jobs. There are French, Spanish, and English editions. The publisher provides a discussion of testing procedures and the applicability of the tests for minorities. Suggested qualification levels are provided for various job categories for which the test is recommended. Research bulletins concerning validation studies can be obtained from the publisher.

Job-Tests Program—Factored Aptitude Series: Sales Terms Test by Joseph E. King; c1948–1960; Adults; Testing Time Approximately 10 Minutes; One Form; Industrial Psychology, Inc. 6MMY: Entry 774a2.

Provides an indication of the ability to understand information pertaining to sales. It is also a measure of intelligence. French, English and Spanish editions are available. The publisher provides a discussion of testing procedures and the applicability of the tests for minorities. Suggested qualification levels are provided for various job categories for which the test is recommended. Research bulletins concerning validation studies are available from the publisher.

Job-Tests Program—Factored Aptitude Series: Tools Test by Joseph E. King; c1948–1960; Adults; Testing Time Approximately 10 Minutes; One Form; Industrial Psychology, Inc. 6MMY: Entry 774a4.

Measures understanding of and aptitude for working with simple tools and mechanical equipment. No reading or writing is required of the examinee. There are Spanish, English, and French editions. The publisher provides a discussion of testing procedures and the applicability of the tests for minorities. Suggested qualification levels are provided for various job categories for which the test is recommended. Research bulletins concerning validation studies can be obtained from the publisher.

Kahn Intelligence Test: Experimental Form by Theodore C. Kahn; c1960; Ages 1 Month–Adults; One Form; Psychological Test Specialists. 7MMY: Entry 411.

An individually administered test of intelligence that requires a minimum of verbalization and is almost independent of differential educational and cultural learning factors. It is designed especially for the culturally disadvantaged or verbally handicapped. In addition to the main scale, there are six optional scales: a Brief Scale, and scales for Concept Formation, Recall, Motor Coordination, a scale for use with the deaf and a scale for use with the blind. Props, available from the publisher, are required for administering the test. Distribution of the test is limited to psychologists, psychiatrists, counselors, and others who have the background to deal with problems related to intelligence testing. Preliminary norms are available. The publisher recommends the development of local norms for specific populations such as the blind, physically handicapped, foreign-born, brain injured, and persons with special educational problems.

Leiter International Performance Scale by Russell Grayton Leiter; c1929–1965; Ages 2–Adults; Testing Time 40–60 Minutes; One Form; Stoelting Company (APA Level C). 6MMY: Entry 525.

An individually administered nonverbal intelligence test that is appropriate for persons with speech and auditory handicaps, illiterates, the foreign-born, the educationally and culturally deprived because it is administered without language. The test consists of a series of subtests that require matching, ranging from the pairing of like colors and objects to more complex relationships of designs and analogies. Among the subtests are: Matching Colors; Block Design; Matching Pictures; Matching Circles and Squares; Four Forms; Picture Completion; Number Discrimination; Form and Color; Eight Forms; Counts Four; Form, Color, Number; Genus; Two Color Circles; Clothing; Analogous Progression; Pattern Completion Test; Matching on a Basis of Use; Reconstruction; Circle Series; Circumference Series; Recognition of Age Differences; Match Shades of Gray; Form Discrimination; Judging Mass; Series of Radii; Dot Estimation; Analogous Designs; Line Completion; Footprints Recognition Test; Concealed Cubes; Similarities, Two Things; Recognition of Facial Expressions; Classification of Animals; Memory for a Series; Form Completion Test; Code for a Number Series; Reversed Clocks, and a Spatial Relations Test. Twelve of the subtests have been selected to form a Brief Scale (1934). This is not a paper-and-pencil test. The objects and apparatus required are provided in a kit available from the publisher. Normative data are reported for normal, mentally retarded, cerebral palsied, Mexican children, unselected white children, middle-class white children, California-born Japanese youngsters, and Chinese and Japanese children in Hawaii. Information concerning the reliability and validity of the test with various populations is provided.

Lorge-Thorndike Intelligence Tests, Separate Level Edition, Nonverbal Battery: Level 4 by Irving Lorge and Robert L. Thorndike; c1954; Grades 7–9; Testing Time Approximately 40 Minutes; Two Equivalent Forms; Houghton Mifflin Company. 5MMY: Entry 350.

Spanish directions are available for use with the Nonverbal Battery, which measures abstract reasoning ability through three subtests: Pictorial Classification, Pictorial Analogy, and Numerical Relationships. The battery yields an estimate of intelligence that is not heavily influenced by reading ability. Only the directions for the test are in Spanish; the test items are pictorial. Norms are not reported separately for Spanish speakers. Reliability and validity data are reported for the general population.

Lorge-Thorndike Intelligence Tests, Separate Level Edition, Nonverbal Battery: Level 5 by Irving Lorge and Robert L. Thorndike; c1954; Grades 10–12; Testing Time Approximately 40 Minutes; Two Equivalent Forms; Houghton Mifflin Company. 5MMY: Entry 350.

Spanish directions are available for use with the Nonverbal Battery, which measures abstract reasoning ability through three subtests: Pictorial Classification, Pictorial Analogy, and Numerical Relationships. The battery yields an estimate of intelligence that is not heavily influenced by reading ability. Only the directions for the test are in Spanish; the test items are pictorial. Norms are not reported separately for Spanish speakers. Reliability and validity data are provided for the general population.

Non-Verbal Reasoning Test by Raymond J. Corsini; c1957–1966; Adults; Testing Time Approximately 15–30 Minutes; One Form; Education-Industry Service. 6MMY: Entry 478.

A test of the ability to think logically through the medium of pictorial problems. The publisher asserts that the test is relatively culture free and is not influenced by language facility. Norms are reported for industrial male employees.

PTI Oral Directions Test.

See *Personnel Tests for Industry: Oral Directions Test, Form S.*

Personnel Classification Test.

See *Wesman Personnel Classification Test.*

Personnel Tests for Industry: Oral Directions Test (PTI–ODT), *Form S* by Charles R. Langmuir; c1945–1954; Adolescents and Adults; Testing Time Approximately 25 Minutes; One Form; The Psychological Corporation. 3MMY: Entry 245.

A wide-range measure of mental ability that minimizes the effects of reading, writing, and written computation skills. It measures the ability to understand what one is told to do. The PTI–ODT was designed for those who have had limited education or who have a foreign-language background. The PTI–ODT is suitable for the selection of employees for maintenance and service work in public institutions, transportation systems, stores, hotels, factories and shops. The test is also useful as a screening test in social agencies concerned with the counseling of adults. Scores on the PTI–ODT can be useful in selecting appropriate batteries for further testing. The test requires only that the candidate be able to write numbers and the alphabet. One form is available. However, the PTI–ODT is available in two formats: either a 33⅓ rpm LP record or a tape recording. The test is also available in a Spanish-American edition, *PTI Instrucciones Orales.* Normative data are reported for textile mill applicants, pharmaceutical manufacturing employees, tannery production workers, electrical assembly work applicants, police force applicants, counselors, and nursing applicants.

Pruebas de Habilidad General.

See the *Cooperative Inter-American Tests: Tests of General Ability: Advanced* and *Intermediate Levels* and the *Inter-American Series: Tests of General Ability: Level 4* and *Level 5.*

Purdue Non-Language Test by Joseph Tiffin; c1957–1969; Adults; Testing Time Approximately 15 Minutes; Two Equivalent Forms; University Bookstore (APA Level B). 7MMY: Entry 377.

A culture-free test of mental ability consisting entirely of geometric forms; there is no verbal content. The publisher recommends the development of local norms. Norms are reported for candidates for a supervisory position at a Midwestern company, die-setter applicants at a Midwestern company, and supervisory personnel at four Midwestern manufacturing companies. A situational validity study of "most effective" and "least effective" clerical-stenographic personnel is described, and data are reported for black females, white females, black and white females, black males, white males, black and white males, and all males and all females.

RBH Industrial Questionnaire; c1953–1963; Adults; Testing Time Approximately 60 Minutes; One Form; Richardson, Bellows, Henry & Company, Inc. 7MMY: Entry 982.

A measure of general ability designed for use in the screening of basic blue-collar employees, unskilled laborers and routine factory workers, operatives and craftsmen, and others involved in the electric utility, paper, ore, and chemical industry. Items cover reading comprehension, arithmetic reasoning, and chemical comprehension. The publisher states that the absence of a formal time limit makes the test useful in borderline cases in which limited education or limited knowledge of the English language handicaps otherwise desirable applicants. Norms and statistical data are based on male mechanical employees, process operators, and industrial employees employed in oil refineries.

RBH Non-Verbal Reasoning Test, Long Form; c1948–1963; Adults; Testing Time Approximately 20 Minutes; One Form; Richardson, Bellows, Henry & Company, Inc. 7MMY: Entry 380.

A nonverbal and nonlanguage test designed for use in batteries for the screening of technicians, engineers, engineering aids, technical salesmen, and any population for which language presents a problem. The examinee must be able to read numbers in order to be tested, since he must identify the illustrations and record his answers. The test measures reasoning and concept formation through the use of symbols and geometric figures. Some of the items are concerned with concepts such as: tangents, angle bisection, vertical-horizontal arrangement, and squareness. Norms are reported separately for males and females. However, reliability and validity data are provided for males only.

RBH Non-Verbal Reasoning Test, Short Form; c1950–1962; Adults; Testing Time Approximately 20 Minutes; One Form; Richardson, Bellows, Henry & Company, Inc. 7MMY: Entry 380.

Measures reasoning and concept formulation through the use of symbols and geometric figures. The publisher asserts that the test is nonverbal and nonlanguage. This shortened version of the *RBH Non-Verbal Reasoning Test, Long Form,* is appropriate for use in the selection of operatives and craftsmen, basic blue-collar and unskilled labor positions, routine factory personnel, and any population for which language is a problem. Consideration has been given to the appropriateness of the items in a variety of foreign countries. For instance, a mirror image of the test is provided for a culture in which reading is done from right to left. Male norms are reported for clerical applicants and employees, for industrial supervisors and for industrial applicants and employees. Female norms are available for clerical and stenographic employees. Reliability and validity studies are reported for male examinees only.

RBH Test of Learning Ability, Forms DS–12, DT–12; c1961–1963; Adults; Testing Time Approximately 20 Minutes; Richardson, Bellows, Henry & Company, Inc. 7MMY: Entry 379.

A measure of three components of intelligence: vocabulary comprehension, arithmetic reasoning, and the ability to perceive spatial relationships. The test is recommended for use in the selection and placement of industrial applicants in almost all job categories. The test content is the same as the *RBH Test of Learning Ability, Forms S and T;* however, the publisher asserts that Forms DS–12 and DT–12 are especially useful with examinees who are relatively unsophisticated in test taking or whenever greater than normal variation is anticipated in the time required to comprehend test directions for a group whose scores will be compared. Norms are reported for a variety of occupational groups, including clerical applicants and employees, secretarial and stenographic applicants and employees, nursing applicants and students, industrial employees and students, industrial foremen and supervisors, service-station dealers and applicants, sales employees and applicants, professional, technical, managerial and executive applicants and employees.

SRA Non-Verbal Form by Robert N. McMurray and Joseph E. King; c1947–1966; Grades 9–12 and Adults; Testing Time Approximately 15 Minutes; One Form Available in a Hand-Scoring and Machine-Scoring Edition; Science Research Associates, Inc. (APA Level B). 4MMY: Entry 318.

Measures reasoning and concept formation independently of language and reading skills. Items consist of a series of drawings of people, objects, or geometric forms, four of which are related. The examinee is required to discover the interrelating principle and indicate the drawing in each series that is most different. The test is recommended for use in screening individuals who have difficulty with reading or language or in screening for jobs in which reading and communication skills have little relationship to successful performance. Intelligence quotients, stanine ranks, and percentile ranks are reported. The range of scores and the average rank for workers in each of 150 occupations are provided. A study of the appropriateness of the *SRA Non-Verbal Form* for use with black adolescents is described in the technical report for the test.

SRA Pictorial Reasoning Test by Robert N. McMurray and Phyllis D. Arnold; c1966–1967; Ages 14–Adults; Untimed Administration Approximately 45 Minutes, Timed Administration Approximately 20 Minutes; One Form; Science Research Associates, Inc. 7MMY: Entry 381.

A measure of reasoning and concept formation that is relatively independent of language and reading skills. Items consist of five drawings or pictures, four of which are related. The examinee must discover the interrelating principle. The test is appropriate for selection and placement. It is especially useful with persons who have language or reading difficulties. The publisher asserts that the test was designed to be as fair as possible to all distinct cultural subgroups in American society. Recommended usage is in the selection of applicants for jobs in which writing and communication skills contribute little to successful performance. The test can also be used by companies and agencies participating in retraining programs for displaced adult workers or school dropouts in order to identify persons most likely to benefit from the program. Norms are presented for a timed and untimed administration of the test. Seven subcultures participated in the norming of the test: Appalachians, Spanish-speaking bilinguals, rural and urban blacks, rural and urban whites, and French-speaking bilingual Canadians. Norms are reported for the total group tested, the urban white group, control group (mainstream Americans), other groups (other subcultures). Reliability data and correlations between the SRA *Pictorial Reasoning Test* and other aptitude and achievements are reported.

Short Test of Educational Ability, Level 4; c1966–1969; Grades 7–8; Testing Time Approximately 30 Minutes; One Form; Science Rsearch Associates, Inc. 7MMY: Entry 382.

A measure of educational ability designed to avoid reliance on achievement concepts and skills acquired in school. Only basic reading skills are required. A single score is obtained from the three subtests: Verbal Meaning, Arithmetic Reasoning and Number Series. Working time for the test is 20 minutes. The test can be administered by the classroom teacher. The test is available in parallel English and Spanish editions. The publisher recommends that the Spanish edition be used only with students who have had at least two years of their formal education in Spanish and can read Spanish with some facility. The directions to be read by the teacher are annotated with Southwestern, Cuban, and Puerto Rican dialects. Separate norms have not been developed for the Spanish edition. Data are provided concerning the equivalence of the Spanish and English editions. Information concerning the reliability of the test is provided.

Short Test of Educational Ability, Level 5; c1966–1969; Grades 9–12; Testing Time Approximately 30 Minutes; One Form; Science Research Associates, Inc. 7MMY: Entry 382.

A measure of educational ability designed to avoid reliance on achievement concepts and skills acquired in school. Only basic reading skills are required. A single score is obtained from the four subtests: Verbal Meaning, Arithmetic Reasoning, Letter Series, and Symbol Manipulation. The test is available in parallel English and Spanish editions. The publisher recommends that the Spanish edition be used only with students who have had at least two years of their formal education in Spanish or who have otherwise demonstrated their ability to read Spanish with some facility. The directions to be read by the teacher are annotated with Southwestern, Cuban, and Puerto Rican dialects. Separate norms have not been developed for the Spanish edition. Information concerning the reliability of the test and the equivalence of the Spanish and English editions is provided.

Survey of Mechanical Insight: Spanish Edition.

See *Examen de Percepción Mecánica: Edición Experimental.*

Test of General Ability: Grades 6–9 by John C. Flanagan; c1957–1960; Grades 6–9; Testing Time Approximately 45 Minutes; One Form; Science Research Associates, Inc. 6MMY: Entry 496.

A measure of general intelligence and basic learning ability independent of school-acquired skills such as arithmetic and reading. For this reason the publisher states that the test is appropriate for students from culturally deprived backgrounds. The first part of the test, the information section, measures the student's ability to grasp meanings, recognize relationships, and understand the basic concepts and underlying principles of the natural and social environment. It also measures his ability to systematize and relate new information to knowledge already possessed. The second part of the test, the reasoning section, tests the ability to understand relationships and to form concepts. An attempt has been made to make the reasoning section as free from acculturation as possible. All items are pictorial. The *Examiner's Manual* has been translated into Spanish. Scores are reported in terms of intelligence quotients and grade expectancy scores.

Test of General Ability: Grades 9–12 by John C. Flanagan; c1957–1960; Grades 9–12; Testing Time Approximately 45 Minutes; One Form; Science Research Associates, Inc. 6MMY: Entry 496.

A measure of general intelligence and basic learning ability independent of school-acquired skills such as arithmetic and reading. For this reason the publisher states that the test is appropriate for students from culturally deprived backgrounds. The first part of the test, the information section, measures the student's ability to grasp meanings, recognize relationships, and understand the basic concepts and underlying principles of the natural and social environment. It also measures his ability to systematize and relate new information to knowledge already possessed. The second part of the test, the reasoning section, tests the ability to understand relationships and to form concepts. An attempt has been made to make the reasoning section as free from acculturation as possible. All items are pictorial. Scores are reported in terms of intelligence quotients and grade expectancy scores.

Test of Mechanical Insights: Spanish Edition.

See *Examen de Percepción Mecánica.*

Test de Comprehensión Mecánica by George K. Bennett; Translated by J. Boulger and M. Najman de Dembo; c1940–1957; Grades 9–12 and Adults; Untimed, Approximately 30 Minutes; Two Equivalent Forms; The Psychological Corporation.

A Spanish edition of the *Bennett Mechanical Comprehension Test,* a measure of the ability to understand mechanical relationships and physical laws in practical situations. The test can be used in the selection of personnel for mechanical work, apprentices, and students for technical and engineering training. The test is untimed, requiring approximately 30 minutes. Two forms are available, AA–S and BB–S. Form BB–S is more difficult than Form AA–S. Some of the normative data reported were obtained from groups tested in the United States with the English edition. Norms based on the Spanish edition are reported for a group of Venezuelan and two groups of Cuban examinees. Reliability data and information supporting the equivalence of Forms AA–S and BB–S are provided. The validity studies reported use data obtained from testing American examinees with the English edition of the test.

See Entry 1049 in the 7MMY for a review of the English edition of the *Bennett Mechanical Comprehension Test.*

Tests de Aptitud Diferencial by George K. Bennett, Harold Seashore, and Alexander Wesman; c1947–1957; Ages 14–Adults; Testing Time Approximately 120 Minutes; Two Equivalent Forms; The Psychological Corporation (APA Level B).

An authorized translation and adaptation of the *Differential Aptitude Tests* for use with Latin American examinees. The subtests included in the battery are: Verbal Reasoning, Numerical Ability, Abstract Reasoning, Space Relations, Mechanical Reasoning, Clerical Speed and Accuracy, Language Usage: Spelling, and Language Usage: Grammar. Normative data are based on American examinees tested with the English edition of the test. Specimen sets of the *Tests de Aptitud Diferencial* can be obtained from The Psychological Corporation. Inquiries concerning the Latin American adaptation should be addressed to Dr. Robert B. MacVean; Colegio Americano de Guatemala; Apartado Postal No. 83; Guatemala City, Guatemala.

The English edition of the test is reviewed in the 7MMY: Entry 673.

Two-Dimensional Space Test, Form I; c1948–1963; Adults; Testing Time Approximately 15 Minutes; One Form; Richardson, Bellows, Henry & Company, Inc. 6MMY: Entry 1097.

Measures the ability to visualize objects in space. Items consist of geometric figures cut into two or three parts and presentation of four whole figures that might be made from the parts. The examinee is required to assemble visually or ideationally the parts and identify the figure that could be formed. The test can be used with individuals who are not fluent in English and those with low educational levels. The test is recommended for use in the selection of mechanical and operating employees, especially those concerned with layout and assembly. Norms are reported for male industrial applicants, clerical employees and applicants, industrial supervisors, and mechanical and operating employees. Reliability and validity data are based on male examinees.

United States Training and Employment Service (USTES) *Nonreading Aptitude Test Battery: 1969 Edition;* 1965–1971; Grades 9–12 and Adults; Testing Time Approximately 190 Minutes; One Form; U.S. Training and Employment Service (APA Level B).

The USTES *Nonreading Aptitude Test Battery* (NATB) was designed to measure the same aptitudes as the USTES *General Aptitude Test Battery* (GATB), which is considered inappropriate for use with disadvantaged individuals. The GATB is inappropriate for use with the disadvantaged because: It was standardized on employed workers, most of whom were not disadvantaged; few validity studies were conducted on disadvantaged groups; four of the subtests require reading skills that many disadvantaged individuals do not have, and there are problems concerning comprehension of instructions and lack of test sophistication.

The nine aptitudes measured by the NATB (and the GATB) are: intelligence, verbal aptitude, numerical aptitude, spatial aptitude, form perception, clerical perception, motor coordination, finger dexterity, and manual dexterity. The tests included in the NATB are: Picture-Word Matching, Oral Vocabulary, Coin Matching, Design Completion, Tool Matching, Three-Dimensional Space, Form Matching, Coin Series, and Name Comparison. The Mark Making, Place, Turn,

Assemble, and Disassemble Tests from the GATB are included in the NATB. These five are performance measures that require the examinee to manipulate test materials such as finger dexterity boards and pegboards. The GATB Screening Exercises provide a basis for determining whether the NATB or GATB should be administered. The GATB Screening Exercises consist of four practice items from the GATB Vocabulary Test and three items from the GATB Three Dimensional Space Test. Approximately ten minutes is required for screening. Examinees who do not pass both sections of the screening measure should be tested with the NATB.

The NATB should be administered by a person experienced in testing the disadvantaged. Examiners must have successfully completed the NATB training program and must be able to establish good rapport with examinees.

Norms are reported in terms of Occupational Aptitude Patterns and Specific Aptitude Test Battery. The Occupational Aptitude Pattern is the combination of patterns of aptitudes and minimum scores required to perform satisfactorily the major tasks of the groups of occupations identified with each pattern. A Specific Aptitude Test Battery is the pattern of aptitudes and minimum scores required to perform the major tasks of an occupation in question. Norms used with the NATB are the same as those developed for the GATB.

The validity of the NATB has been established in terms of its relationship with the GATB. It has not been validated against the criteria of job and training success of disadvantaged individuals. The NATB is not available to the general public. The battery is intended for use by the various state employment service agencies affiliated with the U.S. Training and Employment Service. Authorized nonprofit institutions may also use the NATB for counseling if they use their own facilities for testing and employ trained testing supervisors and counselors. Orders for test materials must be cleared through a state employment service office. Manuals and test accessories are available from the U.S. Government Printing Office. Tests and scoring keys are distributed by National Computer Systems, Inc.

WLW Culture-Fair Inventory by Lynde C. Steckle, Robert W. Henderson, and Barbara O. Murray; c1969; Adults; Untimed, Approximately 45 Minutes; One Form; William, Lynde & Williams. 7MMY: Entry 399.

An untimed, nonverbal measure of intelligence consisting of items that discount the influence of environment and education. The test is designed for use in the selection and placement of minority groups or "hard-core" individuals. One score is obtained from the five sections of the test: Selection of Figure in Five That Is Most Different, Block Counting, Selection of Fifth Figure in a Series, Paper Form Board, and Selection of Figure Which Completes Pattern. There is one form of the test. Preliminary norms are based on male and female college students and for black and white female clerical applicants for jobs in an urban insurance company. Reliability and validity data are based upon earlier experimental forms of the test.

Wesman Personnel Classification Test by Alexander G. Wesman; c1946–1965; Grades 8–16 and Adults; Testing Time Approximately 35 Minutes; 3 Equivalent Forms; The Psychological Corporation.

A test of mental ability designed for use in the selection of employees for clerical, sales, supervisory, and managerial positions. The Verbal subtest requires the use of reasoning through analogy and the perception of relationships in order to correctly respond to the item. The Numerical subtest measures competence in basic arithmetical skills and processes and general facility in the use of numerical concepts. Normative data are reported for female chain-store clerks for whom the tenth grade was the median grade completed; production workers; production and inspection supervisors; male office supervisors; female clerical workers; salaried workers employed as laboratory technicians and office personnel; male shop supervisors; U.S. Air Force Captains; sales trainees; job analysts; and accounting and quality control personnel in a manufacturing company. Norms are also reported for various educational groups: students in an evening high school—adult males, one-fourth to one-third of whom came from a foreign-language (predominantly Spanish) background; 10th-grade students, high school seniors, nursing school applicants, college freshmen, and college sophomores. Average scores on the test are reported according to school level attained.

Western Personnel Test: Spanish by Robert L. Gunn and Morse P. Manson; c1962–1964; Adults; Testing Time Approximately 10 Minutes; One Form; Western Psychological Services.

A Spanish translation of a test of general intelligence designed for personnel screening. Item content includes number series, word meaning, disarranged sentences, and arithmetic reasoning. The Spanish edition of the test uses the same norms as the English edition. Norms are reported for professional workers, college students, clerical workers, skilled workers, unskilled workers, and the general population, which is a total of the five groups tested.

Reviews of the English edition of the test are included in the 6MMY: Entry 512.

Personality, Interests, Attitudes, and Opinions

Activity Vector Analysis by Walter V. Clark; c1948–1963; Ages 16–Adults; Testing Time Approximately 10 Minutes; One for Foreign Language Editions, Three Equivalent Forms in English; AVA Publications, Inc. 6MMY: Entry 58.

> A self-report adjective checklist used to measure the following personality traits: Aggressiveness, Sociability, Emotional Control, Social Adaptability, Intelligent Behavior, and Activity Level. The examinee checks the adjectives he feels that others have used in describing him and those he feels are descriptive of himself. The analysis of responses provides an insight into the individual's self-concepts and social role perceptions. The *Activity Vector Analysis* is designed for use in business and industry. Spanish, Portuguese, French, German, and English editions are available. Test results must be interpreted by a Certified AVA Analyst. Distribution of the test is limited to persons who have completed a training course offered by the publisher. Standard scores are reported.

Adolescent Alienation Index by F. K. Heussenstamm; c1971; Ages 12–19; Testing Time Approximately 20 Minutes; Two Forms; Monitor (APA Level B).

> The *Index* is a measure of identifying emergent or developing alienation. The test may reflect personality disjunctures before the behavioral symptoms of normlessness, meaninglessness, powerlessness, social isolation, and self-estrangement are evident. Two forms of the test are available: Form A for use with answer sheets and Form C, consumable booklets, which are designed for examinees with less sophistication in taking tests and marking answer sheets. Norms are reported separately for suburban white, urban black, rural Mexican-American high school students, and black Job Corps trainees.

Association Adjustment Inventory: Spanish Edition by Martin M. Bruce; c1959–1968; Adults; Testing Time Approximately 15 Minutes; One Form; Martin M. Bruce, Publishers (APA Level B).

> A translation of a multiple-choice word-association test adapted from the *Kent-Rosanoff Free Association Test.* The inventory is designed as an aid in screening for maladjustment and immaturity and as an aid in diagnosing deviate ideation. The test yields 13 scores: Juvenility, Psychotic Responses, Depressed-Optimistic, Hysteric-Non-Hysteric, Withdrawal-Sociable, Paranoid-Naïve, Rigid-Flexible, Schizophrenic-Objective, Impulsive-Restrained, Sociopathic-Empathetic, Psychosomapathic-Physical Contentment, and Anxious-Relaxed. Norms are not reported separately for the Spanish edition. Normative data are provided for institutionalized adults and the adults in the general population.
>
> The English edition of the *Association Adjustment Inventory* is described in *Personality Tests and Reviews:* Entry 413.

California Occupational Preference Survey: Spanish Edition by Robert R. Knapp, Bruce Grant, and George D. Demos; Adapted and Translated by Blanca M. de Alvarez and Guido A. Barrientos; c1966–1970; Grades 8–16 and Adults; Testing Time Approximately 40 Minutes; One Form; Educational and Industrial Testing Service (APA Level B).

> The *California Occupational Preference Survey* (COPS) was designed for use in vocational counseling to assist individuals in defining broad areas of occupational interest. Fourteen occupational cluster scores are obtained from the test. The scores represent clusters of occupational activities at the professional and skilled level within six major occupational areas and two other areas. The scales are: Science; Professional, Science; Skilled, Technical; Professional, Technical; Skilled, Outdoor, Business; Professional, Business; Skilled, Clerical, Linguistic; Professional, Linguistic; Skilled, Aesthetic; Professional, Aesthetic; Skilled, Service; Professional, and Service; Skilled. The occupations classified as professional generally require college training and advanced degrees; those classified as skilled usually require specialized training such as that obtained in on-the-job training, vocational, or trade school. Only the test and answer sheet are available in Spanish. The Spanish edition makes use of the norms based on the English version —percentiles for high school males, high school females, college males, and college females. Evidence of the reliability and validity of the English edition is provided; this information is not reported for the Spanish version.
>
> A review of the English edition is included in the 7MMY: Entry 1012.

Curtis Completion Form: Spanish Edition by James W. Curtis; c1968; Older Adolescents and Adults; Untimed, Approximately 30 Minutes; One Form for Each Language; Western Psychological Services (APA Level C).

A sentence-completion test designed to evaluate emotional maturity and adjustment. The author recommends the use of the test in industrial settings for screening of individuals whose emotional adjustment makes them poor employment risks. The test can also be used in identifying those who would benefit from psychotherapy or psychiatric treatment. Analysis of item responses may yield information concerning the nature of emotional problems and the individual's relationship to his immediate environment. Factors or traits scored are: antagonism, suspicion, jealousy, self-pity and pessimism, insecurity, social inadequacy, environmental deprivation, severe conflict, avoidance responses, and ambiguous and incomplete responses. For score interpretation, there is an expectancy chart for adjustment levels of individuals who obtain various scores on the *Curtis Completion Form*. Individuals are classified as normal, neurotic, and psychotic. Separate expectancy tables are not provided for the Spanish and French editions. Information on reliability and validity is reported for the English edition. These data are not available for the Spanish and French editions. A review of English edition of the test is included in the 5MMY: Entry 128.

Demos D Scale: An Attitude Scale for the Identification of Dropouts by George D. Demos; c1965–1970; Grades 7–12; Untimed, Can Be Completed in 15–40 Minutes; One Form; Western Psychological Services.

Measures Attitudes Toward Teachers, Attitudes Toward Education, Influences by Peers or Parents, and School Behavior. The publisher asserts that the test is appropriate for preventative work with minority and culturally disadvantaged groups. Mean scores are reported for a nondropout Anglo-American group, high school dropouts, and juveniles in a detention facility. No reliability data are provided.

Geist Picture Interest Inventory: 1964 Revision by Harold Geist; c1964–1968; Grades 8–12 and Adults; Testing Time Approximately 40–65 Minutes; One Form for Each Sex; Western Psychological Services. 6MMY: Entry 1054.

Designed for the identification of vocational and avocational interests. The *Geist Picture Interest Inventory* (GPII) is appropriate for use with the culturally and educationally deprived, the verbally handicapped, and a group having limited verbal skills. A minimum use of language is required in testing, since the examinee is required to circle which of three pictures depicting vocational or avocational scenes he prefers. Separate editions are available for males and females. the *GPII: Male* assesses 11 general interest areas: Persuasive, Clerical, Mechanical, Musical, Scientific, Outdoor, Literary, Computational, Artistic, Social Service, and Dramatic. The *GPII: Female* covers the same 11 interest areas as the male edition plus a 12th area, Personal Service. The *Motivational Analysis of Occupational Choices* is an optional qualitative checklist included in the GPII test booklets to provide a means of identifying the motivating forces behind occupational choices. Seven motivational areas are considered on the checklist: Could Not Say, Family, Prestige, Financial, Intrinsic and Personality, Environmental, and Past Experience. Norms for the *GPII: Male* are reported for a U.S. mainland sample, 8th and 9th grades; U.S. mainland sample, 10th and 11th grades; U.S. mainland sample, 12th grade and remedial reading groups, 8th and 10th grade; U.S. mainland sample, trade school and university. Norms are also reported for the following Puerto Rican samples: 8th and 11th grades, 12th grade, and trade school, and university students. Norms are also reported for Hawaiian samples: 10th and 11th grades, 12th grade, remedial reading groups, university students, and attorneys. Norms are also provided for various occupational groups. For the *GPII: Female* norms are reported for 8th, 9th, 10th, 11th, 12th grades, junior college students, and university students. Norms for various occupations are also given. No Puerto Rican norms are reported for the *GPII: Female*.

Geist Picture Interest Inventory for Men (GPII), Spanish Edition by Harold Geist; c1958–1964; Grades 8–12 and Adults; Testing Time Approximately 40–65 Minutes; One Form; Western Psychological Services.

An interest inventory for Spanish-speaking and bilingual males. A minimum use of language is required in testing, since the examinee is required to circle which of three pictures depicting vocational or avocational scenes he prefers. The *GPII: Male* asesses 11 general interest areas: Persuasive, Clerical, Mechanical, Musical, Scientific, Outdoor, Literary, Computational, Artistic, Social Service, and Dramatic. The *Motivational Analysis of Occupational Choices* is an optional qualitative checklist included in the GPII test booklets to provide a means of identifying the motivating forces behind occupational choices. Seven motivational areas are considered on the checklist: Could Not Say, Family, Prestige, Financial, Intrinsic and Personality, Environmental, and Past Experience. Separate scores are not reported for the Spanish edition. Normative data reported for the English edition are used in interpreting the Spanish form. Groups for which norms are reported are: a U.S. mainland sample, 8th and 9th grades; U.S. mainland sample, 10th and 11th grades; U.S. mainland sample, 12th grade and remedial reading groups, 8th and 10th grades; U.S. mainland sample, trade school and university. Norms are also reported for the following Puerto Rican samples: 8th and 11th grades, 12th grade and trade school, and university students. Norms are also reported for Hawaiian samples: 10th and 11th grades, 12th grade, remedial reading groups, university students, and attorneys. Norms are also provided for various occupational groups. No information is reported concerning the reliability and validity of the Spanish edition.

The English editions of the *Geist Picture Interest Inventory* is reviewed in the 6MMY: Entry 1054.

Group Personality Projective Test (GPPT) by Russell N. Cassel and Theodore C. Kahn; c1956–1961; Ages 11–Adults; Testing Time Approximately 45 Minutes; One Form; Psychological Test Specialists (APA Level C).

A measure of basic personality characteristics designed to assess the presence and degree of anxiety-producing tension, unresolved needs, proneness to delinquency, and factors associated with unsatisfactory leadership. Subscales are: Tension, Nurturance, Withdrawal, Neuroticism, Affiliation, and Succorance. The test is designed for use in screening large groups for potentially pathological personality patterns. It can be used with examinees who are able to read English. Teachers and others with training in the administration and scoring of group tests can administer the GPPT. However, the test should be interpreted by psychologists, psychiatrists, counselors, and others who have had specific training in the use of projective tests. Norms are reported for an unselected group of normal individuals, neuropsychiatric patients, delinquents and prisoners, and Spanish Americans.

I.P.E. Juvenil por Sybil B. G. Eysenck. Adapted by Blanca M. de Alvarez and Guido A. Barrientos; c1965–1968; Ages 7–16; Testing Time Approximately 20 Minutes; One Form; Educational and Industrial Testing Service (APA Level B).

A Spanish-language edition of the *Junior Eysenck Personality Inventory*. The test measures extroversion and neuroticism (with emphasis on emotional overresponsiveness and anxiety). A Lie Scale detects response falsification. The publisher recommends that the use of the Spanish edition be limited to research projects. Norms are reported for Mexican-American youngsters. No reliability or validity data are reported for the Spanish edition. The American edition of the test is reviewed in the 7MMY: Entry 96.

Inter-American Series: Inventory of Vocational Interests: Preliminary Edition; c1970; Adolescents and Adults; Testing Time Not Listed; One Form in Each Language; Guidance Testing Associates.

A general vocational interest inventory available in parallel Spanish and English forms. Occupational categories included are: craftsman; machine operator; production or care of plants, animals, and raw materials; service or security; transportation; office worker; buying or selling; professional performer in recreational activities; professional service in communication, public relations, library, or museum; artist; social service, public welfare, or religion; owner, manager or public official; health service; engineering, architecture, and related specialties. Also included is a checklist of 56 subjects for study in school, college, or other educational institutions. Norms, reliability, and validity data are not reported.

Inter-Person Perception Test by F. K. Heussenstamm and R. Hoepfner; c1969; Ages 6–Adults; Untimed, Approximately 25 Minutes; Two Forms; Monitor.

Designed to assess individual and group status on interpersonal perception or social cognition. The test is designed to be largely free of aspects of verbal intelligence and be primarily a measure of social sensitivity. The examinee's task is to select one of four alternative facial photographs that expresses the same thoughts, feelings, and intentions as the stimulus item. Photographs of faces are the only item contact. There are two forms of the test: Form AC has faces of children and youth; Form AA, faces of adults. The items (photographs) are equally divided by sex and ethnicity. Mexican Americans, Oriental Americans, Negroes, and Caucasians are pictured. The publisher states that the items were constructed with the assistance of representatives from each of the ethnic groups. The *Inter-Person Perception Test* is recommended for use in assessing changes resulting from sensitivity training, counseling, and psychotherapy; selecting personnel who must deal with people; teacher training; and cross-cultural, sociological, and psychological research. No norms are available for children. Norms are reported for adult black males, black females, white males, white females, Mexican-American females, Mexican-American males, Oriental-American males, Oriental-American females, and for the total standardization sample.

Inventario de Asociaciones.

   See *Association Adjustment Inventory: Spanish Edition.*

Inventario de Intereses Ilustrado.

   See *Geist Picture Interest Inventory for Men: Spanish Edition.*

Inventario de Intereses Vocacionales.

   See *Inter-American Series: Inventory of Vocational Interests: Preliminary Edition.*

Junior Eysenck Personality Inventory: American Edition by Sybil B. G. Eysenck; c1963–1970; Ages 7–16; Testing Time Approximately 20 Minutes; One Form; Educational and Industrial Testing Service (APA Level B).

   A measure of extroversion and neuroticism (with emphasis on emotional overresponsiveness and anxiety). A Lie Scale is included to detect response falsification. The publisher recommends that the use of the American edition be limited to research projects. Norms are reported for Mexican-American, black, and majority Americans.

Junior Eysenck Personality Inventory: Spanish Edition.

   See *I.P.E. Juvenil por Sybil B. G. Eysenck.*

STS Inventario Juvenil, Form G by H. H. Remmers and Benjamin Shimberg; c1956–1968; Grades 7–12; One Form; Scholasic Testing Service, Inc.

   A Spanish translation of the *STS Youth Inventory, Form G*, a needs and problems checklist so constructed as to provide an indication of the intensity of a problem. Items are arranged under five broad headings: My School, After High School, About Myself, Getting Along with Others, and Things in General. The My School section focuses on problems that prevent the student from achieving as he feels he should or from obtaining a "relevant" education. Difficulties with self-appraisal, educational, and career planning are the major areas of concern in the items grouped under After High School. About Myself deals with self concept and personal adjustment and happiness. Getting Along with Others covers relationships with adults and peers, feelings of adequacy in social situations, and feelings of acceptance or rejection by others. Topics such as social and moral problems are emphasized in the Things in General section. The *STS Inventario Juvenil* uses the norms established for the English edition. The reliability and validity of the inventory have not been determined independently of the English edition.

STS Youth Inventory, Form G by H. H. Remmers and Benjamin Shimberg; c1956–1971; Grades 7–12; One Form; Scholastic Testing Service, Inc.

   A needs and problems checklist so constructed as to provide an indication of the intensity of a problem. Items are arranged under five broad headings: My School, After High School, About Myself, Getting Along with Others, and Things in General. The My School section focuses on problems that prevent the student from achieving as he feels he should or from obtaining a "relevant" education. Difficulties with self-appraisal, educational, and career planning are the major areas of concern in the items grouped under After High School. About Myself deals with self concept and personal adjustment and happiness. Getting Along with Others covers relationships with adults and peers, feelings of adequacy in social situations, and feelings of acceptance or rejection by others. Topics such as social and moral problems are emphasized in the Things in General section. Normative data are reported by grade and sex. The publisher reports the findings of two research studies that have yielded data concerning the responses and the differences in response patterns of students by race, sex, and age.

Speech Appearance Record (SAR) by George K. Bennett and Jerome E. Doppelt; c1967; Ages 16–25; Time Approximately 15 Minutes; Two Forms; The Psychological Corporation. 7MMY: Entry 1074.

   A structured interview procedure and form for use by employment interviewers and job counselors. The SAR provides for the appraisal of the applicant's command of spoken English, his ability to interact in person-to-person situations. An *Appearance Checklist* is included for recording details of the trainee's appearance, dress, and grooming. Two sets of response cards are provided. One set contains reading passages that are presented to the applicant in order to obtain a rapid appraisal of his approximate level of literacy. The second set of response cards are pictorial and are used to elicit spontaneous speech. No norms, reliability, or validity data are reported.

Themes Concerning Blacks by Robert L. Williams; c1972; Adolescents and Adults; Untimed; One Form; Williams and Associates.

Designed to elicit themes of achievement, black pride, awareness, aspiration, identity, etc. from blacks. Negative themes of hate, aggression, depression, or typical clinical themes can also be elicited. The 15 cards depict the black experience in a variety of situations.

William's Awareness Sentence Completion by Robert L. Williams; c1972; Adolescents and Adults; Untimed; One Form; Williams and Associates.

A semi-projective technique designed to elicit from blacks feelings of conflict regarding black pride or hate. The test can also be used to elicit prejudicial and/or positive attitudes of whites toward blacks.

Miscellaneous and Sensory-Motor

Evaluation Measures for Use with Neighborhood Youth Corps Enrollees by Norman E. Freeberg; c1967–1972; Adolescents; Untimed; One Form for Males and One for Females; Norman E. Freeberg, Educational Testing Service for the U.S. Department of Labor.

A battery of 13 tests designed specifically for research and evaluation of adolescents and young adults enrolled in youth work-training programs. The battery includes measures of vocational orientation, attitudes, and job-related reasoning skills. Seven of the tests use pictorial information accompanied by supplementary verbal information; six of the tests are entirely verbal. The difficulty level of the verbal material is the 5th-grade reading level. Slang expressions are used when necessary to clarify item content. Subject matter was selected on the basis of relevance to, and comprehension by examinees from disadvantaged or lower socioeconomic status backgrounds. The battery is administered to small groups (approximately 12 examinees). The directions for the tests, all item stems, and response choices are presented orally by the examiner.

Descriptions of the 13 tests follow: *Job Knowledge* assesses the degree to which the trainee is aware of job requirements (education required, where the work is performed, starting salary, specific major task performed, most common working hours required, and tools required) related to an occupation depicted. *Vocational Plans* measures the degree to which the examinee expects to enter various occupations. Jobs were chosen that would be familiar to the respondent and scorable on a continuum of occupational status. *Vocational Aspirations* is a measure of the degree to which the respondent would like to enter a depicted occupation. *Interests in Vocational Tasks* measures interest patterns based on specific occupational tasks rather than patterns from choices based on occupational titles. In *Attitude Toward Authority* the examinee's responses to scenes showing an adolescent being addressed by an authority figure are scored in terms of the extent to which they are anti- or pro-authority in nature. *Self Esteem* is a pictorial test of the trainee's perception of his competence in interpersonal or social action and his ability to affect his environment. *Deferred Gratification* is a verbal measure of the willingness to delay present reward for future gain. Four subscales are included: Hasty Aggression, Freedom of Spending, Affiliation, and Delay of Reward. *Job Seeking and Job Holding Skills* includes questions concerning where to look for work and how to interpret the information in newspaper want ads and job application blanks. The second part of the test pictures on-the-job behavior related to punctuality, appropriate dress, response to a supervisor's request, and so on. *Motivation for Vocational Achievement* is a verbal test concerned with obtaining and maintaining a job and the willingness to work. *Practical Reasoning—Map Reading* requires the examinee to use a map for traveling to various places. The items are concerned with the number of blocks to be covered and the direction traveled in reaching the destination. *Practical Reasoning—Zip Coding* measures skill in using zip-code-type information in sorting mail in a postal job. *Practical Reasoning—File Card Sorting* requires the examinee to sort applicants for jobs, based upon stated characteristics. The *Enrollee Rating Scale* was developed for the evaluation of the Neighborhood Youth Corps Program by the trainees. A *Counselor Rating Scale* and *Work Supervisor Rating Scale* are included with the battery. These scales are concerned with favorable and unfavorable trainee characteristics.

Mean scores are reported for male, female, urban, and rural trainees. The author cautions that the *Evaluation Measures for Use with Neighborhood Youth Corps Enrollees* is not ready for use in guidance, selection, and placement. At the present, the use of the battery should be limited to research situations.

ADDRESSES

Write directly to the test publisher for specific information and specimen sets of the measures listed in this bibliography.

Ava Publications, Inc.
11 Dorrance Street
Providence, Rhode Island 02903

American Guidance Service, Inc.
Publishers' Building
Circle Pines, Minnesota 55014

CTB/McGraw-Hill
Del Monte Research Park
Monterey, California 93940

Clinical Psychology Publishing Company, Inc.
4 Conant Square
Brandon, Vermont 05733

Counselor Recordings and Tests
Vanderbilt University
Box 6184, Acklen Station
Nashville, Tennessee 37212

Education-Industry Service
1225 East 60th Street
Chicago, Illinois 60637

Educational and Industrial Testing Service
P.O. Box 7234
San Diego, California 92107

Educational Testing Service
Test Development Division
Princeton, New Jersey 08540

Effective Study Materials
P.O. Box 603
San Marcos, Texas 78666

Follett Educational Corporation
1010 West Washington Boulevard
Chicago, Illinois 60607

Norman E. Freeberg
Educational Testing Service
Princeton, New Jersey 08540

General Educational Development Testing Service of the American Council on Education
One Dupont Circle
Washington, D.C. 20036

The Gryphon Press
220 Montgomery Street
Highland Park, N.J. 08904

Guidance Testing Associates
6516 Shirley Avenue
Austin, Texas 78752

Harcourt Brace Jovanovich, Inc.
757 Third Avenue
New York, New York 10017

Houghton Mifflin Company
2 Park Street
Boston, Massachusetts 02107

Industrial Psychology, Inc.
515 Madison Avenue
New York, New York 10022

Institute for Personality and Ability Testing
1602 Coronado Drive
Champaign, Illinois 61820

McGraw-Hill Book Company
1221 Avenue of the Americas
New York, New York 10020

Management Service Company
Benge Associates
354 Lancaster Avenue
Haverford, Pennsylvania 19041

Martin M. Bruce, Publishers
340 Oxford Road
New Rochelle, New York 10804

Monitor
P.O. Box 2337
Hollywood, California 90028

Montana Reading Clinic Publications
517 Rimrock Road
Billings, Montana 59102

The Psychological Corporation
304 East 45th Street
New York, New York 10017

Psychological Test Specialists
Box 1441
Missoula, Montana 59801

Psychologists and Educators Inc.
Suite 212
211 West State Street
Jacksonville, Illinois 62650

Psychometric Affiliates
Box 3167
Munster, Indiana 46321

The Reading Clinic
Eastern Montana College
See Montana Reading Clinic Publications

Revrac Publications
2200 Forest Glen Road
Silver Spring, Maryland 20910

Richardson, Bellows, Henry & Company,
Inc.
1140 Connecticut Avenue, N.W.
Washington, D.C. 20036

Scholastic Testing Service, Inc.
480 Meyer Road
Bensenville, Illinois 60106

Science Research Associates, Inc.
259 East Erie Street
Chicago, Illinois 60611

Stoelting Company
424 North Homan Avenue
Chicago, Illinois 60624

United States Training and Employment
Service
Fourteenth Street and Constitution Avenue, N.W.
Washington, D.C. 20210

University Book Store
360 State Street
West Lafayette, Indiana 47906

Western Psychological Services
12031 Wilshire Boulevard
Los Angeles, California 90025

Williams and Associates
7201 Creveling Drive
St. Louis, Missouri 63130

William, Lynde and Williams
113 East Washington Street
Painesville, Ohio 44077

NAME INDEX

Alley, W., 126
Alpert, R., 88, 89
Anastasi, A., 9, 10, 12, 19, 22, 54, 63, 85, 125, 133, 139, 140, 145
Anderson, S., 13, 15, 16
Angoff, W., 22, 129
Anttonen, R., 8
Armes, W. H., 70
Arnez, N. L., 74
Asher, E. J., 46
Atkinson, J. W., 82, 87, 89, 148
Ausubel, D. P., 75, 97, 98
Ausubel, P., 49, 76, 77, 79

Bachelor, D. R., 139
Bailey, L. L., 136
Banks, J. A., 75
Baratz, J. C., 60, 61, 62, 97 99, 100, 155
Baratz, S. S., 60, 61, 62, 97, 99, 100, 155
Barker-Lunn, J., 103
Bass, A., 125, 126
Baughman, E., 74
Beal, R. M., 50, 98
Beal, V. A., 70
Belcher, L. H., 129
Benjamin, L., 82
Bennett, G. K., 13
Bereiter, C., 94, 95, 99, 100
Bernstein, B., 50, 95, 96, 97, 99
Bernstein, L., 92
Biaggio, A., 14
Binet, A., 11, 25, 26, 31, 32, 63
Birch, H. G., 68
Birdsell, J. B., 51

Black, H., 9, 10
Bloom, B., 54, 63, 145, 146, 150
Bodmer, W. F., 52
Boehm, A. E., 149
Borg, W. R., 104, 105
Boring, E. G., 11, 26, 29
Bouvier, L. F., 54, 55
Boyd, W., 51
Bray, D., 126
Breese, F. H., 47
Brigham, C. C., 34, 120
Bright, H. A., 6
Brookover, W. B., 81
Brophy, J. E., 50, 98
Brown, B., 47, 81
Bryan, M., 101, 103, 104, 106, 109, 111, 115
Burke, B., 70
Burke, H., 138
Burks, B. S., 37, 41, 47
Burt, C., 11, 27, 28, 29, 37, 40, 41, 42

Caldwell, M. B., 6
Campbell, J. T., 126, 129
Canady, H. G., 2, 7, 56, 92
Carroll, J. B., 120
Castaneda, A., 88, 90
Cattell, J. McK., 32
Cattell, R. B., 88, 133, 135
Chow, B. F., 67
Clark, K. B., 14, 59, 62, 74, 75, 77, 78, 79, 80, 126, 132
Clark, M. P., 74, 75, 77, 78
Cleary, A. T., 13, 14, 125, 126, 128, 129
Clemans, W. V., 13

Clinard, M. B., 73
Cloward, R. A., 56, 61
Cody, J. J., 8
Cohen, M., 82
Cole, M. J., 94
Cole, N. S., 125
Coleman, J. S., 1, 2, 9, 79, 81, 113, 115
Coleman, W., 137
Coon, C. S., 50
Collins, J. E., 47
Cooper, J. G., 139
Cooper, R., 38
Cordova, F., 93
Cogswell, J. F., 150, 151
Cornish, R. D., 91
Coulson, J. E., 150, 151
Coursin, D. B., 67
Coyle, F. A., 142
Craighill, P. G., 90
Cronbach, L. T., 126
Crooks, L. A., 125
Crossland, F. E., 117, 118, 119, 121, 122, 123

Darlington, R. B., 13, 125, 127, 128
Darwin, C., 30
Davidson, H. H., 80, 81
Davidson, K., 87
Davis, A., 44, 49, 132, 133
Davis, J. A., 13
De Gobineau, A., 33
Deutsch, C. P., 36, 48
Deutsch, M., 9, 47, 48, 49, 50, 56, 81, 97, 98, 99
Dilley, J. S., 91
Dobbing, J., 67
Dobzhansky, T., 38, 39, 51, 52
Dockrell, W. B., 28
Doppelt, J., 48
Dorsey, G. A., 33
Douglas, 105
Dove, A., 145
Drake, St. C., 44, 45, 55, 57
Dreger, R. M., 2, 6, 83, 111, 139
Drews, E. M., 84
Dubois, P. H., 9, 16
Dunn, L. C., 39, 52
Dunn, L. M., 113
Durost, W. N., 20
Dyer, H. S., 10, 11, 12, 141

Ebel, R. L., 9, 11, 12, 13, 15, 16, 19, 21, 148
Edwards, F. G., 56
Eells, K., 58, 86, 87, 132, 133, 134, 137
Ehlers, H., 110
Einhorn, H. J., 125, 126
Epps, E. G., 92

Erikson, E., 76, 81
Erlenmeyer-Kimling, L., 40, 41

Fein, R., 55, 70
Feldhusen, J. F., 90
Findikyan, N., 9
Findley, W. G., 101, 103, 104, 106, 109, 111, 115
Fishman, J. A., 16, 17, 18, 21, 23, 24, 153
Flaugher, R. L., 125, 126, 129
Fleming, E. F., 8
Ford, S., 22, 129
Fowler, W. L., 137
Freeman, F. N., 37, 40, 47
Fremer, J., 150
French, J. W., 21, 22, 23, 24
Fuller, J. L., 39
Furst, N. F., 89

Gael, S., 126
Galton, F., 28, 29, 30, 31, 33, 34, 35, 37
Gardner, B. B., 44
Gardner, M. R., 44
Garmezy, N., 6
Garn, S. M., 50, 51
Gates, A. I., 68
Geisel, P. N., 74
Georgeoff, P. J., 74
Gibby, R. G., 92
Giddings, M. G., 59, 60
Ginzberg, E., 73
Glaser, R., 148, 149
Glass, B., 52
Goddard, H. H., 10, 27, 37
Goldberg, M. L., 104, 105
Goldman, L., 12, 18
Goldschmid, M., 74
Goldstein, J., 82
Goldstein, S., 97
Good, W. R., 12, 15
Goodman, M. E., 75
Gordon, E. W., 61, 155
Gordon, H., 45, 46
Goslin, D. A., 9, 25
Gottesman, I. I., 38, 39, 51, 53
Gottlieb, D., 80
Gozali, J., 8
Grambs, J. D., 70, 74, 75
Grant, D. I., 126
Gray, S. W., 61
Green, R. L., 56, 78
Greenberg, J. V., 81
Gronlund, N. E., 19
Gross, M. J., 9
Guildford, J. P., 11, 27, 28, 29
Guinn, N., 126

Gulliksen, H., 125
Gussow, J. D., 65, 69, 70, 72

Haber, R. N., 88, 89
Haberman, M., 8
Haggard, E. A., 131, 132
Haggerty, M. E., 47
Hall, G. S., 33
Harleston, B. W., 119
Harper, P., 69
Harrell, R. F., 68
Haubrich, V. F., 56
Hauser, P. M., 54, 55, 71
Havighurst, J., 44, 47, 49
Hawkes, T. H., 89
Heathers, G., 104, 106, 111, 112
Helvétius, 11, 30, 36
Herrnstein, R., 2, 41, 42
Hess, R. D., 50, 98, 100
Hilgard, E. R., 82
Hill, R., 73
Hills, J. R., 14
Hilton, T., 13, 14, 128, 129
Hirsch, J., 38
Hodgkins, B., 74
Hodgson, F., 1
Hoffman, B., 9, 10
Hollingshead, A. B., 44
Holzinger, K. J., 37, 40, 47
Humphreys, L. G., 28
Hunt, J. McV., 11, 31, 33, 39, 60, 62, 97, 98, 99
Hunter, J. E., 127
Hurlock, E., 74
Husek, T. R., 148, 149
Hutcheson, R. H., 70

Irvine, S. H., 129

Jackson, R., 148
Jacobson, R. L., 8, 24, 81, 118
Jarvik, L. F., 40, 41
Jencks, C., 37, 56
Jenkins, M. D., 46, 111
Jennings, H. S., 38
Jensen, A. R., 2, 28, 36, 37, 39, 40, 41, 42
Jiminez, C. K., 142
John, V. P., 97
Johnson, B. C., 75
Jones, J. A., 56, 61
José, J., 8
Justman, J., 104, 105

Kagan, J., 129
Kallingal, A., 126
Karmel, L. J., 13
Katz, I., 79, 81, 82, 86, 87, 92, 93

Katzenmeyer, W. G., 90
Keller, J. E., 137
Keller, S., 49
Kennedy, W. A., 47
Keston, J. J., 142
Key, C. B., 46
Kidd, A. H., 135, 136
Kimble, G. A., 6
Kirk, G. E., 39
Klaus, D. J., 149
Klaus, R. A., 61
Klausmeier, H. J., 90
Klineberg, O., 2, 22, 23, 45, 46, 47, 48, 58, 63, 64, 93, 134
Klock, J. C., 14
Knobloch, H., 65, 69, 75, 92
Kram, K. M., 70

Labov, W., 94, 99, 100, 155
Lambert, N. M., 140
Landreth, C., 75
Larson, R. G., 74
Leahy, A. M., 37, 41
Lee, E. S., 47
Lehman, I. J., 13, 20
Lennon, R. T., 3, 11, 12, 15, 129
LeSage, W., 12
Levin, H. A., 74
Lewis, S., 14
Li, C. C., 52
Lighthall, F., 88
Linden, J. D., 9, 28
Linden, K. W., 9, 28
Linn, R. L., 125, 126
Locke, J., 35
Loeb, M. B., 44
Loretan, J. O., 16
Lorge, I., 141
Loughlin, L. J., 91
Lowell, E. L., 83
Ludlow, H. G., 137, 142
Lunt, P. S., 44
Lynd, H. M., 44
Lynd, R. S., 44

Macfarlane Smith, I., 135
Mackler, B., 59, 60
Malina, R. M., 69
Mandler, G., 88, 89, 90
Manning, W., 9
Marquart, D. I., 136
Maslow, A. H., 24, 25
Maurer, S., 67
Mayer, K. B., 43, 44
Mayeske, G., 115
Mayr, E., 52
McCandless, B. R., 88, 90

McClelland, D. C., 83, 84, 156
McGraw, M. B., 64
McKeachie, W. J., 91
McReynolds, P., 88
Medley, D., 129
Mehrens, W., 13, 20
Mercer, J., 8, 60, 113, 114, 142, 143, 144, 154
Meredith, H. V., 69
Merrill, M., 48
Messick, S., 13, 15, 16
Meyer, E. L., 8
Michael, W. B., 21, 22, 23, 24
Milholland, J. E., 135
Miller, D. B., 92
Miller, K. S., 2, 6, 83, 111
Milner, E., 49
Mitchell, B. C., 47, 70
Montagu, A. M., 34, 51, 53
Moran, R. E., 142
Morland, J. K., 77
Mosteller, F., 82
Moynihan, D. P., 45, 71, 82
Mueller, J. H., 43
Mueller, K. H., 43
Murray, H. A., 83
Mussen, P. H., 85

Nash, H. B., 47
Newman, H. H., 37, 40
Newton, P., 73, 76, 81
Nitko, A. J., 148
Noll, V. H., 138
North, R. D., 2
Nunn, P., 35, 36

O'Connor, H. A., 91
Ogletree, E., 103
Orgel, A. R., 139
Osterhouse, R. A., 91
Owen, G. M., 70

Packard, V., 82
Palmero, D. S., 88, 90
Pandey, R. E., 125
Papania, N., 137
Parsley, K., 91
Pasamanick, B., 64, 65, 69, 75, 92
Pasanella, A., 9
Passow, A. H., 104, 105
Pearson, K., 31, 34
Peterson, J., 2
Pettigrew, T. F., 38, 51, 52, 58
Pfeifer, C. M., 126
Pike, L., 126
Pintner, R., 2
Plotkin, L., 14, 59, 62, 126

Pollie, D., 91
Pollitzer, W. S., 52
Popham, W. J., 148, 149
Porter, A. C., 14, 126
Powell, M., 91
Prescott, G. A., 20
Pressey, S., 47
Proshansky, H., 73, 76, 81

Quirk, T. J., 129

Radke, M., 78
Rainwater, L., 71
Ralston, R., 47
Rex, J., 59
Riccio, A. C., 12
Ricciuti, H. N., 67, 70
Rider, R., 69
Riessman, F., 59
Rist, R. C., 8, 104
Roberts, D. F., 14, 52, 82, 92
Robinson, J. M., 82, 92
Rock, D. A., 129
Roeder, L. M., 67
Rosen, B. C., 82, 84, 85, 86
Rosenberg, P., 78
Rosenblum, S., 137
Rosenthal, R., 8, 24, 81
Roth, R. W., 74
Rulon, P. J., 140

Sacks, E. L., 92
Sarason, S. B., 88, 89, 90
Schaefer, A. E., 70
Scheier, I. H., 88
Schmidt, F. L., 127
Schrag, P., 110
Schwarz, P. A., 143
Seashore, H., 48
Sedlacek, W. E., 126
Seward, G., 76
Sherman, M., 46
Sherman, Matthew, 148
Shields, J., 40
Shimberg, M. E., 7, 46
Shipman, V., 98, 100
Shoemaker, D. M., 148, 150
Shuey, A. M., 2, 92, 111
Simon, G. B., 149
Simon, T., 11, 25, 26, 31, 32, 63
Sinnott, E. W., 39
Skeels, H. M., 41, 47
Skodak, M., 41, 47
Snow, R. E., 8
Sokal, M. M., 32
Sommer, J., 13
Spearman, C., 26, 28

Speisman, J., 91
Spielberger, C. D., 90, 91
Stakenas, R. C., 74
Standiford, P., 48
Stanley, J. C., 14, 125, 126
Stern, W., 25
Stoddard, G. D., 11, 26
Sutherland, J., 78

Taback, M., 69
Tannenbaum, A. J., 136, 141
Tate, M. E., 139
Taylor, J. A., 88
Taylor, O. L., 129
Teahan, J. E., 84
Temp, G., 13
Tenopyr, M. L., 126
Terman, L. M., 11, 16, 33, 48
Thompson, W. R., 39, 83
Thorndike, R. L., 8, 14, 125, 126, 127, 128, 148
Thresher, B. A., 123, 124
Thurstone, L. L., 28
Tsai, L. S., 67
Tupes, E. C., 126
Turnbull, W., 10
Tyler, L., 26, 28

Van de Riet, V., 47
Vega, M., 92
Vernon, P., 11, 27, 28
Veroff, J., 86

Waite, R. R., 88, 90
Walker, E. I., 92
Walters, T., 70
Ward, A. W., 137
Warner, R. L., 44, 132
Watson, J. B., 38
Wechsler, D., 11, 14, 26
Weiner, B., 83
Werts, C. E., 125, 126
Wesman, A. G., 11, 19, 27, 48, 133
West, J., 44
Wheeler, L. R., 46
White, J. C., 47
Whiteman, M., 81, 97
Wickes, T. A., 92
Wilkerson, D. A., 61
Wilks, S. S., 125
Williams, R. L., 7, 145
Winick, M., 66
Wolf, R., 54, 145, 146, 147, 153, 154
Woodyard, E., 68
Woodworth, R. S., 37, 41
Wrightstone, J. W., 89
Wundt, W., 29
Wylie, R., 75

Yates, A., 103
Young, F., 6

Zee, P. T., 70
Zieky, M., 148
Zubek, J., 38

SUBJECT INDEX

Achievement Anxiety Test (AAT), 89
Achievement Motivation. *See* Motivation
American Personnel and Guidance Association (APGA), 3–5
Anxiety, 87–91
  and ethnicity, 89
  as an inhibiting factor, 89–90
  scales, 88–89
  and social class, 90
  as a stimulating factor, 90
  and test performance, 87–88
Association of Black Psychologists (ABP), 3–5

Bias
  cultural, 115
  item, 13–14, 128–29
  test, 14, 125–28
Bilingualism, and test performance, 93
Binet-Simon scale, 31–32
Birthweight
  increase in, 65
  and mental development, 69
  and race, 69
Black English
  as a developed language, 99–100
  as underdeveloped language, 94–95
Black Intelligence Test of Cultural Homogeneity (BITCH), 145
Brown v. *Board of Education of Topeka*, 108, 110, 112

Cattell's Culture-Free Intelligence Test, 134–36, 142

Child-rearing practices, 49, 61
Children's Manifest Anxiety Scale (CMAS), 88
College admission
  testing and, 116–30
  tests of aptitude and, 122–23
College enrollment of minorities, 117–19
Commission on Tests, Report of, 10, 119–20
Committee on Hostile Test Center Environment, 91–92
Compensatory education, 34–35, 42, 61–62
Court cases, 4, 8, 108, 112, 114, 119
Criterion-referenced tests, 147–52
  definition of, 148
Culture-free and culture-fair tests, 133–42
  futility of, 140–42
Culture specific tests, 142–45
Cumulative deficit phenomenon, 8–9, 50

Davis-Eells games, 58, 136–38
Deprivation
  cultural, 16, 45–49
  economic, 45, 54–55
  educational, 55–56
  verbal, 49, 97–98
Desegregation
  adverse effects of, 79
  and intellectual performance of blacks, 79
Diet
  maternal, 65, 68
  and pregnancy, 70
  See also Nutrition

Differences
  cross-cultural, 57–58
  IQ, 1
Dove Counterbalance General
  Intelligence test, 145

Early training project, 61
Environment
  definition of, 63
  influence of deprived, 45–46
  influence of enriched, 46–47
  influence of urban and rural, 46
  measurement of, 54, 145–47, 153–54
  of minorities, 45, 49
Environmentalists, 35–36, 42–43

Fertility, differential, 71
Foster children, 41

"g" factor, 28
Galton's tests, 31
Genes, 37–38, 51–52
Genotype, 37–38
  relationship between phenotype and,
    38–39
Goodenough Draw-a-Man-Test, 139–40
Grouping
  effects of, 104–06, 115
  homogeneous, 102–04
  and scholastic achievement, 101
  and segregation, 111
Guidelines for testing minority group
  children, 16–19, 21

Hereditarians, 35–36, 62
Heredity, 29–30, 35
  and environment, 2–3, 35–37
Heritability
  concept of, 39–40
  estimates of, 37, 41
Hobson v. Hansen, 8, 112
Hostility, 93

Index of social status, 44
Intellectual performance
  class differences in, 47–48
  and examiner race, 92–93
Intelligence
  Binet's definition of, 26, 32
  Cattell's definition of, 32
  concept of, 25–34
  confusion about, 11
  definition of, 26–27, 27f
  as eminence, 30
  fixed, 32, 33
  historical perspective, 29–34
  theories of, 27–29

Intelligence testing
  abolition of, 15–16
  misconceptions about, 11–13
  moratorium on, 4
IPAT Anxiety Scale, 88
IQ
  correlations among relatives, 40–41
  correlations among unrelated persons,
    41
  definition of, 25–26
  of exceptional black children, 46 .
  increase in, 46–47
  as innate capacity, 9, 11
  variation in, 37

Jews, 33–34

Labelling, 53, 114
  grouping and, 106
Language, 93–100
  lower class, 50, 95–96
  maternal, 61–62, 98
  middle-class, 96–97
Larry P. et al. v. Wilson Riles et al., 4, 8, 114
Leiter International Performance Scale,
  139
Lorge-Thorndike test, 6

Malnutrition. See Nutrition
Manifest Anxiety Scale (MAS), 88
Mental age, 25–26
Mental retardation, 8, 113–14
Mercer's pluralistic evaluation, 143–44,
  154
Migration, selective, 47
Motivation, 82–87
  cultural differences in, 85
  definition of, 83
  effects of grouping on, 106
  and ethnicity, 84
  and social class, 82, 84

National Association for the Advancement
  of Colored People (NAACP), 4–5
Nature-nurture, 35
  See also Heredity; Environment
Nutrition, 64–72
  and birth weight, 67
  and intellectual development, 66–67, 72
  and physical development, 66
  and prematurity, 67
  and race, 70–71

Otis-Lennon test, 6

Parental Attitude Scle (PAS), 84
Phenotype, 38–39

relationship between genotype and, 38–39
Prematurity
and mental development, 69
and race, 69, 72
and socioeconomic status, 69
Probability curve, 31, 34–35, 121

Race
concept of, 50–53
of examiner, 23, 92–93
taxonomy of, 51–52
Racial awareness, 75, 77
Racial comparisons, 53–59, 64–65
Racial discrimination
grouping and, 109
Nordic superiority, 34
white superiority, 33, 45
Racial identification, 77
Racial imbalance, 114, 117, 120
Racial preference, 77–78
Raven's Progressive Matrices, 138–39
Regression to the mean, 31, 34–35
Reliability, 19–20
factors influencing, 20–21
Rulon's Semantic Test of Intelligence, 140

"s" factor, 28
Scholastic Achievement and/or Aptitude Tests (SAT), 13, 120–24
School
black, 56
influence of, on self-concept, 78–79
integrated, 78–79
as a middle-class institution, 15, 43, 60–61
Segregation
de facto, 108–11
devastating effects of, 78–79, 111
Self-concept, 72–82
definition of, 75
effects of grouping on, 106
negative, 72–73, 78
and school, 78
and school performance, 81
and teacher attitude, 79–80
positive, 73–74

and parents, 76
Self-fulfilling prophecy, 8, 24, 81, 106
Social stereotypes, 8
Social stratification, 43–45
caste, 43, 58
class, 43
grouping and, 112
Socioeconomic status
and grouping, 107, 112–13
and IQ scores, 47–48
Speed, 23
Standards for development and use of educational and psychological tests, 12, 21
Stanford-Binet test, 5–6, 142
Structure-of-the-intellect model, 28

Teachers
perceptions of students, 8, 24
role of, in formation of student self-concept, 79–80
in slum schools, 56
students' perceptions of, 80–81
Test Anxiety Questionnaire (TAQ), 88
Test Anxiety Scale for Children (TASC), 88
Test criticism, 3, 7, 9, 116, 124, 131–32
Test fairness, 13, 125–28
unfairness, 14–15
Thematic Apperception Test (TAT), 83
Themes Concerning Blacks (TCB), 83
Thurstone's PMA (primary mental abilities), 28
Twin studies, 40–41

U.S. Commission on Civil Rights, 108

Validity, 19, 128
content, 21–22
construct, 24–25
criterion-related, 23–24
Values
classification of, 85
middle-class, 60, 62

Wechsler Intelligence Scale for Children (WISC), 5–6, 142

80 81 82   9 8 7 6 5